W9-CWM-924

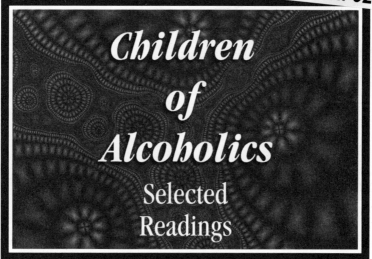

Children of Alcoholics
Selected Readings

Volume II

Robert J. Ackerman

Hoover Adger, Jr.

Claudia Black

Cathleen Brooks

Stephanie Brown

Lewis D. Eigen and David W. Rowden

Jeannette L. Johnson, et al.

Jerry Moe

Ellen R. Morehouse

Emmy E. Werner and Jeannette L. Johnson

Sybil Wolin and Steven Wolin

Robert A. Zucker, et al.

Edited by Stephanie Abbott

National Association for Children of Alcoholics

Foreword

The National Association for Children of Alcoholics is proud to publish this monograph, which represents a variety of perspectives and professional experience. The contributing writers are among the most distinguished clinicians and researchers in the family addiction field, bringing together impeccable research as well as intuitive clinical experience.

In the first section, *RESEARCH*, Lewis D. Eigen and David Rowden give the parameters of the problem, as they introduce us to a methodology for estimating the numbers of children of alcoholics in this country. Jeannette L. Johnson addresses the measurement of premorbid risk factors in COAs. Lastly, Ann W. Price and James G. Emshoff discuss approaches to prevention and intervention.

The second section focuses on *THE YOUNG CHILD*. Jerry Moe shares his strategies that help children build on their own strength and resilience. Ellen R. Morehouse looks at the challenge of matching children of alcoholics to the services available to them. Emmy E. Werner and Jeannette L. Johnson follow the lives of 65 children of alcoholics and note some common factors in those who go on to live productive lives. Lastly, Cathleen Brooks writes directly to the child in *The Secret Everyone Knows*.

The third section addresses the dilemmas of *THE ADULT CHILD*, as Stephanie Brown gives the reader a framework for understanding the concepts of ACA as well as codependency, with an emphasis on the impossibility of reducing the ACA experience to any single category. Claudia Black speaks to the adult child directly about the issues common to ACAs. Finally, Sybil and Steven Wolin look at the challenge of growing up in a family with an addicted parent, with being "overly responsible" as an achievement with a price, rather than a defense.

Our final section is *THE FAMILY*. Hoover Adger reminds health providers that they will see large numbers of patients affected by alcoholism in the family, and they are in a good position to identify problems. Robert A. Zucker, Deborah A. Ellis, C. Raymond Bingham, and Hiram E. Figerald explore the research in the differences in child risk, such as hyperactivity, for children from families with antisocial problems. Robert Ackerman sums it all up with an overview of alcoholism as a systemic problem as he examines how families evolve and the effects on the children at each stage.

Stephanie Abbott
Editor

CONTRIBUTING WRITERS

Robert Ackerman, Ph.D.
Professor of Sociology
Indiana University of Pennsylvania
Indiana, PA

Hoover Adger, Jr., M.D., M.P.H.
Associate Professor of Pediatrics
Johns Hopkins University School of Medicine
Baltimore, MD

C. Raymond Bingham, Ph.D.
Department of Veterans Affairs
Assistant Research Scientist
Department of Psychiatry
University of Michigan
Ann Arbor, MI

Claudia Black, Ph.D., M.S.W.
President, Claudja, Inc.
Bainbridge Island, WA

Cathleen Brooks
Executive Director
Next Step, Institute
Palm Bay, FL

Stephanie Brown, Ph.D.
Director, The Addictions Institute
Menlo Park, CA
Co-Director, The Family Recovery Project
Mental Health Research Institute
Palo Alto, CA

Lewis D. Eigen, Ed.D.
President and CEO
Social & Health Services, Ltd.
Rockville, MD

Deborah A. Ellis, Ph.D.
Assistant Professor
Department of Psychiatry and Behavioral Neurosciences
Wayne State University
Detroit, MI

James G. Emshoff, Ph.D.
Associate Professor
Department of Psychology
Georgia State University
Atlanta, GA

Hiram E. Fitzgerald, Ph.D.
University Distinguished Professor
Department of Psychology
Chair, Applied Developmental Science Graduate Programs
Michigan State University
East Lansing, MI

Jeannette L. Johnson, Ph.D.
University of Maryland at Baltimore
Department of Psychiatry, Division of Alcohol and Drug Abuse
Baltimore, MD

David McDuff, M.D.
University of Maryland at Baltimore
Department of Psychiatry, Division of Alcohol and Drug Abuse
Baltimore, MD

Jerry Moe, M.A.
Director - Children's Program
Betty Ford Center
Rancho Mirage, CA

Ellen Morehouse, ACSW, NCAC II
Executive Director
Student Assistance Services Corp.
Tarrytown, NY

Ann W. Price, Ph.D.
Grady Health Systems
Atlanta, GA

Jon Rolf, Ph.D.
Senior Health Advisor
Prevention Applications Branch
Center for Substance Abuse Prevention
Rockville, MD

David W. Rowden, Ph.D.
Information Systems Security Manager
Caliber Associates
Fairfax, VA

Steven J. Wolin, M.D.
Clinical Professor of Psychiatry
George Washington University Medical School
Project Resilience
Washington, DC

Sybil Wolin, Ph.D.
Project Resilience
Washington, DC

Robert A. Zucker, Ph.D.
Professor of Psychology
Departments of Psychiatry and Psychology
Director, Division of Substance Abuse and Alcohol Research Center
Department of Psychiatry
University of Michigan
Ann Arbor, MI

EDITOR
Stephanie Abbott, MA
Adjunct Professor
Marymount University
Arlington, VA

TABLE OF CONTENTS

SECTION IV: THE FAMILY

SECTION I: RESEARCH

A Methodology and Current Estimate of the Number of Children of Alcoholics in the United States

Lewis D. Eigen, Ed.D. and David W. Rowden, Ph.D.

Introduction

In 1982 a study was conducted for the State of New York which estimated that in 1980 there were one half million children of alcoholics (COAs) in New York and 5.5 million in the United States.[1] Essentially the methodology utilized was to start with the number of adult "alcoholics" in the nation and extrapolate to the number of children under 20 by using the ratio of adults to children in the general population.[2] The methodology was based on an earlier study which estimated the number of COAs for the State of Pennsylvania.[3] In 1982 the estimate of adult alcoholics that was available to the researchers was crude at best, and the researchers did the best[4] that they could with the data and information that was then available. In 1985 the same general methodology was again used[5], this time with 1979 prevalence estimates based upon more than "guesstimates."[6] The number of COAs for the United States was estimated to be 6.6 million. This estimate was considerably larger (20%) than that of the 1982 study. The difference was more striking when one considers that the researchers changed the age definition for COAs to include only those youngsters under the age of 18, rather than the 20 year criterion that had been utilized earlier. The marked increase in COAs was far greater than what could be explained by demographic changes and was almost certainly due to a better prevalence estimate.

Subsequent to these efforts, there has been a substantial leap forward in the epidemiology of alcohol usage and alcoholism. In addition, the demographics of the U. S. population have changed considerably since then. However, heretofore, there have been no new studies estimating the number of COAs. Also, much more is known today about the additional risks to which COAs are exposed.[7] Many private and public agencies are developing policies and programs for protecting COAs and/or ameliorating the problems caused by additional risk factors. To plan, fund and/or implement these policies and programs, reasonable quantitative estimates of the number of COAs are required.

It is the purpose of this paper to produce such contemporary COA estimates. The plural is utilized because the COA estimate is fundamentally dependent upon two definitional issues: the definition of an alcoholic, and the definition of a child of an alcoholic. As this paper will articulate, there are several reasonable definitions of each of these elements, and each produces a somewhat different COA estimate. Therefore, this paper will articulate a methodology and calculate different definitions dependent upon which definitional assumptions are made. It is important to note, however, that under all definitional possibilities, the current estimates are considerably higher than those obtained in the 1982 and 1985 studies. Some of the methodological reasons for these differences will also be discussed.

COA Alternative Concepts

When we speak of the child of an alcoholic, the purpose is generally to examine the risk factors to the child and/or the actions that might be taken to prevent or reduce those risks. When we think of COAs, we might have any of the following concepts in mind.

I.   Children whose biological parents are or have been alcoholics.[8]
II. Children who are currently living with alcoholic parents or caregivers.
III. Children who have ever lived with alcoholic parents or caregivers.

These are not mutually exclusive of course. Many children in today's complex society do not live with both biological parents, and some live with neither biological parent. The presumption is that there is a statistical and likely causal relationship between the well-being and development of the child and the parent's or caregiver's problems with alcohol. The linkage might be hereditary, behavioral, cultural or some combination of these. Therefore, if the purpose of estimating the number of COAs is to estimate the number of children potentially at additional risk, then we should be estimating the number of children in any one or any combination of factors of I, II or III since each are capable of producing risk. The following example illustrates the complexity:

Neither biological parent is alcoholic, but parents are divorced and remarried. The step-parent of the children living in the home of the custodial, natural parent has an alcohol problem.

In the modern, nuclear family, the addition of step-parents or parent surrogates adds significantly to the risk likelihood from non-hereditary factors and adds to the COA estimate. Although the methodology developed and utilized in this paper will allow this type of analysis, the remainder of this paper will confine itself to the COA risk of the biological parents only. Thus all estimates herein will be conservative in this sense. A later analysis in another study will deal with estimates of additional risk if parent surrogates are included as well.

For a COA estimate there are three distinct types of COAs that could be defined. They are:

COCAs: **C**hildren **O**f **C**urrent **A**lcoholics

This includes those children whose parents would be classified as "alcoholic" sometime in a particular year. Excluded would be children, whose parents might have been drinking alcoholics in the previous year or earlier but were no longer so. This is a much more restrictive definition of a COA than were used in the text of the 1982 and 1985 studies where the issue of current, lifetime or parental period prevalence was not directly addressed.

COPPAs: **C**hildren **O**f **P**arental **P**eriod **A**lcoholics

If we are interested in children under the age of 18, there is an 18 year "parental period" during which the child could be exposed to risk from an alcoholic parent. Therefore, an 18 year parental period prevalence of alcohol problem period would define this category. The parent of a COPPA may have been a drinking alcoholic for a single short period during the 18 year parental period or the parent may be classified as an alcoholic for the entire 18 year period or anything in between. Note that the COPPA definition, like the COCA definition, precludes the risk of problem transmitted from parents who may have been alcoholics prior to the birth of the child. Thus, both of these will not account for the risk of genetic effects, Fetal Alcohol Syndrome (FAS) or Fetal Alcohol Effects (FAE), for those children of parents who are in recovery.

COLAs: Children Of Lifetime Alcoholics

Here the child may have a parent who was **ever** a drinking alcoholic. This includes not only the parental period, but also the period before the child was ever born. To the degree that pharmacological and genetic factors transmit additional risk, this COLA definition is critical in that COPPA and COCA definitions would completely ignore this factor, unless the parental problem also manifested itself at some time in the child's developmental years. Also, there are many who believe that there are often dysfunctional behavioral influences on children of sober adult alcoholics in recovery even if they have been abstinent for years.

It follows, therefore, that all COCAs are also COPPAs, and likewise all COPPAs are also COLAs. From a mathematical point of view,

$$\# \text{ COLAs} > \# \text{ COPPAs} > \# \text{ COCAs}$$

This study attempts to provide national estimates for all three definitions. COAs under 18 years of age are considered, as in the 1985 study, rather than under 20 as had been done in the 1982 study. The reasons are several fold. First, 18 has become the age of majority in all states. In addition, many governmental programs directed at children do not apply to young people over the age of 18. It is noteworthy that even with the markedly more narrow definition of child, the COA estimates that are produced herein are considerably larger than the earlier estimates using the 20 year old criterion.

Alcoholism Prevalence

In order to estimate the number of children of alcoholics, one must first have an estimation of the number of alcoholics themselves. There has been much debate over the various possible definitions that could be used to make such an estimate, and it has even been argued that there is no discrete point at which drinkers become alcoholics–that there is a continuum, and that the very concept of an alcoholic is based on a false premise of non-continuity[9]. In the 1982 study the words "alcoholics," "alcoholic homes," "problem drinkers," and "problems in drinking behavior" are utilized somewhat interchangeably. The common thread was to estimate the prevalence of a condition that exposes children to additional health risk.

Recent attempts at measuring alcoholism prevalence center around utilization of the DSM-III and DSM-III-R diagnostic criteria, and estimates of "alcoholics" proceed from that.[10] In this methodology we build upon the seminal surveys conducted by NIAAA utilizing the DSM-III definitions. These are criteria for establishing medical diagnostic conditions. For purposes of determining alcoholism prevalence to estimate the number of children of alcoholics, we used the DSM-III-R criteria for *alcohol dependence* and for *alcohol abuse*. Either condition in a parent[11] may produce the kinds of additional risk factors that COA investigations indicate.[12] It has been argued by some that the definition of alcoholic should be limited to *alcohol dependence* and should not necessarily include *abuse* in the absence of *dependence*. While we have accepted the "either/or" NIAAA definition, we observe that had the alternative been chosen, all estimates herein would have been somewhat reduced.[13] Further, that others using the data of this study be particularly careful in extrapolations of findings to other studies where the alternative definition of alcoholic (or even another definition) might have been utilized.

The most recent and comprehensive estimates have been given by NIAAA as a result of the 1988 NHIS survey. This study estimates the annual prevalence of "alcohol dependence" and "alcohol abuse." But one of the thorniest issues in estimating the number of COAs is which prevalence to use for the definition of parental alcohol problem. Monthly prevalence? Weekly? Yearly? Lifetime prevalence? The answer, of course, depends on the COA definition chosen: COLA, COPPA or COCA.

Since the COA concept involves the risk of influence of parents with alcohol problems, annual (or less) prevalence **underestimates** the number of COLAs or COPPAs. A parental alcohol problem, which may not have existed through the first 8 years of a child's life, may be present for the next 10 years or vice versa. Even if a parental alcohol problem existed before the birth of a child and not after, there is still the possibility that genetic or other familial/social influences might affect the child. However, a lifetime prevalence would overestimate the appropriate prevalence for all three of our definitions since it would include those parents who had alcohol problems **only after** the children were grown. The point is somewhat moot in that there are no reliable studies of lifetime prevalence of

DSM-III-R diagnoses. What ideally is needed is a concept of **parental age prevalence**–the lifetime prevalence of the parent **only** up to the point that the children are no longer children, which for this purpose we will consider to be 18 years. So the **parental age prevalence is clearly *less* than lifetime prevalence but *greater* than annual prevalence**. If a parental age prevalence were known, it would be ideal for calculating the number of COLAs. Then if a pre-parental age prevalence could be calculated (the lifetime prevalence of the parent up to the point at which the child is born), then there would be a sound prevalence estimate for using the COPPA definition – namely, subtracting the pre-parental age prevalence from the parental age prevalence. There are no known, national, direct studies of parental age prevalence or pre-parental age prevalence, as there are none of lifetime prevalence, but there are ways of making reasonable estimates.

COLA Estimate

The COLA estimate is the easiest of the three definitional estimates to obtain. The methodology proposed in this study, regardless of COA definition, involves three distinct steps. First, is obtaining the appropriate estimate of the prevalence that matches the COA definition. Second, is utilizing that prevalence to calculate the COA *probability*, the likelihood that a particular child would have an alcoholic parent. And third, applying the COA probability to the demographics of the nation (or subdivision thereof.)

Table 1 shows the annual prevalence rates for the different age groups for "alcohol dependence," or "alcohol abuse," as estimated by NIAAA in 1988.

Table 1
Annual 1988 Prevalence of DSM-III-R Alcohol
Abuse or Dependence[14]

Sex	Ages 18-29	Ages 30-44	Ages 45-64	Age 65 +
Male	23.50%	14.30%	7.24%	2.77%
Female	10.10%	4.07%	1.73%	0.37%

For the COLA definition, we would want a lifetime prevalence rate for the parent up to the parental age when the child becomes 18. Since it is rare that a person over the age of 65 would have a child under 18, a 0-64 year parental prevalence would be appropriate. There is no such measure available from the NIAAA survey or anywhere else. However, the annual prevalence for each of the age groupings under 65 is always a lower bound of the 0-64 year prevalence. For each sex there are three annual prevalence figures (depending on age group under 65), and the maximum becomes the greatest lower bound for the 0-64 prevalence. For males, this is 23.50%, and for females, 10.10%[15]. Utilization of these prevalence rates will be a very conservative technique in that they **always underestimate** the 0-64 prevalence rate. This concludes step 1 for COLAs.

Estimating the COA Probability

Previous attempts to calculate the number of COAs from adult prevalence rates utilized methods of extrapolating the ratio of children to adults from the general population to the sub-population of alcoholics.[16]

There is an alternative and somewhat simpler and straight forward method of estimating the number of COAs given the alcoholism prevalence rates. Specifically, every child has both a male and female parent. Straight probability analysis can be used to answer the relatively simple question: *What is the probability that, for a particular child, at least one of the two parents is an alcoholic?* Essentially we call this the COA probability. If the male and female prevalence rates are P_m and P_f respectively, then the probability for a particular child would be given by:

$$P_{coa} = P_m + P_f - P_m P_f$$

But this assumes that P_m and P_f are independent – that the likelihood that an alcoholic would marry and/or have a child with another alcoholic is no different from chance. This assumption is certainly not tenable, given the well established cultural set of influences on both marriage and drinking patterns. If the probability that a particular alcoholic female would marry an alcoholic male were simply random, it would be the male prevalence, P_m. Clearly, it is higher

than that, however. If it were given by M, then
$$P_{coa} = P_m + P_f - MP_f$$
Since $M > P_m$, then $(P_m + P_f - MP_f) < (P_m + P_f - P_m P_f)$

In the most extreme case **all** female alcoholics could be assumed to marry male alcoholics and therefore $M = 1$. Then

$$P_{coa} = P_m + P_f - MP_f \text{ or simply}$$
$$P_{coa} = P_m$$

Therefore an upper bound for Pcoa would be
$$P_m + P_f - P_m P_f$$
and a lower bound would be given by P_m.

Utilization of the lower bound would be a very conservative process and would always somewhat underestimate the actual number of COLAs. However, as will be seen, even utilizing this lower bound, the estimates are considerably higher than previous estimations.

Since for the COLA definition, $P_m = .235$ and $P_f = .101$,
$$.235 < P_{coa} < .235 + .101 - (.235)(.101), \text{ or}$$
$$.235 < P_{coa} < .312$$

The COLA Estimate

In 1988 there were 63.8 million children under 18 years of age in the United States.[17] Utilizing the COA probability range for COLAs just computed, the envelope of COLAs in the United States in 1988 was

$$15.0 \text{ million} < \# \text{ COLAs} < 19.9 \text{ million}$$

The difference between the 15.0 million estimate and the 19.9 million estimate lies in the proportion of female alcoholics who bear children fathered by male alcoholics. The 15.0 million number assumes all of them do, and the 19.9 million assumes that a female alcoholic is no more likely to have a child sired by a male alcoholic than any other woman. Reality lies somewhere in between.

COPPA Estimate

A similar process can be followed to obtain the COPPA estimate except that the prevalence rate is different. The highest male prevalence rate as shown in Table 1 is for the 18 to 29 year age group. That prevalence was appropriate for COLA estimates but for COPPA estimation, the 23.50% prevalence is only appropriate for those males who father their children before the age of 30. Therefore, what is needed for the COPPA estimate is an age prevalence weighted by the proportion of children fathered at the different age ranges. Fortunately, data to produce such a weighting is available. Figure 1 shows the male fertility by age of father. Table 2, which is derived from the Figure 1 fertility data, shows the proportion of children that are fathered by men in the same age ranges as is used by NIAAA in the DSM-III-R 1988 prevalence analysis.

Figure 1 Male Fertility Rate[18] (Births per 10,000)

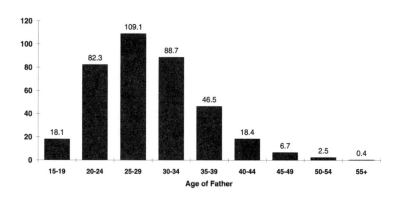

Table 2
Percentage of Children Fathered By Men of Different Ages[19]

	Ages 18-29	Ages 30-44	Ages 45-64	Age 65+
% of Children Fathered	53.3%	41.2%	2.6%	0

If the male prevalence rates are weighted proportionately the combined rate is 18.6%. And if the same proportions are applied to the female rate, it is 8.0%. This process assumes that the fertility rates for both male and female alcoholics are not substantially different from those of their non-alcoholic age counterparts.[20] Therefore, for calculating the COA probability for COPPAs, P_m = .186 and P_f = .080. When these numbers are applied,

$$.186 < P_{coa} < .186 + .080 - (.186)(.080), \text{ or}$$
$$.186 < P_{coa} < 0.251$$

This in turn, when applied to the 63.8 million children under 18 years of age, produces

$$11.9 \text{ million} < \# COPPAs < 16 \text{ million}$$

Just like the COLA estimates, the difference between the ends of the range are a function of the alcoholic male/female marriage and breeding pattern. Also, the conservative nature of dealing with the prevalence issue assures that the range itself is an underestimate of the true number, just like the COLA estimate, in that an average, weighted, annual prevalence was utilized rather than a multi-year prevalence for the 18 year COCA exposure period.

COCA Estimate

In the COLA and COPPA estimating procedure previously described, we chose lower bound estimates of prevalence by utilizing the annual prevalence survey by NIAAA. Ideally we would not have utilized annual prevalence which underestimates the results. However, for the COCA estimate we do want the actual annual prevalence. The problem is that the NIAAA data present average prevalence figures by age group and for the population as a whole, but what is needed for the COCA estimate is a prevalence weighted for the parental period only – not the general population prevalence. This is not immediately available from the NIAAA data, but can be reasonably estimated.

Figure 2
% of Children Born By Paternal Age

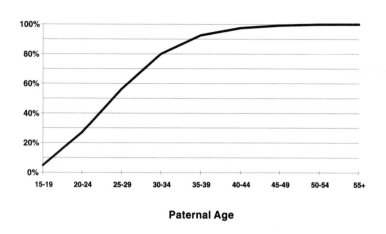

Paternal Age

The data from Figure 2 demonstrate that 28 years is currently the approximate, median age of paternity in America. Also, that over 97% of the children are born before the father has reached the age of 45. Extending this by the 18 year parental period essentially means that only 3% of the fathers ever reach the age of 65 during the parental period. Likewise, approximately only 50% even reach the age of 45 during the parental period. Therefore, when weighting the COCA paternal prevalence, we should eliminate 97% of the over 65 population and 50% of the over 45 group. Likewise, 44% of the males under the age of 29 have not yet fathered a child; nor have 3% of those men under the age of 44. Therefore, equivalent proportions of these age groups should be ignored for weighting purposes. Table 3 shows the figures utilized for the male weighting procedure.

After adjusting the weighting for these removals, the weighted, male, annual prevalence rate is 15.05%.

Table 3
Weighting for Males (in Millions)

	Age 18-29	Age 30-44	Age 45-64	Age 65+	Total
Male Population	24,677	28,441	22,042	12,355	87,515
Proportion Included	53.30%	100.00%	50.00%	2.60%	
Prevalence	23.50%	14.30%	7.24%	2.77%	15.05%
Population Included	13,153	28,441	11,021	321	52,936
Alcoholics Included	3,091	4,067	798	9	7,965

If a similar weighting system is utilized for females, there will be a slight underestimate of the proper prevalence in that females marry and become parents at a slightly earlier age than the males. However, the error thus induced is relatively small, and the COA probability estimate is much more heavily controlled by the male rate than the female anyway.[21] Table 4 shows the parallel weighting for females.

The female weighted prevalence rate is, by this analysis, 4.96%.

Table 4
Weighting for Females (in Millions)

	Age 18-29	Age 30-44	Age 45-64	Age 65+	Total
Female Population	24,239	28,779	22,843	18,018	94,897
Proportion Included	53.30%	100.00%	50.00%	2.60%	
Prevalence	10.10%	4.07%	1.73%	0.37%	4.96%
Population Included	12,919	28,779	11,922	468	54,088
Alcoholics Included	1,305	1,171	206	2	2,684

Therefore, for calculating the COA probability for COCAs, $P_m = .1505$ and $P_f = .0496$. When these numbers are applied,

$$.1515 < P_{coa} < .1515 + .0496 - (.1515)(.0496), \text{ or}$$
$$.1515 < P_{coa} < 0.1936$$

This in turn, when applied to the 63.8 million children under 18 years of age produces

$$9.66 \text{ million} < \# COCAs < 12.35 \text{ million}$$

COA Estimate Summary

Thus far, we have produced a range for each of the three COA definitions. Where in the range the best estimate falls is a function of the intra-alcoholic childbearing and marriage patterns. There is insufficient knowledge at this time to know with any degree of certainty what the M value should be to make an ideal estimate.[22] However, it is not unreasonable to assume a value of .5. This would mean that one half of the alcoholic women who bear children would have done so with an alcoholic man. If it were left completely to chance, the proportion would equal the male prevalence rate. As can be seen in Table 1, the assumption that M = .5 would indicate that the intra-alcoholic breeding pattern was over 2 to 3 times greater than chance for the high fertility ages. The lower bound assumes that all female alcoholics interbreed with male alcoholics, while the upper bound assumes that the inter-breeding is completely random—an equally unrealistic assumption in the other direction. Table 5 provides all these estimates.

Table 5
COA Estimates (in Millions)

	Lower Bound $M = 1$	Estimate $M = .5$	Upper Bound Random
COCA	9.6	11.0	12.4
COPPA	11.9	14.0	16.0
COLA	15.0	17.5	19.9

Table 6
COA Estimates as a Percentage of the Youth Population

	Lower Bound *M = 1*	Estimate *M = .5*	Upper Bound *Random*
COCA	15%	17%	19%
COPPA	19%	22%	25%
COLA	24%	27%	31%

Therefore, we believe that the best estimates that can be given at this time are:

There are 11 million COCAs in the United States, 14 million COPPAs and 17.5 million COLAs.

17% of our youth are COCAs, 22% are COPPAs, and 27% are COLAs.

Differences From Earlier Estimates

The estimates obtained in this study are substantially higher than those obtained in the 1982 and 1985 studies. This is especially dramatic in light of the fact that the methodology utilized herein underestimates for the COLA and the COPPA definitions. There are several possible reasons for this apparent discrepancy. What might be thought to be one of the apparent factors, a demographic change in the number of children, is not a factor. As a matter of fact, the number of children under the age of 18 actually decreased from 1980 to 1988–to 63.8 million. There are several factors however that do account for most of the differences.

Age Definition Change

Some difference is due to the fact that the 1982 study counted children up to age 20 while the 1985 and this study limits the COAs to children under the age of 18.

Ratio of Adults to Children

Both the 1982 and 1985 studies utilized the approach, developed by Booz-Allen in the 1974 study, of calculating the ratio of adults to children and applying this ratio to the number of adult alcoholics estimated for the population as a whole. This methodological approach, while seemingly appropriate in the abstract, always seriously underestimates the number of COAs. The reason lies with the alcohol and fertility characteristics of the older people in our society. Alcoholism prevalence decreases markedly for both sexes as age increases. At the same time, very few older Americans are in a position to any longer influence the behavior of their children under 18 (or 20 as in the 1982 study). This is not to say that they are not influential. Their children are usually grown and are no longer under 18. They cannot influence a child who would be counted as a COA only because the child has passed the critical age. The overwhelming majority of children (over 97%) are born to parents under 46 years of age. Thus, there are only a minuscule handful of children under 18 with parents over 65. In using the ratio method, these mature adults were counted in the pool of adults. They, however, no longer can affect any of the factors impinging on children under 18 since their children have already passed that age. They also add very little to the number of DSM-M-R alcoholics since the over 65 prevalence is so low. By being included in the sample, they increase the ratio that is utilized but are neither parents nor alcoholics to any great extent. Therefore, they artificially decrease the Booz-Allen method, ratio derived estimates. In 1980 there were 25.5 million Americans 65 years or older, and this represents about 16% of all the adults over the age of 18 (an even greater proportion of those over 20.) Conceptually, they should be removed from the ratio calculation, and their contribution to the number of alcoholics should likewise be removed. The former is very large, while the latter is very small. The result of not doing so is to deflate the COA estimate. A rough calculation of this type was performed on the 1985 study data (data for 1980), and it showed that the over 65 factor alone accounted for an underestimate of about 20%. It is worth noting that by 1988, the over 65 year proportion of the adult population had increased significantly over 1980, and therefore, this underestimate increases in proportion and magnitude as the proportion of mature Americans increases in the population as a whole.

The same principle should be applied to the over 45 year old group as well. For the 45 to 65 year age group as parents, **approximately half** of their children have already passed 18. And, while the DSM-111-R alcoholism prevalence for this range is not as low as the over 65 group, it is lower than the average for the younger, parental period age groups. If half of this population were removed from the ratio, along with the corresponding reduction in the number of adult alcoholics, there would be far more COAs added to the estimate. So the Booz-Allen ratio method alone causes a substantial undercount of COAs.

Prevalence Estimates

It is certainly the case, as the authors acknowledge, that the 1982 study had little more of an alcoholism prevalence estimate than a "guesstimate." The 1985 study had a better estimate. In this study, we had the advantage of utilizing the results of NIAAA's substantial biometry efforts of the last few years. It is more than likely that these different prevalence estimates may have accounted for a substantial part of the estimation difference between this study and the two earlier ones.

Prevalence Period

In both the 1982 and 1985 study reports, the authors clearly indicate that they were concerned with congenital factors, FAS, FAE, cultural influences and the like. Although they do not explicitly distinguish among the COLAs, COPPAs and COCAs, the language of the reports indicated that these researchers had a COLA concept in mind. Yet the prevalence figures they had to work with were only annual prevalence figures. So, while they were likely thinking COLA, or certainly COPPA, they were actually calculating COCA and as we have already shown,

$$\# \text{ COLAs } > \# \text{ COPPAs } > \# \text{ COCAs}$$

and this inevitably led to an underestimate.

Psychological / Political Factors

The 1985 study was performed by individuals who were among the earliest leaders in bringing the attention of the nation, in general, and the health establishment, in particular, to the nature and implications of the COA problem. Their work was supported by the Children of Alcoholics Foundation which was not an entirely disinterested party. At the same time, there was not the national recognition of the COA problem that there is today. It is possible that the researchers and the COA Foundation "bent over backwards," as it were, to avoid being "alarmist" or appearing to exaggerate the magnitude of the problem. The methodology that was chosen, at each step, would underestimate rather than overestimate. The number of children at risk that were estimated was already, clearly, a serious problem of national significance, and there may have been great reluctance to utilize more complex, less traditional methodology or innovative methodology which would increase the estimate, lest they be accused of trying to magnify the problem. In particular, the choice to use the Booz-Allen ratio method, the only published method in the literature at that time, virtually guaranteed a substantial undercount.

In a sense, we have also been somewhat conservative, only to a lesser extent. We have chosen lower bounds throughout, so that to the degree there is error in the methodology, it is on the side of caution and underestimation.

Recent Parallel Results

Recently, the National Center for Health Statistics has reported an analysis of the 1988 NHIS national survey data in which over 40,000 Americans were asked whether they grew up in a household with a parent who was an alcoholic.[23] This survey was not designed to project the number of COAs and had other purposes driving the design and instrument. It only queried adults—not children under the age of 18. Further, the survey depended on self-definition and subjective perception, with the concomitant risk of denial or exaggeration and memory problems of the respondent in terms of whether the parent was an alcoholic, as opposed to some more objective measure such as DSM-III-R. This survey produced an 18.1% prevalence estimate for current adults who report growing up in alcoholic homes. If this proportion were extrapolated downward to the 1988 under 18 year old population of 63.8 million, the estimate of children would be approximately 11.5 million. This estimate, produced by a much different methodology with different definitional criteria as well, is much larger than the estimates of the 1982 and 1985 studies. It is right in the middle of our COCA estimate range as given in Table 5 and somewhat less than our COLA and COPPA estimates. The latter, in particular, is conceptually closer to the questions as posed to the survey recipients. Therefore, this study would support the contention that the 1982 and 1985 studies were underestimates, but would not suggest the same size underestimate as our study did.

Implications

There are certainly enough COAs in the nation, even under the 1982 and 1985 estimates, to constitute a major public health problem. The fact that there are many more than previously thought does not change the fundamental fact that there are children at risk. However, in addition to the academic exercise of having more precise estimates, there are major public policy implications of the difference in order of magnitude of the problem. To the degree that COAs require more educational, social or medical costs to the society, the number of COAs who could potentially benefit from programs is an important factor in making cost-benefit analyses of different prevention and intervention strategies. Such analyses and extrapolations should be performed with great care, however. In studies heretofore there has been relatively little attention paid to the possible range of COA definitions as well as different definitions of "alcoholics." In a health cost study, for example, it is possible that the higher medical costs of COAs applies disproportionately less to COLAs than to COCAs, or to either differentially to the COAs utilizing the definition in that study. It is, therefore, recommended that future studies involving COAs try, to the extent possible, to be as precise as possible, not only in involving COLAs, COPPAs or COCAs, but also in using DSM-III-R definitions of "alcoholics."

Given the broadest COA definition, the COLA estimates herein, one in four American children is at additional, potentially preventable, health risk. And under the most narrow definition, COCA, almost one in five children has a parent who is a drinking alcoholic which poses an increased health risk. The consequences of that additional risk, while primarily borne by the children themselves, impact every American, fiscally and otherwise.

Notes

*This study was performed pursuant to Contract #277-90-4002 of the Center for Substance Abuse Prevention, SAMHSA, Public Health Service of the U. S. Department of Health and Human Services. The authors wish to acknowledge the assistance of Dr. Bridgit Grant of NIAAA, Ms. Judi Funkhouser of the Center for Substance Abuse Prevention, Mr. George Marcelle of Social and Health Services Ltd, Ms. Migs Woodside, Dr. Sheila Blume and Mr. Basil Henderson of the National Foundation for the Children of Alcoholics, and Ms. Lynn Hadley, Ms. Cathy Crowley and Ms. Peggy Williams of the National Clearinghouse for Alcohol and Drug Information whose invaluable assistance in this endeavor is gratefully acknowledged.

1   Migs Woodside, Children of Alcoholics: A Report to Hugh L. Carey, Governor, State of New York, New York State Division of Alcoholism and Alcohol Abuse, 1982.

2   In 1980, this ratio was 1.8 for the nation and 2.3 for New York.

3   Booz-Allen and Hamilton, Incorporated, An Assessment of the Needs of and Resources for Children of Alcoholic Parents, National Institute on Alcohol Abuse and Alcoholism, 1974. This study utilized a 14 million national estimate of alcoholics. The 1982 researchers observed in applying the ratio of adults to children that the Booz-Allen study made a mathematical error. The estimate with this "error" was 1.2 million COAs in Pennsylvania.

4   The researchers utilized the 10 million estimate provided by "Facts on Alcoholism and the Family" of the New York City National Council on Alcoholism. The researchers report that there had been a very crude estimate given earlier by NIAAA of approximately 9 million.

5   Marcia Russell, Cynthia Henderson and Sheila B. Blume, Children of Alcoholics: A Review of the Literature, Children of Alcoholics Foundation, 1985.

6   W. B. Clark and L. Midanik, "Alcohol Use and Alcohol Problems Among U. S. Adults: Results of the 1979 National Survey," Monograph No. 1: Alcohol Consumption and Related Problems, DHHS Publication No. (ADM) 82-1190, 1982.

7   See Children of Alcoholics Foundation, Inc., Children of Alcoholics in the Medical System: Hidden Problems, Hidden Costs, 1990, and Migs Woodside, Children of Alcoholics: A Report to Hugh L. Carey, Governor, State of New York, New York State Division of Alcoholism and Alcohol Abuse, 1982.

8   While it is common terminology for many in the alcohol field to refer to
     a person who may have previously had an alcohol problem but is
     currently in recovery as an "alcoholic," this is not the sense in which
     the currency of "alcoholic" is used herein. Rather, the term is used to
     indicate one who manifests current symptoms of alcohol dependence or
     alcohol abuse.

9   Michael E. Hilton, "What I Would Most Like To Know: How Many
     Alcoholics are there in the United States?" British Journal of Addiction
     84:459-460, 1989.

10   B. S. Grant and T. C. Harford, The Relationship Between Ethanol Intake
     and DSM-III Alcohol Reporting, Journal of Studies on Alcohol, v. 51, #5,
     1990.

11   The DSM-III-R definition of "alcohol dependency" includes "alcohol
     abuse." Therefore the two terms are not mutually exclusive; "alcohol
     abusers" are therefore a subset of those who are "alcohol dependent."

12   It could be argued that to be an "alcoholic" one would, strictly speaking,
     have to meet the alcohol dependency DSM-III-R criteria, but the alcohol
     abuse criteria alone would not qualify. This latter category would, under
     this argument, represent abusive drinking patterns at some stage of life,
     but do not necessarily amount to, or develop into, alcoholism, per se.
     However, the additional health risk factors to children can and are
     produced by a parent meeting the alcohol abuse criteria are potentially
     just as significant. Thus, we have used an either/or criterion of
     inclusion. This appears to be conceptually consistent with the attempts
     of the 1982 and 1985 researchers.

13   The authors are in the process of calculating the COA estimates as
     reported herein for the alternative definition as well, and these will be
     reported in a separate study.

14   B. S. Grant, et. al., "Prevalence of DSM-III-R Alcohol Abuse and
     Dependence: U. S., 1988," Epidemiological Bulletin #27, Alcohol Health
     & Research World, 15-1, (In Press). The "or" is inclusive.

15   The NIAAA data given by Table 1 are significant to the two decimal places
     as they are presented. However, given the differ ent methodologies of
     estimating parental period prevalence, number of children in different
     ranges and the other factors in this study, the reader should draw no
     implication from the number of "significant" figures provided that this
     methodology or our calculations have that degree of precision.

16   e.g. Migs Woodside, op. cit. and Booz-Allen and Hamilton, Incorporated,
     op. cit.

17   United States Census Bureau, "Total Population Estimates: 1988."

18 National Center for Health Statistics, *Vital and Health Statistics: Supplement to the Monthly Vital Statistics Report: Advance Reports, 1986, Public Health Service, March 1990. The data are for 1986 whereas the prevalence and population data are for 1988. The fertility numbers are relatively stable and this disparity produces little error.*

19 *The sum is less than 100% in that a few children are born to fathers under age 18.*

20 *If the alcoholic fertility rate were greater than the non-alcoholic, then this methodology would underestimate the COA estimate. If less, there would be an overestimate. There is no definitive research that we have been able to find on this subject. There is anecdotal research evidence that young alcoholic males divorce and remarry at a rate that exceeds the non-alcoholics and also are more fertile. There is also evidence that as alcoholism progresses sterility and impotence increases and fertility thereby decreases. Since most children are fathered by relatively young men, it is possible that the behavioral pattern of the young and middle age alcoholic male increases fertility more than the physiological effects of the alcoholism diminishes it in the later stages. Generally marriage rates of alcoholics do not seem to differ than those of non-alcoholics, however divorce rates are higher. When one considers the remarriage factor and the fact that the divorce may have taken place after children have been conceived and/or born. See Thomas J. Paolino, Jr. et al., "Statistics on Alcoholic Marriages: An Overview," The International Journal of the Addictions, 13(8), 1285-1293, 1978.*
    Charles M. Unkovic and Gloria K. Irrgang, Double of Nothing: The Double Alcoholic Marriage, University of Central Florida, Orlando, January 1981.

21 *It is possible to estimate the weighted female prevalence more precisely by following a maternal age analysis similar to the male one that has been done. This would require much more detailed analysis of the NIAAA survey unpublished data in order to match the age categories for maternal fertility. The gain in precision was considered much to small to be worth the effort.*

22 *In the 1988 NHIS survey, raw data that could likely produce a relatively accurate measure was obtained, but it has not yet been analyzed.*

23 *Charlotte A. Schoenborn, Exposure to Alcoholism in the Family: United States, 1988, National Center for Health Statistics, Advance Date Number 205, September 30, 1991*
    Page 17

Developmental Assessment of Children of Alcoholics

**Jeannette L. Johnson, Ph.D., Jon E. Rolf, Ph.D.,
Stuart Tiegel, L.C.S.W., David McDuff, M.D.**

I. Introduction

Reviews of the research conducted during the last several decades on studies of the prevalence of alcoholism in the United States, such as Russell's (1991), substantiate the belief that the children of alcoholics (COAs) are at high risk for alcoholism. A great many questions, however, remain unanswered about how to measure premorbid risk factors in the children of alcoholics and how to demonstrate their causal roles. These questions about risk assessment and function for children of alcoholics are debated by clinical, applied and basic research disciplines; depending upon the discipline, different approaches are used to answer them. All too frequently, the approaches to these questions about risk are contradictory; subsequently, so are the answers. Searles and Windle (1991) address this dilemma by stating that:

> *"One reason for this [conflict between disciplines] is that good science requires experimental rigor at the expense of what sometimes appears to be ecological validity, while clinical data can be easily compromised with respect to empirical validity and reliability but retain substantial real-world meaning for specific individuals. Similarly, clinicians, and to some extent researchers, tend to ignore or reinterpret research findings that do not fit their theoretical orientation or personal world view, and researchers often dismiss clinical reports as uncontrolled or riddled with theoretical over interpretation" (page 2).*

Gaining better understanding of the etiological functions of risk as well as skill in risk assessment in COAs would represent important scientific progress. Such progress, at the same time, could well enhance clinical practice by pointing to more effective prevention and early treatment methods.

An important first step towards making scientific progress in moving from speculations about risk factors to testable risk models involves coming to grips with the need for a common language of risk factors and a common understanding of available and to-be-developed assessment methods. Our answers to clinical, applied, or basic scientific questions about COAs depend upon the quality of the data obtained from our assessments. This is true whether the assessment is a paper and pencil questionnaire, a laboratory performance test, a clinical interview, or a mere conversation. Progress in cataloging and understanding the assessment process can serve as an important building block for a common language with which to communicate better progress in COA risk research. Practically, if researchers understood different assessments, or at best used common assessment instruments in standard ways, they would be able to compare findings and discuss, with confidence, reasons for commonalities and differences.

Assessment for purposes of description or testing causal linkages involve complicated tasks, ones that are not easily met without considerable effort. Each discipline struggles to apply sensitive and specific assessments to test their theories of risk for children of alcoholics. However, assessing any child, and especially a child who may be at risk for an assortment of traits, states, or attributes hypothesized to underlie (or mark) a developmental risk factor, is a complex undertaking. Which domain do you assess with what instrument, at what age (or stage of risk expression), and how often? These are thorny questions.

It is the primary goal of this paper to wrestle with some of these issues and to provide a framework for assessing children of alcoholics that would be useful to both researchers and service providers working with COAs. Hopefully, this paper will provide the impetus for a continuing discussion on assessment strategies so that a consensus might emerge on optimal assessment plans for children at risk for alcoholism.

A secondary goal of this paper is to present the issues related to assessment within the context of a developmental framework. Through proper assessment of the child's behavior, and within the context of understanding normal developmental attempts at mastery, we can track the developmental trajectories of both adaptive and maladaptive behaviors. Within this developmental framework, we argue that normal childhood behavior includes the child's innate drive to experience their world by attempting to master the objects, events, and people in their environment. For COAs, we may observe that developmentally normal attempts at mastery are adaptive behaviors in a dysfunctional environment. Nevertheless, these behaviors may become the beginnings of habits which, in a different context and at a different age, might become maladaptive and which some might label 'codependent' in adulthood.

We have organized our review into three sections. We start by presenting a review of the behavioral assessments that have been done on children of alcoholics in the United States within the past three decades. The assessments of COAs across psychophysiological and biological functional domains, while important, have been reserved for another review. It is beyond the scope of this paper to address all these assessment domains. This paper, therefore, is limited to those issues relevant to the behavioral assessment of school-aged children of alcoholics. The second section critiques the current assessment procedures against the background of developmental theory and the relevance of understanding developmental methodology as part of the assessment process. The final section presents recommendations for a comprehensive assessment battery for children of alcoholics and discusses the need for new assessment techniques with these children. It is hoped that these recommendations will be the beginning of a discussion that will foster a consensus on the most appropriate assessment battery for children of alcoholics.

II. Review of the Assessments of Children of Alcoholics

In this section we review three decades of published reports on the behavioral assessment methods applied to school-aged children of alcoholics. This is not a review of the literature on the differences between children of alcoholics and children of non-alcoholics. Over 20 reviews, some quite excellent, of the literature on these differences exist (Adler & Raphael, 1983; Austin & Prendergast, 1991; Chafetz, Blane, & Hill, 1971; Corder, McRee, & Rohrer, 1984; el-Guebaly, 1986; el-Guebaly & Offord, 1977, 1979; Galanter, 1991; Johnson & Bennett, 1988; Johnson & Rolf, 1990; Johnson, Sher, & Rolf, 1992; Plant, Orford, & Grant, 1989; Russell, Henderson, & Blume, 1985; Searles & Windle, 1991; Sher, 1991; Thalinger & Kovanek, 1988; von Knorring, 1991; Warner & Rosett, 1975; Watters & Theimer, 1978; West & Prinz, 1987; Wilson & Orford, 1978; Windle, 1989).

The following criteria were used for inclusion in the review of behavioral assessments of school-aged children of alcoholics:

Sample Definition:

1. Studies of COAs were included if their parents had a primary diagnosis of alcoholism; parents with secondary diagnoses of alcoholism were not included.

2. School-aged children of alcoholics are defined as those between the ages of 5 and 18. Studies of infants, pre-schoolers, or college-aged youth are not included.

3. Studies reviewed were those published samples of children from the United States. This review strategy was used to alleviate problems associated with the translation of English tests into foreign language equivalents. However, some excellent studies from other countries are available, i.e., Scandinavia (Aronson et al. 1985; Cloninger, Sigvaardsson, & Bohman, 1988; Knop et al. 1985; Nylander & Rydelius, 1982; Rydelius, 1981; Zetterstrom & Nylander, 1985), Portugal (de Mendonca et al. 1985), France (Lemoine et al. 1968), Russia (Shurygin, 1974), Puerto Rico (Rubio-Stipec et al. 1991), Yugoslavia (Miketic, 1972), Canada (el-Guebaly et al. 1978), Germany (Steinhausen, Nestler, & Huth, 1982), Great Britain (Bell & Cohen, 1981), Australia (Callan & Jackson, 1986), and Czechoslovakia (Matejcek, 1981).

4. The sampling source (i.e., parental alcoholism, childhood treatment status) was overlooked. Thus, some of the samples of children of alcoholics are of children whose alcoholic parents are in treatment, some children of alcoholics are in treatment themselves, and some children of alcoholics are also juvenile delinquents.

5. Composition of the COA sample is presented with regard to size, sex, and age. Since this is a review of assessment procedures and not group differences, control group composition is not described.

Extent of Assessments:

6. Only studies utilizing a battery of tests assessing behavior were included. Behavioral assessment was not limited to performance, but also included self-reports and informant reports of behavior. This review does not include neurophysiological or biological assessments. Consequently, studies using primarily neuropsycho-

logical assessment techniques were not included; however, the studies that included behavioral assessment along with a neuropsychological battery were reviewed.

Table 1 presents the results of the review of 36 studies which met these six inclusion criteria. They are listed in the chronological order of their appearance in the scientific literature. These studies were gathered by two means: (1) through computerized literature searches accessing several psychological databases, and (2) with 'hands on' literature searches in journals that were not included in the computerized databases. We acknowledge that this review may be incomplete because it excludes those studies that have not been published in the scientific literature.

Our review reveals that since behavioral assessment began on children of alcoholics in the early 1960's, over 2000 children of alcoholics have been tested in the United States when you combine the samples of published studies. It is difficult to derive a precise count of the COAs who have been sampled because some of the published studies probably used the same sample of children in more than one publication.

We found a wide variety of behavioral assessments in the COA literature used over the past three decades. Although the earliest behavioral assessments of COAs were usually developed by the authors of those early studies, attempts have been made across time to use standardized assessments with normed reference groups. Table 2 lists over 70 different behavioral measures which were used to assess children of alcoholics (derived by taking a frequency count of those assessments listed in Table 1). Eighty percent of these measures were used only once and only in one particular study. The most frequently used tests (at least three or more times) are the Wide Range Achievement Test (reading, spelling, arithmetic), WISC-R/WAIS-R (verbal, performance, and full scale IQ), Child Behavior Checklist (parental reports of behavior problems; includes externalizing and internalizing syndromes), Children of Alcoholics Screening Test (children's report of concerns about their parent's drinking), Connors Teacher Rating Scale (teacher ratings of behavior problems), Family Environment Scale (parent reports of family functioning variables, such as family cohesion), Hopkins Symptom Checklist (behavioral symptomatology), Peabody Individual Achievement Test, and the Rosenberg Self-Esteem Scales.

Table 1: Testing Children of Alcoholics: A Review of Childhood Behavioral Assessments in Chronological Order of Appearance in the Literature

Reference	Sample	Assessments
Aronson & Gilbert, 1963	41 male COAs; Age range=7 to completion of grammar school.	Personality Questionaire developed by authors (T).
Haberman, 1966	142 COAs	Childhood Symptom Checklist developed by author(P).
Cork, 1969	115 male(59) and female(56) COAs; Age range=10 to 16, mean=15.	Child Interview developed by author (C).
Kammeier, 1971	65 male(2) and female(45) COAs; Mean age=15.4(1.2).	Minnesota Counseling Inventory(C); Personal Orientation Inventory(C); Iowa Tests of Educational Development(C); Lorge-Thorndike Intelligence Tests(C).
Chafetz, Blane, & Hill, 1971	100 male(60) and female(40) COAs;	Hospital chart review (demographics, illness, Age range=2 to 19, mean=11.6. accident, school problems, and problems with the law).
Fine, Yudin, Holmes, Heinemann, 1976	39 male(21) and female(18) COAs;	Devereux Child or Adolescent Behavior Rating Age range=8 to 18, mean=12.1 Scale(P); Symptom Rating Scale(P); Examination of school records(E).
Herjanic, Herjanic, Penick, Tomelleri, 1977	82 COAs; Age range=6 to 17.	Herjanic Diagnostic Interview for Children(C); PPVT(C); WRAT(C); Other psychological tests not described; Developmental Questionnaire(P); School reports(T).

Hughes, 1977	50 COAs (25 from Alateen); Self-Age range=12 to 19; mean=15.44.	Profile of Mood States(C); Rosenberg Esteem Scale(C); Self report of problems with the law or school(C).
Miller & Jang, 1977	147 male and female COAs.	Interviews for parents and children developed by authors.
Prewett, Spence, & Chaknis, 1981	15 male(8) and female(7) COAs; Age range=7 to 12.	Nowicki-Strickland Locus of Control (C).
Kern, Hassett, Collipp, Bridges, Nowicki-Solomon, & Condren 1981	20 male(10) and female(10) COAs; Age range=8 to 13.	Otis-Lennon Mental Abilities Test (C); Strickland Locus of Control (C).
Moos & Billings, 1982	50 male(25) and female(25) COAs from recovering parents (Mean age=14(5.7); 23 male(11) and female(12) COAs from relapsed parents; (Mean age=10.8(6)).	Health and Daily Living Form(P); Family Environment Scale(P); Child Functioning questionnaire (P).
Ervin, Little, Streissguth, & Beck, 1984	50 male(25) and female(25) COAs; Age range=infancy to over 15 years; 66% of sample between 3 and 14 years of age.	Bayley Scales of Infant Development(C); Stanford Binet(C); WISC-R or WAIS(C); WRAT(C).
Tarter, Hegedus, Goldstein, Shelly, & Altterman, 1984	16 male COAs; Mean age=16(1.2).	WISC-R(C); PINTS(C); Detroit Tests of Learning Aptitude(C); PIAT(C); Matching Familiar Figures Test(C); MBD Checklist(C); MMPI(C).
Hegedus, Alterman, & Tarter, 1984	16 male COAs; Mean age=16(1.2).	PIAT(C); PINTS(C); MMPI(C); Family Environment Scale(C); Devereux Adolescent Behavior Scale(P).

Study	Sample	Measures
Tarter, Hegedus, & Gavaler, 1985	16 male COAs; Mean age=16.	Childhood History MBD Checklist(C).
Jacob & Leonard, 1986	100 male(56) and female(44) COAs; Age range=10 to 18.	CBCL(P); Conners Teacher Rating Scale(T); Myklebust Pupil Rating Scale(T).
anning, Balson, & Xenakis, 1986	Study 1: 46 male(26) and female(20) COAs; Age range=5 to 17.	Matthews Youth Test for Health(P); Jenkins Activity Survey(P).
	Study 2: 95 COAs; Age range=5 to 17, Mean age=9.9.	same as above
Marcus, 1986	40 male(15) and female(25) COAs; Age range 7 to 12.9.	PIAT(C).
Werner, 1986	49 male(22) and female(27) COAs tested longitudinally from birth to age 18.	At 10 years of age: Primary Mental Abilities Test (C); Bender-Gestalt(C).
		At grade 12: California Psychological Inventory(C); Nowicki-Strickland Locus of Control (C); needs assessments done by clinical team; Standardized tests available from school.
Rhodes & Blackham, 1987	32 male(11) and female(21) COAs; Mean age=16.6.	CAST(C); demographic information; Children of Alcoholics Family Role Instrument.
Earls, Reich, Jung, & Cloninger, 1988	38 male(22) and female(16) children of 1 alcoholic parent(Mean age=11.1); 12 male(7) and female(5) children of 2 alcoholic parents(Mean age=13.9); Age range=6 to 17.	Home Environment Interview for Children(P,C);Diagnostic Interview for Children and Adolescents(P,C); Coopersmith Self-Esteem Inventory(C); Dimensions of Temperament Survey(C);Peabody Picture Vocabulary Test(C); Wide Range Achievement Test(C); Behavior Screening Questionnaire(P).

Bennett, Wolin, & Reiss, 1988	64 male and female COAs; Age range=6 to 18, mean age=12.08(3.4).	WISC-R or WAIS-R(C); PIAT(C); Piers Harris Children's Self Concept Scale(C); Herjanic Diagnostic Interview for Children and Adolescents (C); CBCL(P); Conners Parent Symptom Rating Scale(P).
Roosa, Sandler, Gehring, Beals, & Cappo, 1988	Study 1: 10 male and female COAs; grades 9-12	CAST(C); Children of Alcoholic Life-Events Schedule(C).
	Study 2: 56 male(16) and female(40) COAs; Age range=14 to 18.	CAST(C); Children of Alcoholic Life-Events Schedule(C); Hopkins Symptom Checklist(C);demographic questions and other measures not reported.
Johnson & Rolf, 1988	50 male(26) and female(24) COAs; Age range=6-18, mean age=13(8.6).	WRAT(C); WISC-R or WAIS-R(C); Perceived Competence for Children(C); Project Competence Child Interview(C); CBCL(P); Connors Parents Symptom Rating Questionnaire(P); Perceived Competence for Children(P).
Drake & Vaillant, 1988	174 male COAs; Mean age=14(2).	Wechsler-Bellevue IQ(C); Emotional problem scale; Boyhood Competence Scale; Physical Health Scale; Feelings of Inadequacy Ratings(P,T, or CI); School behavior problems and truancy (T).
Roosa, Sandler, Beals, & Short, 1988	Study 1: 38 male and female COAs; Age range=14 to 19.	Depression and anxiety subscales of the Hopkins Symptom Checklist(C); Rosenberg Self-Esteem Scale(C); Adolescent Alcohol Involvement Scale(C).
	Study 2: 32 male and female COAs; Age range=14 to 18.	same as above

Rolf, Johnson, Israel, Baldwin, & Chandra, 1988	50 male(26) and female(24) COAs; Age range=6-18, mean age=13(8.6).	Center for Epidemiological Studies Depression Scale(P); CBCL(P); Childrens Depression Inventory(C); Beck Depression Inventory(CYouth Self Report(C).
Johnson, Leonard, & Jacob, 1989	33 male and female COAs; Age range= 10 to 18, mean age=14.3(2).	Questionnaire on drinking experience and drinking style(C); Williams Temperance and Intemperance Scales(C); Reasons for Drinking Scale(C); Questionnaire on what child would do to obtain alcohol and drug use(C).
Pandina and Johnson, 1989	Time 1: 276 male(128) and female(148) COAs; Age range=12 to 18.	Self-report questionnaires designed by the Rutgers Health and Human Development Project (use of drugs index, age of onset, frequency of use, reasons for use, consequences of use)(C).
	Time 2: 270 male(124) and female(146) COAs; Age range=15 to 21 (same subjects as Time 1 but older).	
Tarter, Jacob, & Bremer, 1989	33 male COAs; Mean age=12.12(2.33).	Detroit Tests of Learning Aptitude(C) (plus 13 neuropsychological tests).
Tarter, Kabene, Escallier, Laird, Jacob, 1990	37 male COAs; Mean age=15.	Dimensions of Temperament Scale(C); Family Environment Scale(P).
Roosa, Beals, Sandler, & Pillow, 1990	43 male(13) and female(30) COAs; Mean age=15.6.	Hopkins Symptom Checklist(C); CAST(C); Children of Alcoholics Life Events Schedule(C); General Life Events Schedule for Children(C). CBCL(P); Straus Conflict Tactics Scale(P);

Study	Sample	Tests
Ballard & Cummings, 1991	13 male(5) and female(8) COAs; Age range=6 to 10, mean age=7.6(1.3).	Children viewed videotapes of angry and positive adult interactions and then interviewed regarding their feelings and perceptions about the videotape
Whipple & Noble, 1991	18 male COAs; Age range=10 to 15, mean age=12.3.	Personality Inventory for Children(P); High School Personality Questionnaire(C); Junior Eysenck Personality Inventory(C): Tridimensional Personality Questionnaire(C).
Stern, Kendall, & Eberhard, 1991	16 COAs, grades 1 to 5 (from special and regular education classes).	CAST(C); Friel Co-Dependency Assessment(taken by parent about themselves).

Sample Notes: Mean age=years(SD)

Test Abbreviations: CBCL=Child Behavior Checklist; CAST=Children of Alcoholics Screening Test; PIAT=Peabody Individual Achievement Test; PPVT=Peabody Picture Vocabulary Test; WRAT=Wide Range Achievement Test; PINTS=Pittsburgh Neuropsychological Test System.

Test Informants: C=Child; P=Parent; T=Teacher; E=Experimenter Rating; Cl=Clinician

We recognize that clinicians and researchers choose assessments for different reasons, but with such a wide variety of tests used, it makes comparisons between even more studies difficult, if not impossible. Clearly there is a great need to use instruments to help between-study comparisons and to aid our understanding of the implication of the findings for further research and intervention services.

After reviewing the variety of measures used to test COAs, it appears that while some of these assessments may be necessary, they are not sufficient. The importance of understanding developmental processes in COAs and the child's active role in this process cannot be underestimated. It is possible that some COAs may experience a subtle, yet important, divergence from normal developmental pathways that has yet to be measured with existing assessment techniques. Against the background of a developmental framework, we contend below that existing assessment strategies have not adequately explored the predictive aspects of the developmental process in COAs.

II. Exploring a Developmental Framework for Assessing COA's Codependency

Developmental research shows that children of different ages think, feel, and act according to differences in cognitive and affective stages of development (Cowen, 1978; Flavell, 1977; Nannis, 1988; Piaget, 1955, 1963). Measuring these processes requires an assessment procedure that attends to normal individual differences in behavior during development; however, as the previous review demonstrated, this has rarely been done in studies of COAs. In Table 1, examination of the subject age ranges within studies shows little attention to normal developmental differences in the research design. Frequently, a single assessment instrument was used for mixed age and stage groups of subjects and, typically, only overall group mean scores and between-group mean differences were reported. Describing children in this manner conflicts with acceptable standards for testing developmental processes and differences between groups of children.

Many behavioral scientists and laypersons are familiar with Piaget's explanatory model of cognitive development during childhood (Piaget, 1951, 1955, 1963, 1970). We can outline his model here and speculate how the cognitive processes of children developing in families headed by alcoholics might develop into codependency.

Table 2: Assessments used on Children of Alcoholics 1963-1991

Adolescent Alcohol Involvement Scale-2
Bayley Scales of Infant Development-1
Beck Depression Inventory-1
Behavior Screening Questionnaire-1
Bender-Gestalt-1
Boyhood Competence Scale-1
California Psychological Inventory-1
Center for Epidemiology Studies-Depression-1
Chart Review-1
Child Functioning Questionnaire-1
Child Behavior Checklist (CBCL)-3
Childhood History MBD Checklist-2
Childhood Symptom Checklist-1
Children of Alcoholics Screening Test-4
Children of Alcoholics Family Role Instrument-1
Children of Alcoholic Life-Events Schedule-2
Children's Depression Inventory-1
Connors Teacher Rating Scale-3
Coopersmith Self-Esteem Inventory-1
Detroit Tests of Learning Aptitude-2
Developmental Questionnaire-1
Devereux Child/Adolescent Behavior Rating Scale-2
Diagnostic Interview for Children/Adolescents-1
Dimensions of Temperament Survey-2
Drinking Experience/Style Questionnaire-1
Emotional Problem Scale-1
Family Environment Scale-3
Feelings of Inadequacy Ratings-1
General Life Events Schedule for Children-1
Health and Daily Living Form-1
Herjanic Diagnostic Interview for Children/Adolescents-2

Law problems, self report-1
Lorge-Thorndike Intelligence Tests-1
Matching Familiar Figures Tests-1
Matthews Youth Test for Health-2
Minnesota Multiphasic Personality Inventory-2
Minnesota Counseling Inventory-1
Myklebust Pupil Rating Scale-1
Needs Assessment-1
Nowicki-Strickland Locus of Control-3
Otis-Lennon Mental Abilities Test-1
Peabody Picture Vocabulary Test(PPVT)-2
Peabody Individual Achievement Test(PIAT)-4
Perceived Competence for Children-2
Personal Orientation Inventory-1
Personality Inventory for Children-1
Personality Questionnaire-1
Physical Health Scale-1
Piers-Harris Children's Self Concept Scale-1
Pittsburgh Initial Neuropsychology Test System-2
Primary Mental Abilities Test-1
Profile of Mood States-1
Project Competence Interview-1
Reasons for Drinking Scale-1
Rosenberg Self-Esteem Scales-3
Rutgers Health and Human Development Questionnaire-1
School records or problems-5
Stanford Binet-1
Strauss Conflict Tactics Scale-1
Tridimensional Personality Questionnaire-1
Videotapes of Angry and Positive Interactions-1
Wechsler-Bellevue IQ-1

High School Personality Questionnaire-1
Home Environment Interview for Children-1
Hopkins Symptom Checklist-4
Interviews developed by author for the study-2
Iowa Tests of Educational Development-1
Jenkins Activity Survey-2
Junior Eysenck Personality Inventory-1

What child would do to use AOD questionnaire-1
Wide Range Achievement Test-4
Williams Temperance and Intemperance Scales-1
WISCR or WAISR-4
Youth Self Report-1

This is a list of assessment instruments used on CoAs which were derived from the studies in Table 1. The numbers after the instrument indicate how many studies reported using it in their study.

Further, we can speculate how such adaptations are both normal (i.e., common) and predictable products of typical cognitive processes.

A Cognitive Developmental Framework

Piaget describes how the different ways of knowing and acting on the environment (e.g., cognitive development) change in a systematic fashion as children grow older. In his model, cognitive development is viewed as a natural progressive process, one motivated by the child's innate tendency to organize experiences and adapt to predictable environmental events according to the typical cognitive structures of each developmental stage. As described by Piaget, cognitive developmental stages occur in a hierarchical sequence: sensorimotor, preoperations, concrete operations, and formal operations.

While most people remember best Piaget's (1963) sequence of stages, he described the **process** of cognitive change that influences the ways children come to know about themselves and their world. To Piaget it is the mechanism of change, the movement from and through each stage, that is crucial to understanding the developmental course. Measuring this progress across and through stages is difficult and while it may be convenient to divide development into stages, development is a continuum that may not be linear, but instead consist of minor oscillations. These minor oscillations propel the course of cognitive progress, which proceeds by self-regulation, coordination, and equilibrium (Flavell, 1963). Equilibrium refers to the tendency for children to adapt to events, people, and objects in the environment to create a balance between oneself and the environment. When a child experiences an unfamiliar or unpredicted event, the motivation for regaining equilibrium propels change as the child experiences a 'beneficial perturbation' (Flavell, 1977), or disequilibrium. For example, a child can experience disequilibrium when his/her alcoholic parent behaves in a deviant way. Disequilibrium produces a state of cognitive conflict, which the child resolves by cognitively restructuring reality: parents are people who get mad, scare their own children, or fall down and go to sleep.

Adapting to the objects, events, and people in the environment through cognitive organization and reorganization occurs with two complementary processes: assimilation and accommodation. Assimilation and accommodation happen simultaneously and often without the conscious awareness of the individual. When children assimilate something, they adapt the external stimuli to their own existing cognitive structures (or patterns of reality); when they accommodate, they adapt their cognitive structures (i.e., reality) to include the new stimuli. Thus, through assimilation, the events, people, or objects in the environment are interpreted according to the ways one already thinks about things (Flavell, 1977). For example, when children first encounter objects or events never before experienced, they will try to change them into something they have already experienced and are familiar with, regardless of the properties of the object. For example, an alcoholic parent who has drunk him or herself into unconsciousness is thought to be asleep due to fatigue. In this way, the child acts on the object or event in a manner that is already familiar to their repertoire.

In the process of accommodation, however, existing cognitive structures must be adjusted to new experiences that don't 'fit in'. In the case of the child experiencing a new object, event, or person, their behavioral repertoire is adjusted; if the adult reacts unexpectedly due to the child's actions (e.g., a drunk parent who slaps a child who approaches seeking attention), the child learns about new properties of this person and adjusts his or her behavioral repertoire to include new ways of acting (e.g., when a parent has been drinking alcohol and looks or talks in a different way, the child learns to avoid the parent).

In summary, assimilation and accommodation, occurring simultaneously in order to establish equilibrium in the face of cognitive conflict (disequilibrium), happen with each familiar and unfamiliar experience of an object, event, or person. Disequilibrium, or cognitive conflict, produces a state of cognitive tension which the child is driven to resolve through further cognitive exploration. Each time a child confronts an experience, the way in which they understand the event is, in part, shaped by their current cognitive structures. That is, they bend (or even distort) reality so as to make it fit within current modes of cognitive organization. Healthy children, including COAs, can even come to create a reality that cannot be shared or understood by children who have a different experiential history. In this way a balance is maintained in their representation of the world. However, as objects, events, or people are physically or mentally manipulated, current modes of cognitive organization are also modified by the experience. Hence, although we alter reality to fit with our present cognitive structures, our cognitive structures can be altered slightly to fit with new aspects of the world.

Constructivism in COAs

In Piaget's model, development is seen as a self-generated cycle. Children therefore are not seen as passive recipients of information, but rather actively construct or build their conception of the world through both physical and mental manipulations. The child, while constructing reality, is not passively absorbing an adult's conceptualization of reality nor passively replicating it, but actually constructing it according to his or her own interpretation and particular stage of cognitive development. Depending upon the stage of development and the sequence of experiences, children's concepts of things vary according to the characteristics of that stage. Different stages of cognitive development are characterized by some types of thinking that often appear illogical, inaccurate, and fanciful; yet this type of thinking is quite normal (i.e., Piaget, 1951). For example, a preschooler may interpret a drunk parent's talking to an unseen person as the same kind of imaginary friend that preschoolers like to play with.

The imagination and fanciful thinking of childhood serves many purposes. In general, though, imagination (or fanciful thinking) is one way children mentally explore the attributes of potential events without actually acting them out. Such cognitive exploration can serve as an expression of cognitive mastery, the feeling of accomplishment derived from engaging in and mastering difficult problem solving tasks. The importance of this activity has been repeatedly emphasized in the literature (Asarnow, Carlson & Guthrie, 1987; Freedman et al. 1978). The ability to problem solve is also considered to be an essential part of resilience; it is the ability to recover effective functioning after experiencing negative consequences of living (Rolf et al., 1990). Werner (1986) describes resilient children as those children who actively solve problems in the face of considerable adversity. Werner (1984) also suggests that one of the four central characteristics of resiliency is an active, evocative approach toward solving life's problems which enables the child to successfully understand and reinterpret emotionally hazardous experiences during development.

Active problem solving is expressed differently at different ages and its measurement would require different tools across stages. Six to 12 year old children think things out concretely; they'll try to work out complex problems with specific examples and not hypothetical constructs symbolic of a generalized category of a problem. For example, when COAs in the stage of concrete operations want to solve the problems of their alcoholic parents, they will do so concretely. They pour the wine out of the bottle so there is none to drink; they may clean the house or cook the food when the parents neglect caretaking duties. These COAs become problem solvers through physical activities. In the stage of formal operations (12 years and older), however, COAs are able to hypothesize about the problems resulting from parental behaviors and therefore are able to mentally manipulate a range of possible causes and solutions for the problems; they are not tied to the here and now of concrete solutions. COAs in this stage may try to listen to the parents' interpretations of their problems and suggest numerous 'what if' problem solving solutions. Their minds become a workshop of problem solving strategies (Siegler & Jenkins, 1989).

Active problem solving is one of the most important self-regulated protective processes available to a child in a truly dysfunctional household. Active problem solving helps the child in his/her attempts to cope with adversity. When problem solving is successful, it resolves cognitive conflict, which, in turn, establishes internal equilibrium, if only for a little while. The generalization of a successful problem solving strategy learned during childhood in an alcoholic household to other situations may prove maladaptive or dysfunctional. Not all problem solving strategies that COAs learn will be appropriate to generalize to non-alcoholic environments. Compensating for an alcoholic parent's behavior may have been necessary for a young COA to grow up, but continuing this behavior into adulthood may prove problematic. For example, an adult COA who compensates for a new companion's problematic behaviors may reinforce 'codependency' and prevent further development of competence in both individuals.

The point being made is that cognitive activity, and hence, problem solving, is necessary for the resolution of cognitive conflict. The **absence** of problem solving activity in childhood may be a risk factor for future depression. All children need to discover which strategies work effectively, which don't, and where newly discovered strategies are appropriate and inappropriate (Siegler & Jenkins, 1989). The structure of cognitive activity for children of alcoholics and non-alcoholics is the same; the challenge is to discover the appropriate assessment methods that demonstrate that it is the functionality of the problem solving strategy that is different.

III. Applying a Developmental Framework to the Assessment of COAs

This review of the literature suggests that the assessments used on COAs, to date, have been somewhat deficient in their relevance to developmental processes associated with hypothesized risk factors for future psychopathology and substance abuse. The good news, however, is that the assessment process has recently become more scientifically systematic and less anecdotal. This is partially a result of evolving progress in the assessment field, and partially a result of examining the available information on COAs and recognizing the complexity of etiological processes. The next steps in deciding on adequate assessment strategies for COAs will most likely consider complex issues related to the embeddedness of problem behaviors in different contexts at different ages.

How to do it: Caveats

Zucker and Fitzgerald (1991) suggest that adopting a developmental methodology will help us understand adaptive functioning in COAs, how early maladaptive behaviors are created, and the contexts in which they appear, linger, and diminish. However, how does one adequately and operationally define a source of risk for a COA given the possibility of the existence of multiple genetic processes and environmental changes that may interact at any point? We list five consequences of adopting a developmental framework for assessing COAs:

1. **Individual Differences** Through the individual and systematic assessment of COAs, individual patterns, styles, or strategies of cognitive organization may be identified that differentiate COAs from children of non-alcoholics within or across developmental stages. Thus, measuring the individual child's adaptability or adaptation to objects, events, and people, and not necessarily with norms and group averages, is necessary.

2. **Attention to Developmental Assessment** Children who come from dysfunctional homes may respond differently to problem solving tasks, interview questions, and people, depending upon where the assessment is performed or the perceived threat of the alcoholic parent's interpretation of the elicited response. Developmental

change precludes simple and unitary assessment procedures in children of different stages and ages; a particular test appropriate at one age is not necessarily appropriate at another. Younger children do not understand tests using abstract symbolic concepts. Similarly, younger children must be asked questions with simpler language. Furthermore, assessments purporting to measure the feelings and behaviors through the child's verbal responses are not always sufficiently representative of the target phenomena that may occur in their natural environment.

3. **Continuity and Discontinuity** It may be necessary to evaluate the dynamic process of developmental continuity and discontinuities of the target behavior being assessed. How many assessment occasions are adequate to measure stability and instability of behaviors across time or circumstance? Assessing behavior many times would also allow us to look at the turning points of certain behaviors and answer the question of whether or not critical periods exist.

4. **Interacting Risk Factors** Converging evidence about social, behavioral, and health problems has suggested that many negative behavioral outcomes are interrelated (Donovan & Jessor, 1985; Hundleby, 1987; Jessor & Jessor, 1977). Be cautious in believing that the chosen sub-set of promising variables selected for measurement will be sufficient to test an etiological model adequately. Much depends upon knowledge of previously significant findings, our own training and biases, and the theoretically based hypotheses influencing the research procedures (Johnson & Rolf, 1990). Since adaptation involves complex processes resulting from the interplay of personal and environmental factors, a good assessment would include the assessment of many domains of behavior over time.

5. **Resilience** Many clinicians and researchers are seeking to understand the meaning of resilience, especially in the lives of children of alcoholics (Cowen et al. 1991; Cowen & Work, 1988; Garmezy & Tellegen, 1984; Rolf et al. 1990; Werner, 1989; Werner & Smith, 1982). With the exception of work of Emmy Werner, measurement of resilience in COAs has been overlooked. The writings of Garmezy and Werner provide useful clues to assessment.

What to Assess?

Zucker and Fitzgerald (1991) suggest that the literature has shown six separate areas that indicate causal links of risk for alcoholism among adolescent children of alcoholics. Perhaps it is to these areas we should first look:

1. Antisocial behavior or aggressive activity;

2. Difficulty in achievement-related activity, such as poorer school performance or less productivity in high school;

3. Diminished or deficient affiliative behaviors. For example, males who later become alcoholic are more loosely connected to others. The data has shown interpersonal deficits (less dependent, less considerate, less accepting of dependency), greater likelihood of leaving home early, and being more indifferent to mothers and siblings as a teenager;

4. Presence of increased marital conflict in the parental home;

5. Dysfunctional parent-child interaction (e.g., inadequate or lax parental supervision, lack of parental interest or affection for child, or inadequate contact) and

6. Inadequate role models.

In addition to measuring degree of risk, we also need to examine the emergence and development of protective processes and problem solving strategies that COAs use in the face of adversity. Cowen and his colleagues (1991) suggest that a triad of protective factors is associated with stress resilient children that include: (1) the child's positive temperament and disposition; (2) a close, warm family relationship; (3) extrafamilial support (e.g., teachers, clergy). Perhaps, again, it is to these three areas we should look to examine the potential protective factors among COAs.

What to Use?

On a more technical level, assessment of children of alcoholics requires a thoughtful selection from available assessment tools. Achenbach and McConaughy (1987) recommend the following psychometric principles to aid in measurement decisions: (1) employ standardized procedures; (2) use multiple, aggregate items to sample each targeted aspect of functioning; (3) use measures permitting normative age appropriate reference groups; and (4) use psychometrically sound measure which have demonstrated reliability and validity within the targeted subject's developmental stage and specific age group. To these we add:

(1) Follow the principles set forth in the Standards for Educational and Psychological Testing (APA, 1986);

(2) Leave test construction to those who know how to implement proper psychometric procedures. Even though new measures and assessments for children appear with regularity in the literature (Cowen et al. 1991; Rohrbeck, Azar, & Wagner, 1991; Silverman et al. 1991), it is best to wait for reports on validity and reliability before using them.

(3) Use trained personnel to perform the assessment. As Johnson and Rolf (1990) suggest, interpersonal interactions with the COA could confound the results of any test. In a good testing session, it is the child's response to the task at hand, and not their response to the ability of the experimenter, that is desired.

(4) Listen without prejudice. In an area that attends so closely to what the child and the parent has to say, it is important to listen without giving away answers; thus, when interviewing children, probe their thinking without making their verbal reports something you want or expect to hear.

Broadband Screening Tools

The National Institute on Drug Abuse has developed the Adolescent Assessment/Referral System (AARS) (NIDA, 1987), an assessment tool limited to youth aged 12 to 19 (see Tarter, 1990 for a complete description). The first phase consists of a problem screening tool, the Problem Oriented Screening Instrument for Teenagers (POSIT), a 139 item screen designed to identify problems in need of further assessment in ten functional areas (substance use, behavior patterns, health status, psychiatric disorder, social skills, family system, school adjustment, work, peer relationships, and leisure/recreation). It is a good screen, but the POSIT itself does not provide comprehensive assessment; instead, it will indicate if further, in-depth assessment is required in any of the ten functional areas.

Comprehensive Assessment Battery

The AARS has compiled a Comprehensive Assessment Battery, a battery of instruments for each of the ten areas selected on the basis of recommendations of national experts in adolescent assessment and treatment. Table 3 presents the CAB recommended assessment tools for each of the ten functional areas addressed by the AARS. The AARS manual provides descriptions of the instruments, along with information on how to obtain them, administration time, and cost.

The Need for Alternative Approaches to Creating an Assessment Package for COAs

Findings from published research have generally pointed to the insufficiency of single cause explanatory accounts of problem behaviors in children (Searles and Windle, 1991). Multifactorial models appear more relevant but require more and better measurement of their constructs. Other than the tests recommended in the AARS, several others are specific to the problems of COAs and also fulfill the criteria of Achenbach and McGonaughy (1987). Using their developmental framework for assessment, five axes are proposed in Table 4, Appendix A: parent reports, teacher reports, cognitive assessment, physical assessment, and direct assessment of the child. For COAs, we add a sixth axis, the assessment of processes contributing to resiliency. In Appendix A we present some measures for consideration for these six axes relevant to the latter two stages of cognitive development: concrete operations (6 to 12 year-olds) and formal operations (12 year-olds and older). We also recognize that defining any assessment battery is a considerable task requiring consideration of many viewpoints; we present this as a preliminary framework for starting purposes only.

What is needed are consensus building workshops with COA researchers, clinicians, and expert advisors to outline the ideal assessment battery for COAs. Understanding the COA's construction of reality, the process of change, problem solving strategies used in the resolution of cognitive conflict, and the child's adaptation to a dysfunctional household will need to be explored with developmental techniques. The laboratory assessment process ignores the contextual embeddedness of the child's responses (Zucker and Fitzgerald, 1991). Contextual embeddedness, referring to the interweaving of context and child, is an important variable in understanding how and where the COA's behavior is stable or unstable. This is especially important in trying to understand the behavior of children who might change the way they behave according to the context of their response; more specifically, COAs may change their responses

Table 3: Comprehensive Assessment Battery Tools from the AARS

Functional Area	Specific Measures
Substance Use/Abuse	Personal Experience Inventory Adolescent Diagnostic Interview
Physical Health Status	Physical examination and lab work Physician Report Form
Mental Health Status	Diagnostic Interview Schedule for Children Brief Symptom Inventory
Family Relationships	Family Assessment Measure Parent-Adolescent Relationship Questionnaire
Peer Relations	Piers Harris Self-Concept Scale Behavior Problem Checklist
Educational Status	WAIS-R, WISC-R Woodcock-Johnson Psychoeducational Test Battery
Vocational Status	Career Maturity Inventory Generalizable Skills Curriculum
Social Skills	Social Skills Rating System Matson Evaluation of Social Skills with Youngsters
Leisure and Recreation	Social Adjustment Inventory for Children and Adolescents Leisure Diagnostic Battery Physical Activity Assessment
Aggressive Behavior/ Delinquency	Youth Self-Report National Youth Survey Delinquency Scale

Table 4: Multiaxial Assessment

Age Range	Axis 1	Axis 2	Axis 3	Axis 4	Axis 5	Axis 6
	Parent Reports	Teacher Reports	Cognitive Assessment	Physical Assessment	Direct Observation	Resilience
6 to 11	CBCL Dev. Hx. DICA HEIC LEQ-P	TRF School Records PIAT	WISC-III WRAT-R (Level 1)	Modified Physician-Report Form	Jr. Eysenck LEQ-C Perceived Comp. YSR (11 year olds) CDI (8 to 15) STAIC DICA Alcohol/Drug Hx.	HEIC
12 to 18	CBCL Dev. Hx DICA HEIC LEQ-P	TRF School Records	WISC-III (to 16) WAIS-R (after 16) WRAT-R (Level 2) PIAT	Physician-Report Form	HSPQ LEQ-A (14 to 19) Perceived Comp. YSR (11 to 18) BDI (after 16) STAIC DICA PEI	HEIC

according to the context of the alcoholic parents' behavior or expectation in order to avoid trauma or abuse. We believe that a novel assessment for COAs is necessary that will integrate the clinician's understanding of the COA's behavior according to the context of the alcoholic home and the researcher's need for proper psychometrics.

References

Achenbach, T.M. (1978). *The Child Behavior Profile, I: boys aged 6-11. Journal of Consulting and Clinical Psychology, 46, 478-488.*

Achenbach, T.M., and Edelbrock, C.S. (1979). *The Child Behavior Profile II: boys aged 12-16 and girls aged 6-11 and 12-16. Journal of Consulting and Clinical Psychology, 47, 223-233.*

Achenbach, T.M, and Edelbrock, C. (1987). *Manual for the Youth Self-Report and Profile. Burlington, VT: University of Vermont Department of Psychiatry.*

Achenbach, T.M., and Edelbrock, C. (1986). *Manual for the Teacher's Report Form and Teacher Version of the Child Behavior Profile. Burlington, VT: University of Vermont, Department of Psychiatry.*

Achenbach, T.M. and McConaughy, S.H. (1987). *Empirically based assessment of child and adolescent psychopathology: Practical applications. Newbury Park, CA: Sage Publications.*
Adler, R., & Raphael, B. (1983). *Children of alcoholics. Australian and New Zealand Journal of Psychiatry, 17, 3-8.*

American Psychological Association. (1986). *Standards for Educational and Psychological Testing. Washington, DC: American Psychological Association.*

Aronson, H., and Gilbert, A. (1963). *Preadolescent sons of male alcoholics. Archives of General Psychiatry, 3, 235-241.*

Aronson, M., Kyllerman, M., Sabel, K.G., Sandin, B., and Olegard, R. (1985). *Children of alcoholic families. Acta Paediatrica Scandinavica, 74, 27-35.*

Asarnow, J., Carlson, G., and Guthrie, D. (1987). *Coping strategies, self-perceptions,hopelessness, and perceived family environments in depressed and suicidal children. Journal of Consulting and Clinical Psychology, 55, 361-366.*

Austin, G., & Prendergast, M. (1991). *Children of substance abusers. Prevention Research Update, 8(Winter), 1-67.*

Ballard, M., and Cummings, E.M. (1991). Response to adults' angry behavior in children of alcoholic and nonalcoholic parents. Journal of Genetic Psychology, 151(2), 195-209.

Beck, A.T. and Beamesderfer, A. (1974). Psychological measurements in psychopharmacology. In P. Pichot (ed.), Modern problems in pharmacopsychiatry, 7, (pp. 151-169), Paris:Karger.

Beck, A.T., and Beck, R.W. (1972). Screening depressed patients in family practice: A rapid technique. Postgraduate Medicine, 52, 81-85.

Bell, B., and Cohen, R. (1981). The Bristol Social Adjustment Guide: Comparison between the offspring of alcoholic and non-alcoholic mothers. British Journal of Clinical Psychology, 20, 93-95.

Bennett, L.A., Wolin, S.J., and Reiss, D. (1988). Cognitive, behavioral, and emotional problems among school-age children of alcoholic parents. American Journal of Psychiatry, 145(2), 185-190.

Callan, V.J., and Jackson, D. (1986). Children of alcoholic fathers and recovered alcoholic fathers: Personal and family functioning. Journal of Studies on Alcohol, 47(2), 180-182.

Cattell, R.B., Cattell, M.D., and Johns, E. (1984). Manual and norms for the High School Personality Questionnaire. Champaign, Ill: Institute for Personality and Ability Testing.

Chafetz, M.E., Blane, H.T., and Hill, M.J. (1971). Children of alcoholics: Observations in a child guidance clinic. Quarterly Journal of Studies on Alcohol, 32, 687-698.

Cloninger, C.R., Sigvardsson, S., and Bohman, M. (1988). Childhood personality predicts alcohol abuse in young adults. Alcoholism: Clinical and Experimental Research, 12(4), 494-505.

Corder, B.F., McRee, C., and Rohrer, H. (1984). A brief review of literature on daughters of alcoholic fathers. North Carolina Journal of Mental Health, 10(20), 37-43.

Cork, R.M. (1969). The Forgotten Children: A Study of Children with Alcoholic Parents. Toronto, Addiction Research Foundation: Don Mills, General Publishing.

Cowen, P.A. (1978). Piaget with Feeling: Cognitive, Social, and Emotional Dimensions. New York: Holt, Rinehart and Winston.

Cowen, E.L., and Work, W.C. (1988). Resilient children, psychological wellness and primary prevention. American Journal of Community Psychology, 16, 591-607.

Cowen, E.L., Work, W.C., Hightower, A.D., Wyman, P.A., Parker, G.R., and Lotyczewski, B.S. (1991). *Toward the development of a measure of perceived self-efficacy in children. Journal of Clinical Child Psychology, 20(2), 169-178.*

de Mendonca, M.M., de Matos, A.P., da Costa Matta, A. (1978). *Poor scholastic performance in children of alcoholic fathers. Joral da Sociedade de Ciencias Medicas de Lisboa, 142(1-2), 67-96.*

Drake, R.E., and Vaillant, G.E. (1988). *Predicting alcoholism and personality disorder in a 33-year longitudinal study of children of alcoholics. British Journal of Addiction, 83, 799-807.*

Donovan, J.E., and Jessor, R. (1985). *Structure of problem behavior in adolescence and young adulthood. Journal of Consulting and Clinical Psychology, 53, 890-904.*

Dunn, L.M. (1965). *Peabody Individual Achievement Test. American Guidance Service, Inc.*

Earls, F., Reich, W., Jung, K.G., and Cloninger, C.R. (1988). *Psychopathology in children of alcoholic an antisocial parents. Alcoholism: Clinical and Experimental Research, 12(4), 481-487.*

el-Guebaly, N. (1986). *Risk research in affective disorders and alcoholism: Epidemiological surveys and trait markers. Canadian Journal of Psychiatry, 31, 352-361.*

el-Guebaly, N., and Offord, D.R. (1977). *The offspring of alcoholics: A critical review. American Journal of Psychiatry, 134, 357-365.*

el-Guebaly, N., and Offord, D.R. (1979). *On being the offspring of an alcoholic: An update. Alcoholism: Clinical and Experimental Research, 3(2), 148-157.*

el-Guebaly, N., Offord, D., Sullivan, K., & Lynch, G. (1978). *Psychosocial adjustment of the offspring of psychiatric inpatients. Canadian Psychiatric Association Journal, 23, 281-291.*

Ervin, C.S., Little, R.E., Streissguth, A.P., and Beck, D.E. (1984). *Alcoholic fathering and it's relation to child's intellectual development: A pilot investigation. Alcoholism: Clinical and Experimental Research, 8(4), 362-365.*

Eysenck, S.B.G. (1968). *Manual for the Junior Eysenck Personality Inventory. San Diego, CA: Educational and Industrial Testing Service.*

Fine, E., Yudin, L., Holmes, L., and Heinemann, S. (1976). Behavioral disorders in children with parental alcoholism. Annals of the New York Academy of Sciences, 273, 507-517.

Flavell, J. (1963). The Developmental Psychology of Jean Piaget. New York: D. Van Nostrand Company, Inc.

Flavell, J. (1977). Cognitive Development. Englewood Cliffs, New Jersey: Prentice-Hall.

Freedman, B., Donahoe, C., Rosenthal, L., Schlundt, D., and McFall, R. (1978). A social-behavioral analysis of skill deficits in delinquent and nondelinquent boys. Journal of Consulting and Clinical Psychology, 46, 1448-1462.

Galanter, M. (1991). Recent Developments in Alcoholism, Volume 9, Children of Alcoholics. New York:Plenum Press.

Garmezy, N. (1985). Revision of the Life Events Questionnaire. Unpublished manuscript, University of Minnesota.

Garmezy, N. (1987). Scoring the Adolescent Life Events Questionnaire. Unpublished manuscript, University of Minnesota.

Garmezy, N. and Tellegen, A. (1984). Studies of stress-resistant children: Methods, variables and preliminary findings. In F. Morrison, C. Ford, and D. Deating (eds.), Advances in applied developmental psychology (Vol. 1) (pp. 1-52). New York: Academic Press.

Haberman, P.W. (1966). Childhood symptoms in children of alcoholics and comparison group parents. Journal of Marriage and the Family, 28(2), 152-154.

Harter, S. (1985). Manual for the Self-Perception Profile for Children. University of Denver.

Hegedus, A., Alterman, A., and Tarter, R. (1984). Learning achievement in sons of alcoholics. Alcoholism: Clinical and Experimental Research, 8(3), 330-333.

Herjanic, B., and Campbell, W. (1977). Differentiating psychiatrically disturbed children on the basis of a structured interview. Journal of Abnormal Child Psychology, 5, 127-134.

Hundleby, J.D. (1987). Adolescent drug use in a behavioral matrix: A confirmation and comparison of the sexes. Addictive Behaviors, 12, 103-112.

Hughes, J.M. (1977). Adolescent children of alcoholic parents and the relationship of Alateen to the children. Journal of Consulting and Clinical Psychology, 45, 946-947.

Jacob, T., and Leonard, K. (1986). Psychosocial functioning in children of alcoholic fathers, depressed fathers, and control fathers. Journal of Studies on Alcohol, 47(5), 373-380.

Jastak, S., and Wilkinson, G.A. (1984). The Wide Range Achievement Test-Revised. Wilmington, DE: Jastak Associates.

Jessor, R., and Jessor, S.L. (1977). Problem Behavior and Psychosocial Development: A Longitudinal Study of Youth. New York: Academic Press.

Johnson, J.L., and Bennett, L.A. (1988). School-aged children of alcoholics: Theory and research. Center of Alcohol Studies Pamphlet Series, Alcohol Research Documentation, Inc, New Brunswick, NJ.

Johnson, J.L., and Rolf, J.E. (1988). Cognitive functioning in children from alcoholic and non-alcoholic families. British Journal of Addictions, 83, 849-857.

Johnson, J.L., and Rolf, J.E. (1990). When children change. In: Collins, R.L., Leonard, KE, Searles, J5 (eds)., Alcohol and the Family Research and Clinical Perspectives. New York, Guilford Press, pp. 162-193.

Johnson, J.L., Sher, K.J., Rolf, J.E. (1991). An overview of models of vulnerability to psychopathology in children of alcoholics. Alcohol, Health, and Research World, 15(1).

Johnson, S., Leonard, K.E., and Jacob, T. (1989). Drinking, drinking styles and drug use in children of alcoholics, depressives and controls. Journal of Studies on Alcohol, 50(5), 427-431.

Kammeier, M.L. (1971). Adolescents from families with and without alcohol problems. Quarterly Journal of Studies on Alcohol, 32(2), 364-372.

Kern, J.C., Hassett, C.A., Collipp, P.J., Bridges, C., Solomon, M., Condren, R.J. (1981). Children of alcoholics: Locus of control, mental age, and zinc level. Journal of Psychiatric Treatment and Evaluation, 3, 169-173.

Knop, J., Teasdale, T., Schulsinger, F., and Goodwin, D. (1985). A prospective study of young men at high risk for alcoholism: School behavior and achievement, Journal of Studies on Alcohol, 46, 273-278.

Kovacs, M. (1983). The children's depression inventory: A self-rated depression scale for school-aged youngsters. (Unpublished manuscript, University of Pittsburgh School of Medicine).

Kovacs, M. and Beck, A.T. (1977). An empirical clinical approach toward a definition of childhood depression. In J.G. Schulterbrandt & A. Raskin (Eds.), Depression in childhood: Diagnosis, treatment, and conceptual models. New York: Raven Press.

Lemoine, P., Harousseau, H., Borteyru, J.P., and Menuet (1968). Children of alcoholic parents: Abnormalities observed in 127 cases. Paris, Ouest Medical, Vol 21, 476-482

Marcus, A.M. (1986). Academic achievement in elementary school children of alcoholic mothers. Journal of Clinical Psychology, 35, 63-78.

Manning, D.T., Balson, P.M., and Xenakis, S. (1986). The prevalence of Type A personality in the children of alcoholics. Alcoholism: Clinical and Experimental Research, 10(2), 184-189.

Miketic, B. (1972). The influence of parental alcoholism in the development of mental disturbances of children. Alcoholism, 8, 135-139.

Miller, D., & Jang, M. (1977). Children of alcoholics: A 20-year longitudinal study. Social Work Research Abstracts, 13(4), 23-29.

Moos, R., & Billings, A. (1982). Children of alcoholics during the recovery process: Alcoholic and matched control families. Addictive Behaviors, 7, 155-163.

Nannis, E.D. (1988). Cognitive-developmental differences in emotional understanding. In: Nannis, E.D., and Cowan, P.A. (eds). Developmental Psychopathology and its Treatment. San Francisco:Jossey Bass, pp. 31-50.

National Institute on Drug Abuse (1987). The Adolescent Assessment/ Referral System Manual. Unpublished manuscript available from L. Rahdert, NIDA, Division of Clinical Research, 5600 Fishers Lane, Room 10A-30, Rockville, MD, 20857.

Nylander, I., and Rydelius, P.A. (1982). A comparison between children of alcoholic fathers from excellent versus poor social conditions. Acta Paediatrica Scandinavica, 71, 809-813.

Pandina, R.J., and Johnson, V. (1989). Familial drinking history as a predictor of alcohol and drug consumption among adolescent children. Journal of Studies on Alcohol, 50(3), 245-253.

Piaget, J. (1928). Judgment and Reasoning in the Child. New York: Harcourt & Brace.

Piaget, J. (1951). Play, Dreams, and Imitation in Childhood. New York:Norton.

Piaget, J. (1955). The Child's Construction of Reality. New York: Routledge and Kegan Paul.

Piaget, J. (1963). The Origins of Intelligence in Children. New York: Norton and Company.

Piaget, J. (1970). Genetic Epistemology. New York: Norton and Company.

Plant, M.A., Orford, J., and Grant, M. (1989). The effects on children and adolescents of parents excessive drinking: An international review. Public Health Records, 104(5), 433-442.

Prewett, M.J., Spence, R., and Chaknis, M. (1981). Attribution of Causality by Children with Alcoholic Parents. The International Journal of the Addictions, 16(2), 367-370.

Reich, W., and Earls, F.J. (1982). The Home Environment Interview for Children. Child and Parent Versions. St. Louis, Washington University.

Reich, W., Herjanic, B., Wilner, Z., and Ghandy, P.R. (1982). Development of a structured psychiatric interview for children. Agreement on diagnosis comparing child and parent interviews. Journal of Abnormal Child Psychology, 10, 325-336.

Rhodes, J., and Blackham, G.J. (1987). Differences in character roles between adolescents from alcoholic and nonalcoholic homes. American Journal of Drug and Alcohol Abuse, 13(1 & 2), 145-155.

Rohrbeck, C.A., Azar, S.T., and Wagner, P.E. (1991). Child self-control rating scale: Validation of a child self-report measure. Journal of Clinical Child Psychology, 20(2), 179-183.

Rolf, J.E., Masten, A.S., Cicchetti, D., Nuechterlein, K.H., Weintraub, S. (1990). Risk and Protective Factors in the Development of Psychopathology. New York: Oxford University Press.

Rolf, J., Johnson, J.L., Israel, E., Baldwin, J., and Chandra, A. (1988). Depressive affect in school-aged children of alcoholics. British Journal of Addiction, 83, 841-848.

Roosa, M.W., Beals, J., Sandler, I.N., Pillow, D.R. (1990). The role of risk and protective factors in predicting symptomatology in adolescent self-identified children of alcoholic parents. American Journal of Community Psychology, 18(5), 725-741.

Roosa, M.W., Sandler, I.N., Beals, J., and Short, J.L. (1988). Risk status of adolescent children of problem-drinking parents. American Journal of Community Psychology, 16(2), 225-239.

Roosa, M.W., Sandler, I.N., Gehring, M., Beals, J., and Cappo, L. (1988). The Children of Alcoholics Life-Events Schedule: A stress scale of children of alcohol abusing parents. Journal of Studies on Alcohol, 49(5), 422-429.

Rubio-Stipec, M., Bird, H., Canino, G., Bravo, M., and Alegria, M. (1991). Children of alcoholic parents in the community. Journal of Studies on Alcohol, 52(1), 78-88.

Russell, M. (1991). Prevalence of alcoholism among children of alcoholics. In Windle, M., Searles, J.S. (eds) Children of Alcoholics: Critical Perspectives. New York: Guilford Press, pp 9-38.

Russell, M., Henderson, C., and Blume, S. (1985). Children of alcoholics: A review of the literature. New York: Children of Alcoholics Foundation, Inc.

Rydelius, P.A. (1981). Children of alcoholic fathers: Their social adjustment and their health status over 20 years. Acta Paediatrica Scandinavica: Supplement 286 to Vol. 70, 1-89.

Searles, J.S., and Windle, M. (1991). Introduction and overview: Salient issues in the children of alcoholics literature. In: Windle, M., Searles, J.S. (eds). Children of Alcoholics: Critical Perspectives, New York: Guilford Press, 1-8.

Sher, K.J. (in press). Children of Alcoholics. Chicago: Chicago University Press.

Shurygin, G.I. (1974). Characteristics of the mental development of children of chronic alcoholic mothers. Pediatriya, VII, 71-73.

Siegler, R.S., and Jenkins, E. (1989). How Children Discover New Strategies. Hillsdale, NJ: Lawrence Erlbaum Ass.

Silverman, W.K., Fleisig, W., Rabian, B., and Peterson, R.A. (1991). Childhood Anxiety Sensitivity Index. Journal of Clinical Child Psychology, 20(2), 162-168.

Speilberger, C.D. (1973). State-Trait Anxiety Inventory for Children: Preliminary Manual. Palo Alto, CA: Consulting Psychologists Press.

Steinhausen, H.C., Nestler, V., and Huth, H. (1982). Psychopathology and mental functions in the offspring of alcoholic and epileptic mothers. Journal of the American Academy of Child Psychiatry, 21(3), 268-273.

Stern, R., Kendall, A., Eberhard, P. (1991). Children of alcoholics in the schools: Where are they? Their representation in special education. Psychology in the Schools, 28, 116-123.

Tarter, R.E. (1990). Evaluation and treatment of adolescent substance abuse: A decision tree method. American Journal of Drug and Alcohol Abuse, 16(1 & 2), 1-46.

Tarter, R.E., Jacob, T., and Bremer, D.A. (1989). Cognitive status of sons of alcoholic men. Alcoholism: Clinical and Experimental Research, 13(2), 232-235.

Tarter, R.E., Hegedus, A.M., Gavaler, J.S. (1985). Hyperactivity in sons of alcoholics. Journal of Studies on Alcohol, 46(3), 259-261.

Tarter, R.E., Hegedus, A., Goldstein, G., Shelly, C., and Alterman, A. (1984). Adolescent sons of alcoholics: Neuropsychological and personality characteristics. Alcoholism: Clinical and Experimental Research, 8, 216-222.

Thalinger, D.J. and Kovanek, M.E. (1988). Children of alcoholics-At risk and unserved. A review of research and science roles for school psychologists. School Psychology Review, 17(1), 166-191.

von Knorring, A.L. (1991). Annotation: Children of alcoholics. Journal of Child Psychology and Psychiatry, 32(3), 411-421.

Warner, R.H., and Rosett, H.L. (1975). The effects of drinking on offspring. Journal of Studies on Alcohol, 36(11), 1395-1420.

Watters, T.S., and Theimer, W. (1978). Children of alcoholics: A critical review of some literature. Contemporary Drug Problems, Summer, 195-201.

Werner, E. (1984). Resilient children. Young Children, 40, 68-72.

Werner, E. (1989). High risk children in young adulthood: A longitudinal study from birth to 32 years. American Journal of Orthopsychiatry, 59, 72-81.

Werner, E.E. (1986). Resilient offspring of alcoholics: A longitudinal study from birth to age 18. Journal of Studies on Alcohol, 47, 34-40.

Werner, E.E., and Smith, R.S. (1982). Vulnerable but invincible: A study of resilient children. New York: McGraw-Hill.

West, M.O., and Prinz, R.J. (1987). Parental alcoholism and childhood psychopathology. Psychological Bulletin, 102(2), 204-218.

Whipple, S.C., and Noble, E.P. (1991). Personality Characteristics of alcoholic fathers and their sons. Journal of Studies on Alcohol, 52(4), 331-337.

Wilson, C. and Orford, J. (1978). Children of alcoholics: Report of a preliminary study and comments on the literature. Journal of Studies on Alcohol, 39, 121-142.

Windle, M. (1989). Children of alcoholics: A comprehensive bibliography. New York State Division of Alcoholism and Alcohol Abuse, Research Institute on Alcoholism.

Winters, K.C., and Henly, G.A. (1989). Personal Experience Inventory test and manual. Los Angeles: Western Psychological Services.

Zetterstrom, R., and Nylander, I. (1985). Children in families with alcohol abuse. In: U. Rydberg et al. (Eds). Alcohol and the Developing Brain. New York:Raven Press, 153-159.

Zucker, R.A., and Fitzgerald, H.E. (1991). Early developmental factors and risk for alcohol problems. Alcohol, Health, and Research World, 15(2), in press.

Appendix A

<u>From the child's perspective:</u>

1. Diagnosis

Diagnostic Interview for Children (DICA) (Reich, Herjanic, Wilmer, Ghandy, 1982). This interview elicits psychiatric symptoms in children and adolescents that permit 16 diagnoses to be made according to DSM-III criteria (ADD, oppositional disorder, conduct disorder, alcohol abuse, drug abuse, depression, separation anxiety disorder, over anxious disorder, phobia, gender, identity disorder, anorexia, bulimia, enuresis, encopresis, possible psychosis). There is also a parallel parent version.

2. Home Environment

Home Environment Interview for Children (HEIC) (Reich, Earls, Powell, 1988). This assesses the child's relationships with parents, siblings, relatives, and peers, and involvement in activities in and outside the home environment. It covers the child's school performance, discipline in the home, parents as role models, psychosocial stressors, and relationship to alcoholic parent.

3. Personality

High School Personality Questionnaire (HSPQ) (Cattell et al. 1984). The HSPQ addresses 14 primary personality characteristics.

Junior Eysenck Personality Inventory (Eysenck, 1963). This provides extraversion and neuroticism scales. It also has an adult analog.

4. Self Perception of Competence

Perceived Competence Scale for Children (PCSC) (Harter, 1979). This questionnaire produces six subscales: cognitive, physical, social, academic, and global.

5. Academic Performance

Wide Range Achievement Test-Revised (WRAT-R) (Jastak and Jastak, 19xx). Provides standardized grade level and age-normed percentiles scores for reading, spelling, and arithmetic.

6. Stress

Life Events Questionnaire-Child's Version (LEQ-C) (Garmezy, 1981). The LEQ is a questionnaire designed to measure the child's perception of stress in his/her life.

7. Intellectual Functioning

The Wechsler Intelligence Scale for Children-III or the Wechsler Adult Intelligence Scale-Revised (age 16 and above)

8. Self Perception of Behavior

Youth Self Report (YSR) (Achenbach and Edelbrock, 1987). A self report filled out by 11 to 18 year olds designed to assess competence and behavior problems.

9. Affect

Children's Depression Inventory (CDI) (Kovacs, 1983; Kovacs and Beck, 1977). The CDI is a self report of depression for youths aged 8 to 15.

Beck Depression Inventory (BDI) (Beck and Beck, 1972; Beck and Beamesderfer, 1974). A self report of depression for those aged 16 and older.

From the parent's perspective:

1. Child Behavior Checklist (CBCL) (Achenbach & Edelbrock, 1983). This checklist is comprised of 113 behavior problems and 20 competence items designed to be reported by parents of children ages 4 to 16 years. The items on the CBCL have been factor analyzed separately by sex for the age strata corresponding to preschool, grade school, and high school ages and have been normed according to clinic and non-clinic samples. The CBCL's factoring according to sex and age provides primary and secondary factor T-scores which are interpreted according to their percentile deviations from the reference groups. The CBCL measures the empirically derived syndromes listed in Table x.

2. Life Events Questionnaire-Parent's Version (LEQ-P) (Garmezy, 1981). The LEQ is a questionnaire designed to measure the parent's perception of stress in their child's life.

Breaking the Cycle of Addiction:
Prevention and Intervention with Children of Alcoholics

Ann W. Price, Ph.D.
James G. Emshoff, Ph.D.

Abstract

Research with children of alcoholics (COAs) has been used to design prevention and treatment programs for COAs. School programs are the most common intervention for COAs. Broad-based community programs are understudied, but have shown promise in alcohol and other drug prevention. Screening measures such as the CAST and the CAGE have been developed but are not widely utilized. Currently, most programs utilize a short-term, small group format. Interventions typically include information about alcoholism, problem and emotion-focused coping skills, and social and emotional support. COA interventions are reviewed, several of which demonstrate increased knowledge of program content, social-support, coping skills and emotional functioning among participants. Future research should include more rigorous studies that examine factors that mediate the exposure-adjustment relationship. The dissemination of research findings is an important, though often overlooked, step in the cycle between basic and applied research.

Factors Influencing Stress-Adjustment in COAs

Of the estimated 26.8 million COAs in the United States, nearly one-half are under the age of 18 (National Association for Children of Alcoholics (NACoA), 1998). COAs are at greater risk for a host of behavioral and emotional problems, including addiction. An estimated 13 to 25% of all COAs are likely to become alcoholic themselves (NACoA, 1998). Furthermore, children of alcoholics are at risk of developing a variety of behavioral and emotional problems including higher-than-normal rates of depression, anxiety, school problems, delinquency, and drug abuse.

While there is a strong genetic component to alcoholism, other psychosocial factors influence transmission, as not all COAs become alcoholic. Therefore, prevention and intervention should focus on those variables which influence the transmission of alcoholism or increase the risk for other problems.

Researchers have identified three types of factors that have been found to influence the stress-adjustment relationship in children. First, personality characteristics such as activity level, reflectiveness, cognitive skills, and positive responsiveness to others may influence this relation. For example, positive self-esteem predicted resiliency in COAs (Werner, 1986) and has been found to buffer the relation between stress and anxiety (Ayers, Short, Beals, Sandler and Roosa, 1988). Second, family factors provide another set of promising variables (Sher, 1991; West and Prinz, 1987; Wolin, Bennett, and Jacobs, 1998). Finally, environmental factors such as external support from a teacher, neighbor, parent of peers, or even an institutional structure such as a school or church have been identified as possible protective factors (Garmezy, 1983; Rutter, 1979; and Werner, 1986). Research has shown that support in the form of peers or an adult outside the home can be either helpful in the coping process or reduce the need for coping (Beals, Roosa, Sandler, Short, and Gehring, 1986; Rutter, 1979; Werner, 1986). A good relationship with the non-alcoholic parent has previously been suggested as a factor that protects the child from the negative effects of parental alcoholism (Clair and Genest, 1987; Moos and Billings, 1982; Rutter, 1985).

Hawkins and colleagues (Hawkins, Catalano, and Miller, 1992) provided a comprehensive review of the research including individual, interpersonal, and contextual factors that contribute to the risk of substance abuse among adolescents and young adults. Selection of prevention content should be guided by scientific knowledge about these factors and a recognition that the presence of multiple risk factors increases the risk for substance abuse (Nastasi and DeZolt, 1994).

Prevention Models

In approaching the primary prevention of emotional problems, Albee (1978) suggests that risk for behavioral problems is increased by the presence of organic causes and environmental stress and reduced by the presence of social support, competency, and self-esteem. The implication of this model is that appropriate goals for primary prevention with COAs would include the reduction of stress and the development of self-esteem, social competence, and a strong social support system.

Two primary prevention models have been proposed. The first is the "distribution of consumption model" which aims at the societal control over the availability of alcohol. This involves raising the drinking age, increasing prices, and limiting sale hours, as well as other strategies. The second model is the "sociocultural model" which focuses on education and enhancement of individuals' competencies through information, values clarification, and skill-building techniques. These types of prevention programs can be community-wide through media campaigns, or targeted at schools, recreational centers, or physicians' offices (Williams, 1990). Community-wide programs target all children, thus avoiding the stigmatizing effects of labeling.

Definitions

In response to the individual and environmental risk factors discussed earlier, several types of programs have been developed for COAs. "Universal prevention" programs are designed for the general population. "Selective prevention" programs are designed specifically for identified or self-identified children of alcoholics. "Indicated prevention programs" are designed for children with addicted parents who also have specific emotional or behavioral problems. Using another framework, prevention programs target children as the result of the behavior of an adult caregiver, rather than their own behavior, while intervention programs, usually target children who, themselves, exhibit some symptomology. While each may have a primary focus of one or the other, most COA programs include both prevention and intervention components.

The Family CAGE: An Alcoholic ScreeningTest

The CAGE is perhaps the most widely used screening test for alcoholism. This tool has been adapted to reflect concerns for a parent's drinking through the four questions:

1. **Do you think your parent needs to CUT down on his/her drinking?**

2. **Does your parent get ANNOYED at comments about his/her drinking?**

3. **Does your parent ever feel GUILTY about his/her drinking?**

4. **Does your parent ever take a drink early in the morning as an EYE opener?**

Screening and Identification

Many COAs never receive intervention services. COAs are usually identified incidentally when the child's parent enters alcoholism treatment. This type of identification and recruitment is ineffective in reaching the majority of COAs, because most alcoholics never receive treatment (Emshoff and Anyan, 1989). In addition, few children seek help voluntarily because family denial puts pressure on the child to keep the family's secret (Dies and Burghardt, 1991).

Identification of COAs, therefore, requires a process of active screening. To this end, Dies and Burghardt (1991) describe certain behavior patterns that suggest a child may have an alcoholic parent. Some of these behaviors reflect lack of parental supervision, such as frequent tardiness, absence from school, or carelessness in dress or personal hygiene. Other possible indicators of COA status include emotional instability, immaturity, conflict with peers, isolation from other children, academic problems, or physical complaints (e.g., headaches and stomach aches). Many people who work with children are not trained to recognize these subtle signs; in addition, these signs are not specific to COAs. Therefore, researchers have developed questionnaires to identify COAs who do not display obvious behavior problems (Dies and Burghardt, 1991).

One commonly used screening instrument is the CAGE, a set of four questions regarding the respondent's concern over his or her own drinking behavior. The Family CAGE is slightly reworded to reflect a respondent's concern for the drinking habits of a relative. This questionnaire is intended to screen, not diagnose, family alcoholism: a positive finding on the Family CAGE should be followed by a complete diagnostic assessment (see box).

The Children of Alcoholics Screening Test is a longer screening tool (Jones, 1982; Sheridan, 1995) developed to identify older children, adolescents, and adult children of alcoholics. It is a 30-item (though a short form has been developed) self-report measuring a respondent's attitudes, feelings, perceptions, and experiences related to his/her parent's drinking behavior. The main goal of these measures is to identify youngsters who do not display obvious behavior problems (Dies and Burghardt, 1991). As yet, such measures are not routinely used to identify COAs.

Target Groups and Settings

Target groups might be general—as in broad-based community prevention programs—or specific to particular high-risk groups. High-risk groups such as abused or neglected children, youth with academic problems, or those with gang affiliations are easier to identify and contain a large percentage of COAs. COA prevention and intervention services can then be offered as part of a comprehensive program.

An example of a community-based program targeted to COAs is that of Alateen, a program based on the Alcoholics Anonymous 12-Step Program of Recovery. Alateen is a self-help program that normally meets in various community settings such as churches or community centers. Unfortunately, very little evaluation data on the effectiveness of Alateen is available. Exceptions include a study which showed that Alateen participants had more positive scores on a mood state and self-esteem scale than COAs who did not participate in Alateen (Hughes, 1977). Peitler (1980) compared Alateen to group counseling and a no-treatment control group in sons of alcoholics aged 4-16 and found that group counseling had more positive effects than Alateen in improving self-worth.

In general, group settings (usually within schools), appear to be the main mode of program delivery. Children are available at schools for long periods of time and in large numbers, making it a logical setting for intervention. It is also the setting in which problems relating to parental alcoholism will be most consistently discernible (Dies and Burghardt, 1991). An added benefit is that programs within schools ease access to needed information and services. Finally, it is difficult and/or embarrassing for children and adolescents to attend programs at an outside agency or treatment center, particularly in settings that may have a negative stigma attached (e.g., mental health centers).

Information about alcohol and other drugs and their impact on the family is often included in school curricula. These classes provide a context in which teachers may witness other indices of parental alcoholism. Children may be extremely negative or apprehensive about alcohol and drinking or have changes in attendance or interest levels during alcohol and other drug education. While it is recognized that educational settings are logical prevention settings, few school-based programs designed specifically for COAs have been described in the literature (Dies and Burghardt, 1991).

Prevention Format

While not all COAs require treatment, some will need treatment (e.g. for depression or substance abuse) beyond what can be provided through prevention and intervention programs. For most

COAs, education and support given in a primary prevention program as outlined here is the appropriate level of intervention.

The objective of prevention groups for COAs is to reduce the probability of drinking and other problem behaviors by targeting risk factors associated with drinking problems or other dysfunctional behaviors. Groups may be designed for COAs only, or for those who have been identified on the basis of other behaviors or risk factors, or for those concerned about a loved one's drinking. Groups have been highly recommended by many experts in the field (Emshoff, 1990) because they reduce feelings of isolation, shame, and guilt (Dies and Burghardt, 1991) and capitalize on the importance of peer influence and mutual support to adolescents (Dies and Burghardt, 1991). As an additional benefit, there is some empirical evidence that group interventions allow participants to both receive and give support. Groups may be structured and closed-ended, with a specific beginning and end-point, or open-ended with participants joining and terminating in a fluid manner.

Program Content

Program content is often based in social learning theory and emphasizes role-playing, modeling, practice of resistance skills, and feedback. These techniques have produced significant effects on the reduction of the use of cigarettes, alcohol, and marijuana in general prevention programs (Erickson and Bell, 1990; Pentz, 1985).

While each intervention is unique, there are several intervention strategies which are relatively common across programs. These strategies include: information, training in skill development, a focus on social support and the socioemotional needs of children, and an emphasis on alternatives to substance use. These strategies have been developed for prevention efforts with diverse populations, but are applied (and sometimes adapted or customized) to groups of COAs.

Many recent primary prevention models concentrate on correcting misperceived social norms about drug use and expectations about drug use consequences. Social norms and related social influences are significant predictors of adolescent drug use and significant mediators of primary prevention programs (MacKinnon, Johnson, Pentz, Dwyer, Hansen, Flay and Wang, 1991).

The influence of the child's developmental stage must be considered during program design. For example, elementary-aged children do not always have realistic perceptions of relationships and causal links and, thus, often feel responsible for the drinking parent. The middle school years are often the period of time in which many children make decisions about beginning to drink alcohol and use other drugs. Older adolescents often experience both self-esteem and mental health problems. A consideration of these developmental issues is necessary to appropriately target prevention and intervention efforts in order to obtain desired outcomes.

Information and Education

Most programs provide some amount of information regarding alcohol and alcoholism in order to reduce misconceptions and to provide an accurate basis for education throughout the intervention. COAs are more likely to have misconceptions about the positive effects of drinking on cognitive and social performance (Brown et al., 1987; Mann, Chassin and Sher, 1987). The disease model is most commonly promoted as a means of understanding the behavior of the alcoholic parent. Understanding concepts such as tolerance, blackouts, and withdrawal helps the child to reduce self-blame and guilt about parental drinking. Finally, it is important that COAs understand that they are at risk for a variety of psychosocial problems, especially alcoholism. COAs who are aware of their risk status drink significantly less than COAs who are unaware of their risk status (Kumpfer, 1989).

Competence and Coping Skills

Competencies can be viewed as protective factors that help children cope with stress, thereby reducing their risk status. Most prevention and intervention programs teach specific emotion-focused and problem-focused coping skills (Nastasi and DeZolt, 1994). Emotion-focused coping is a process by which the child seeks social support or uses strategies such as distancing or reframing the negative aspects of the situation to emphasize the positive.

Problem-focused coping involves strategies to change or to manage the problems related to living in an alcoholic home. This might include specific survival skills such as how to handle situations such as riding home with a drunk parent or explaining parental behavior to friends. Specific information and practice with decision-making, problem solving, communication, and peer-resistance skills are typically included. Emotion-focused and problem-focused skills are not mutually exclusive and children who learn both skills are better equipped to manage their lives.

Personal-Social Competencies

Personal-social competencies can improve COA functioning despite vulnerability and lack of control over stressors (Albee, 1978; Dohrenwend, 1978). Examples of the competencies include self-esteem, self-efficacy, the ability to establish and maintain intimate relationships, and the development of effective strategies for expressing feelings and solving problems (Nastasi and DeZolt, 1994).

Social support is a natural by-product of group participation. Often children learn for the first time that others are in similar situations. Many children benefit from sharing their experiences and emotions in a safe environment with other children. Through mutual exchange, children learn survival skills from the experiences of their peers, gain practice in expressing feelings, and build their social support networks.

Increasing self-esteem and self-efficacy is often a goal of COA interventions. Many COAs attempt to achieve perfection in everything they do as a means of acquiring self-esteem. This focus sets the stage for inevitable failure. Therefore, interventions should emphasize alternative ways to acquire self-esteem and self-efficacy.

Many COAs only appear to be coping well. Properly trained facilitators are aware that denial serves a protective function. Group facilitators need to exercise patience and sensitivity as children adjust to their changing awareness about their parent's drinking. Group leaders should also recognize that COAs may have problems with interpersonal boundaries, a characteristic common in alcoholic families. Leaders should be sensitive to feelings of abandonment children may experience when the group terminates.

Alternative Activities

Alternative activities provide opportunities for COAs to participate in activities that exclude alcohol, tobacco and other drugs. Healthy alternative activities (e.g. sports activities, peer leadership training institutes, experiential programs such as Outward Bound) can help build a sense of self-efficacy, increase self-esteem, provide a positive peer group, and increase life skills such as problem-solving and communication. Programs may be exclusively focused on alternative activities, but are preferably part of a comprehensive prevention program.

Evaluation Findings

The examples below are among the few prevention programs targeted towards COAs that provide evaluation data. These programs exemplify the prevention components discussed in this paper.

Stress Management and Alcohol Awareness Program

Roosa, Gensheimer, Ayers, and Short (1989) developed a competency building intervention called the Stress Management and Alcohol Awareness Program (SMAAP). SMAAP is an 8 week, school-based preventative intervention focused on self-esteem, alcohol-related education, and emotion and problem-focused coping strategies.

Recently SMAAP (Short, Roosa, Sandler, Ayers, Gensheimer, Braver and Yein, 1995) was revised to include information to correct misconceptions COAs often have about the effects of alcohol use on cognitive ability and social competence (Brown, Creamer, and Stetson, 1987; Mann, Chassin, and Sher, 1987). The revised curriculum included additional practice using coping skills and the use of a "Personal Trainer" who met weekly with the participants to reinforce the personal and social skills children learned through the program.

Recent evaluation showed that program participants were more likely than controls to report increased knowledge, social-support, and emotion-focused coping behavior. Teachers reported increased problem solving and social competence among participants. However, teachers were not blind to group membership. The results also showed an unintended negative side effect: an overall significant increase in the expected tension reduction resulting from alcohol consumption. Additional research is needed to clarify this finding as past research has found a significant relation between positive alcohol expectancies and greater alcohol use by adolescents (Christansen, Smith, Roehling, and Goldman, 1989; Mann et al., 1987). Finally, there were no differences between groups which received and did not receive the Personal Trainer component.

Students Together And Resourceful

Students Together And Resourceful (STAR) is an intervention designed to provide students accurate information concerning alcoholism and its effects on the family and to increase participants' social competence skills and both the quantity and quality of peer relations. Group exercises were designed to help students recognize and express their feelings and to practice specific skills such as problem-solving, decision-making, stress management, and refusal skills.

The evaluation used a randomized design to compare participants and non-participants over time. Results indicated that participants were successful in establishing stronger social relations, a sense of control, and improved self-concept. In addition, participants reported increases in the number of friends, peer involvement, and perceived social support. Participants also reported decreased loneliness and depression (Emshoff, 1990).

Strengthening Families Program

The Strengthening Families Program (SFP) is a family intervention consisting of a parent training program, social skills training for the children, and a family relationship enhancement program. Typically the program is conducted in churches or community centers in brief sessions of two or three hours. The program has been found to reduce risk factors, increase resilience, and decrease alcohol, tobacco and other drug use among children of substance abusers.

The Strengthening Families Program has been modified for a variety of cultural groups including rural and urban African American COSAs, Hawaiian COSAs, Hispanic COSAs, and rural preteens (Kumpfer, Molgaard, and Spoth, 1996). Evaluation studies showed that the basic program with minor cultural revisions was more effective than a substantially revised program. The authors concluded that the core content of the program should not be deleted when making cultural revisions. As a result of positive outcomes of SPF replications, NIDA has chosen SFP as one of three model substance abuse prevention programs for dissemination.

CASPAR

The Cambridge and Somerville Program for Alcoholism Rehabilitation (CASPAR) offers a range of prevention and intervention services including programs for COAs. Groups are conducted by adult staff in school and community settings and by trained peer leaders in after-school groups in junior high schools (Davis, Wolfe, Orenstein, Bergamo, Buetens, Fraster, Hogan, MacLean, and Ryan, 1994). Participants are either self-referred or referred by parents, teachers, community agencies, other students, or CASPAR personnel.

A recent evaluation examined outcomes in participants in either a COA-specific group or a basic education group. COAs in the basic alcohol education group reported that they intended to drink differently and were drinking less as a result of participation than either non-COAs or participants in the COA group. However COAs reported more positive learning experiences. COAs were also more willing to attend the basic education group thus avoiding self-identification as a COA (DiCicco, Davis, Tarvis, and Orenstein, 1984).

Conclusions

Despite their risk status, most COAs are remarkably well-adjusted (Nastasi and DeZolt, 1994; Serrins, Edmundson, and Laflin, 1995; Sher, 1991). However, many children are adversely affected by exposure to parental drinking and its related problems. Delineation of factors influencing the relation between COA status and outcomes will point the way to modifiable points of intervention.

In order to increase our knowledge base, more stringent methods of program design and evaluation are needed. Future research can move our understanding further through the use of better sampling procedures, random assignment, control groups, appropriate sample sizes, the use of developmentally and culturally appropriate instruments, and precise definitions of parental alcoholism.

Emshoff and Anyan (1989) called for the use of action research in working with COAs, a model that emphasizes an interactive relationship between research and intervention. This approach would include more longitudinal evaluations which would contribute to our knowledge base and provide practitioners information regarding program effects. As part of the action research model, the dissemination of evaluation results is an important step leading to improved services for COAs. Evaluation data also indicate the need for future research, thus contributing to the continual cycle between basic and applied research.

Evaluation research with children of alcoholics indicates several levels of intervention and several basic prevention program components. Basic alcohol and drug education should be included in public school curricula. Parental and family training is a promising area that has been shown to reduce child and adolescent risk factors (Dishion and Andrews, 1995; Webster-Stratton, Kolpacoff and Hollingsworth, 1988). Comprehensive community programs that target social norms regarding alcohol and other drugs is another promising, yet under-utilized area. Preventive intervention programs should include the basic components of information and education, skill building in the areas of coping and social competence, social support and an outlet for the safe expression of feelings, and lastly, healthy alternative activities.

References

Albee, G. (1978). A competency model to replace the deficit model. *Vermont Conference on Primary Prevention.*

Ayers, T.S., Short, J.L., Beals, J., Sandler, I.N., and Roosa, M.W. (1988). Stress, self-esteem, and symptomatology in children of problem drinking parents. *Paper presented at the Western Psychological Association annual conference, San Francisco.*

Baer, P.E., McLaughlin, R.J., Burnside, M.A., and Porkorny, A.D. (1988). Alcohol use and psychosocial outcome of two preventive classroom programs with seventh and tenth graders. Journal of Drug Education, 18(3):171-184.

Beals, J., Roosa, M.W., Sandler, I.N., Short, J.L., and Gehring, L. (1986). Social support among children of alcoholics. *Paper presented at the American Psychological Association Convention, Washington, D.C.*

Brown, S.A., Creamer, V.A., and Stetson, B.A. (1987). Adolescent alcohol expectancies in relation to personal and parental drinking patterns. Journal of Abnormal Psychology, 96:117-121.

Christansen, B.A., Smith, G.T., Roehling, P.V., and Goldman, M.S. (1989). Using alcohol expectancies to predict adolescent drinking behavior. Journal of Consulting and Clinical Psychology, 57:93-99.

Clair, D.J. and Genest, M. (1987). Variables associated with the adjustment of children of alcoholics. In J.F. Lotterhos and M.E. McGuire (Eds.), Nurse care planning on alcoholism: A resource guide. East Carolina University, Alcoholism Training Program.

Davis, R.B., Wolfe, H., Orenstein, A., Bergamo, P., Buetens, K., Fraster, B., Hogan, J., MacLean, A., and Ryan, M. (1994). Intervening with high risk youth: A program model. Adolescence, 29(116):763-774.

DiCicco, L., Davis, R.B., Hogan, J., MacLean, A., and Orenstein, A. (1984). Group experiences for children of alcoholics. Alcohol Health and Research World, 8:20-24.

Dies, R.R. and Burghardt, K. (1991). Group interventions for children of alcoholics: Prevention and treatment in the schools. Journal of Adolescent Group Therapy, 1(3):219-234.

Dishion, T.J., and Andrews, D.W. (1995). Preventing escalation in problem behaviors with high-risk adolescents: Immediate and 1-year outcomes. Journal of Consulting and Clinical Psychology, 63:538-548.

Dohrenwend, B.P. (1978). Social stress and community psychology. American Journal of Community Psychology, 6:1-14.

Ellickson, P.L. and Bell, R.M. (1990). Drug prevention in junior high: A multisite longitudinal test. Science, 247:1299-1305.

Emshoff, J.G. (1990). A preventive intervention with children of alcoholics. Prevention in Human Services. 7(1):225-253.

Emshoff, J.G., and Anyan, L.L. (1989). From prevention to treatment: Issues for school-aged children of alcoholics: In M.Galanter (Ed.), Recent Developments in Alcoholism: Volume 9. Children of Alcoholics. New York: Plenum Press.

Gramezy, N. (1983). Stressors of childhood. In N. Garmezy and M. Rutter (Eds.), Stress, coping, and development in children. New York: McGraw-Hill.

Hawkins, J.D., Catalano, R.F. and Miller, J.Y. (1992). Risk and protective factors for alcohol and other drug problems in adolescence and early adulthood: Implications for substance abuse prevention. Psychological Bulletin, 112(1):64-105.

Hughes, J.M. (1977). Adolescent children of alcoholic parents and the relationship of Alateen to these children. Journal of Consulting and Clinical Psychology, 45:946-947.

Jones, J. (1982). Preliminary test manual: The children of alcoholics screening test. Chicago, IL: Family Recovery Press.

Kumpfer, K.L. (1989). Promising prevention strategies for high-risk children of substance abusers. OSAP High Risk Youth Update. 2(1):1-3.

Kumpfer, K.L., DeMarsh, J.P., and Child, W. (1989). Strengthening families program: Children's skills training curriculum manual, parent training manual, children's skill training manual, and family skills training manual (Prevention Services to Children of Substance-abusing Parents). Social Research Institute, Graduate School of Social Work, University of Utah.

Kumpfer, K.L., Molgaard, V., and Spoth, R. (1996). The strengthening families program for the prevention of delinquency and drug use. In: Peters R.D. and R.J. McCahon (Eds.), Preventing Childhood Disorders: Substance Abuse and Delinquency. Newburg, CA: Sage Publications.

MacKinnon, D.P., Johnson, C.A., Pentz, M.A., Dwyer, J.H., Hansen, W.B., Flay, B.R. and Wang, E.I. (1991). Mediating mechanisms in a school-based drug prevention program: First year effects of the Midwestern Prevention Project. Health Psychology, 10(3):164-172.

Mann, L.M., Chassin, L., and Sher, K.J. (1987). Alcohol expectancies in relation to personal and parental drinking patterns. Journal of Abnormal Psychology, 96:117-121.

Moos, R., and Billings, A. (1982). Children of alcoholics during the recovery process: Alcoholic and matched control families. Addictive Behaviors, 7:155-163.

Nastasi, B.K. and DeZolt, D.M. (1994). School interventions for children of alcoholics. New York: The Guilford Press.

National Institute for Alcohol Abuse and Alcoholism (1995). Children of alcoholics: important facts. Rockville, MD: National Clearinghouse for Alcohol Information.

Peitler, E.J. (1980). A comparison of the effectiveness of group counseling and Alateen on the psychological adjustment of two groups of adolescent sons of alcoholic fathers. Dissertation Abstracts International, 41:1520-B.

Pentz, M.A. (1985). Social competence and self-efficacy as determinants of substance abuse in adolescence. In: S. Shiffman and T.A. Wills (Eds.), Coping and Substance Abuse. Orlando, Fl: Academic Press.

Roosa, M.W., Gensheimer, L.K., Ayers, L.K., and Shell, R. (1989). A preventive intervention for children in alcoholic families: Results of a pilot study. Family Relations, 38:295-300.

Rutter, M. (1979). Protective factors in children's responses to stress and disadvantage. In: J.M. Joffe, G.W. Albee, and L.D. Kelly (Eds.), Readings in primary prevention of psychopathology: Basic concepts. Hanover, NH: University Press of New England.

Rutter, M. (1985). Resilience in the face of adversity: Protective factors and resistance to psychiatric disorder. British Journal of Psychiatry, 147:598-611.

Serrins, D.S., Edmundson, E.W., and Laflin, M. (1995). Implications for the alcohol/drug education specialist working with children of alcoholics: A review of the literature from 1988 to 1992. Journal of Drug Education, 25(2):171-190.

Sher, K.J. (1991). Psychological characteristics of children of alcoholics: Overview of research findings. In: M. Galanter (Ed.). Recent Developments in Alcoholism: Volume 9. Children of Alcoholics. New York: Plenum Press.

Sheridan, M.J. (1995). A psychometric assessment of the Children of Alcoholics Screening Test (CAST). Journal of Studies on Alcohol, 36:117-126.

Short, J.L., Roosa, M.W., Sandler, I.N., Ayers, T.S., Gensheimer, L.K., Braver, S.L., and Yein, J. (1995). Evaluation of a preventive intervention for a self-selected subpopulation of children. American Journal of Community Psychology, 33(2): 223-247.

Springer, J.F., Phillips, J.L., Phillips, L., Cannady, L.P., and Kerst-Harris, E. (1992). CODA: A creative therapy program for children in families affected by abuse of alcohol or other drugs. Journal of Community Psychology, OSAP Special Issue, June:55-74.

Webster-Stratton, C., Kolpacoff, M., and Hollingsworth, T. (1988). Self-administered videotape therapy for families with conduct-problem children: Comparison with two cost-effective treatments and a control group. Journal of Consulting and Clinical Psychology, 56(4):558-566.

Werner, E.E. (1986). Resilient offspring of alcoholics: A longitudinal study from birth to age 18. Journal of Studies on Alcohol, 47(1):47-65.

Werner, M.J., Joffe, A., and Graham, A.V. (1997). Screening, early identification, and office-based intervention with children and youth living in substance abusing families. (In press).

Williams, C.N. (1990). Prevention and treatment approaches for children of alcoholics. In M. Windle and J. S.Searles (Eds.), Children of Alcoholics. New York: Guilford Press.

Wolin, S.J., Bennett, L.A., and Jacobs, J.S. (1988). Assessing family rituals in alcoholic families. In: E. Imber-Black, J. Roberts, R. Whitney (Eds.), Rituals in Families and Family Therapy. New York: WW Norton and Com.

This paper was adapted from the authors' article of the same title published by the National Institute on Alcohol Abuse and Alcoholism in ALCOHOL HEALTH AND RESEARCH WORLD, Vol. 21, No.3, 1997, pp. 241-246.

SECTION II: The Young Child

Small Steps Becoming Large: Effective Strategies to Assist Children of Alcoholics in the Healing Process

Jerry Moe

For the past eighteen years there has been a growing and encouraging emergence of programs and practitioners to assist youngsters living in alcoholic and other drug addicted families. While prevention continues to lag far behind intervention and treatment, these scattered attempts to reach children, some as young as four, do acknowledge the accepted truth that everyone in the family, <u>especially the children</u>, is adversely impacted by substance abuse. These efforts are also grounded on the hypothesis that significant risk for future addiction may be greatly reduced by working with these children now.

In recent years the scope of these efforts has widened further to include children in other families that also experience the same silence and suffering that children of substance abuse endure. In their families, addiction to food, work, gambling, and relationships, and co-dependency create a similarly stifling environment of tension, fear, isolation, and pain. Youngsters living in violent and abusive households, as well as those in families challenged by mental health problems, often experience similar dynamics.

Despite the huge disparity between the need and what we have been able to provide, the last eighteen years have brought considerable quality and hope to the undertaking, manifested primarily by the wealth of knowledge and understanding we have gained to more effectively assist these youngsters. The evolution of programs, research and effective evaluation methodology have magnified our capacity to empower children and their families in creating a new legacy of health and wellness.

Building Strengths and Resilience

Despite the fact that children from addicted families are at risk for a variety of problems as they grow and develop, research shows the majority of these children become successful, productive, and functioning adults. How did these youngsters beat the odds and overcome adversity? Many children of addiction build a variety of strengths and resilience to successfully cope with the varied challenges they face. Werner, in her longitudinal study, and other researchers have found many traits of resilient individuals, including:

> social competence,
> problem - solving skills,
> the development of autonomy,
> and a sense of purpose and future.

Wolin has cited the importance of family rituals as an important protective factor to assist youngsters.

This growing body of research has created a paradigm shift with a focus on health, wellness, and prevention instead of damage and sickness. While it doesn't deny that children can be scarred by growing up in addicted families, it sheds light on how they can build resilience. Children don't develop these skills in a vacuum, but in the context of creating relationships with nurturing adults. Such relationships can be fostered in family, school, and community settings where such traits as caring and support, high expectations, and active youth participation are all present. Helping youngsters to build these relationships and develop life skills are key to creating that new legacy.

This paper will explore a variety of ways to help children of addiction deepen their strengths and resilience. It will emphasize that proper attention to both the process and the content of our work is essential. Inherent in both of these is, of course, the recruitment and training of people who can successfully implement and facilitate the work. This chapter will state and describe five principles of process that my own experience, and that of others, illuminate as cornerstones to effectively reach these children. It will then take four (of a number of possible) content domain/spheres and provide examples of activities that can be used to exemplify and teach the desired content for those domains. Our work is still so limited as compared to the need that it is essential that we do it effectively. The process principles and the kind of content given as examples here will serve as foundations on which to make the most of the money and resources we have available.

Basic Process Principles

There are many essential ingredients to empowering young children from alcoholic and other high stress families, especially in the group setting. Consistently combining these principles creates an atmosphere conducive to trusting, talking, and feeling. The group setting becomes a safe place for so many who thought they were all alone.

1. Enter the Children's World
2. Create a Safe and Nurturing Environment
3. Beyond Words . . . Experiential Learning
4. Acknowledge Children's Learning Styles with Varied Activities
5. Have Fun

Enter the Children's World

Facilitators may possess the latest tools and techniques yet be rendered fairly ineffective without a "heart to heart" connection with the children. This can only take place if the group leaders enter the children's world by giving them focused attention and love. Sometimes this simple fact is forgotten in the process of getting the job done.

There are many ways to enter the children's world. First of all, facilitators need to be an integral part of group -- if youngsters sit on the floor, so do the facilitators; if youngsters are involved in a self - worth exercise, so are the facilitators. Secondly, it's helpful for facilitators to learn the name of each group participant and call everyone by his or her name. The Children Are People program offers a fun way to accomplish this task by the "Name Game" activity. Children thoroughly enjoy coming up with a fun name beginning with the first letter of their first name. Over the years I've become known as "Jellybeans Jerry" to hundreds of kids. This word association helps facilitators remember names and use them, thereby according the youngsters dignity and respect.

It is also highly helpful for facilitators to know a few things about each participant. The "Share Square" activity will garner important facts as kids respond to such questions as what is their favorite TV show, cartoon character, hobby or game, and reveal a favorite wish. Facilitators can write down the "Name Game" names and pertinent "Share Square" data on three-by-five cards for easy review and reference before each session. Many children of addiction aren't used to being addressed by their appropriate name and asked questions about meaningful and relevant things in their lives. Above all, it's vital for facilitators to be "real" - i.e. consistently exhibit

- Who is your favorite cartoon character?
- What food would you like to be on a hot day?
- If you were king or queen of the world for a day, what one thing would you change?
- What kind of animal do you feel like today?
- What is one special thing about your best friend?
- What is ht ebest present you've ever gotten?
- If you could go anywhere on vacation, where would you go?
- Where is a safe place you can go?
- What famous person would you like to meet?
- What is your favorite dessert?
- If you were stuck on a desert island, and only one person or thing could be brought to you, who or what would it be?
- What kind of food do you not like to eat?
- If you could have two wishes, what would they be?
- What is a feeling you have trouble talking about?
- What is something special about you?
- What would you like to be doing twenty years from now?
- What's something that really makes you laugh?
- What's your favorite day of the year?
- What's something you'd like to know more about?
- If you could be famous, what would you be famous for?

congruence between what they say and do in group. When facilitators take the time to show they truly care, the "heart to heart" connection deepens. Children don't care about how much adults know until they know about how much adults care.

Create a Safe and Nurturing Environment

Entering the children's world goes a long way to establishing a nurturing environment. Warm, personable, and open facilitators enhance and deepen this process, as youngsters feel cared for and valued in special ways. A basic group structure provides consistency and predictability for children who often live in chaotic and unpredictable environments. Group members derive a certain comfort from this as the safety allows them to take more risks and open up in group. Lastly, clear rules and consistently enforced consequences when the rules get broken establish expectations, limits and boundaries which protect children and deepen the safety that the group offers in an on-going fashion.

Beyond Words . . . Experiential Learning

All too often words have virtually no meaning for youngsters from addicted family systems. "I'll quit tomorrow", "Mommy will be right back", and "If your Dad stays out one more night I'm gonna divorce him", are familiar messages that children hear again and again. Broken promises, inconsistency, and family denial, shrouded in secrecy, can leave children with a strong impression that words are hollow. It is essential to get beyond words in assisting young children of addiction.

When the session began, Jimmy's hand shot into the air to go first. This ten year-old had experimented with many different voices as he spoke through the "Confused Connie" feeling puppet. After a few silly comments these words tumbled out of Jimmy's mouth, "Why do men marry women and have kids and say they love the kids only to hit and hurt them?" The group fell silent as Jimmy's eyes filled with tears. Now talking with his own voice he uttered, "I hate Dad when he does that, but I still love him. What's wrong with me?" Jimmy sobbed as the group rallied around him with support and encouragement. He'd taken a huge step in the process of his own recovery.

Instead of merely talking about feelings or addiction (Jimmy had made a breakthrough by using a puppet), facilitators can bring the concepts to life through specially designed games and activities that get kids involved and illustrate key points through the experience. A Chinese proverb says it best :

> When I hear something, I forget it;
> When I see something, I remember it;
> When I do something, I understand it.

Acknowledge Children's Learning Styles With Varied Activities

Youngsters learn in a variety of ways. Some learn best visually, others by ear, and still others kinesthetically. Facilitators can most effectively reach a group of children by utilizing varied activities. These may include skits, art, music, movement, dance, role plays, films, puppets, and "game shows" that stimulate different learning styles. After youngsters have experienced different activities, the ensuing discussion often has added depth and insight.

Have Fun

Many children of addiction grow up way too fast. Some take on adult roles and responsibilities while others shoulder worries, burdens, and concerns which block the spontaneity, joy, magic, and wonder of being a kid. Facilitators can assist youngsters to learn and grow and also provide an opportunity for the children to be kids. By setting a mood which inspires creativity, joy, and laughter, group leaders provide a healing atmosphere conducive to talking, trusting, and feeling. Fun is healing and essential.

These tips can enhance the quality and effectiveness of the group process. Youngsters who feel safe, respected, cared for, and are given the opportunity to feel, learn, and grow in various ways will reach out, take risks, and allow themselves to become vulnerable in miraculous ways. Properly trained facilitators, benefitting from on-going supervision and in-services, are the key to balancing these process principles in a consistent and loving manner (See <u>Conducting Support Groups for Elementary K-6 Children : A Guide for Educators and Other Professionals</u>, Johnson Institute, 1991).

Content Areas

Most groups for young children of addiction utilize an educational support group format. Each session provides specific information on important life skills as well as the support and practice youngsters need to integrate this data into their daily lives. Some children, especially in cases of abuse, abandonment, and other trauma, need much more assistance and guidance than an educational support group offers. Individual therapy may be warranted in such cases.

Educational support groups, usually meeting on a weekly basis, offer a specific theme for each session. While programs across the country feature a variety of topics, including Defenses, Alcohol and Other Drugs, Family, Problem Solving, Risks and Choices, and Making Friends, both research and experience point to four content areas critical to helping children from addicted family systems.

1. Feelings (All my feelings are okay)
2. Alcohol, Other Drugs and Addiction (It's not my fault)
3. Self - Care (It's important to take care of myself)
4. Self - Worth (I am special)

The rest of this paper will explore these content areas and feature a specially designed game or activity relevant to each.

Feelings

Many children of addiction survive by learning not to feel. The prospect of talking, let alone sharing feelings, can raise youngsters' guilt and anxiety, as they fear betraying their parents and the family secrets. A small group often serves as the first safe place they have ever had to be open and explore feelings. Children learn that all feelings are okay. Group becomes a safety net where youngsters deepen their skills in identifying, expressing, and owning their feelings. "Stuffed Feelings and Problems" is an activity which facilitates this process.

"Stuffed Feelings and Problems" is a kinesthetic experience which helps children understand the consequences of holding problems and feelings inside. With the group sitting in a circle, the facilitators place a tote bag, full of brightly colored rocks, in the middle. Each rock has a problem (such as "addiction". "depression", "co-dependency", and "family secrets") or a feeling (such as "anger", "scared", "hurt", "shame", "guilty", and "sad") painted on it. One by one the youngsters pick up the bag and carry it around the room. The facilitators ask, "How does it feel carrying all this stuff?", or "Can you be free to be a kid and laugh and play when you've got that bag with you?", and "When you carry such a heavy load what are you often thinking about?".

After a brief discussion, the facilitators put the bag back in the middle of the circle. Each child takes a rock out of the bag and reads the problem or feeling on the rock. They then have the opportunity to share a time when they felt that feeling or had that particular problem. Group members quickly come to see that they are not alone; everyone has problems and feelings. Before long the bag is empty, and everyone has the chance to carry it around again. There is amazement at how much lighter it is because they talked about their problems and feelings -- they got them out. The facilitators explain that this is the actual function and work of group -- to better understand problems by talking about them and to share feelings to let go of their weight and intensity. Afterward, young children often say, "You let go of a couple more rocks today!", after a group member has disclosed a particularly tough problem and shared his or her painful feelings.

Addiction

Youngsters living in addicted families may be confused about what is going on in a home often shrouded in silence and secrecy. Educational support groups can help youngsters learn about addiction, especially that it's not their fault and they are not alone, in age appropriate ways. It is essential to help children differentiate themselves from their parent's problems and realize they didn't cause the problems and can't make them better. There are many excellent stories, films, and activities[1] which bring this cunning and baffling disease to within understanding for children. Music can also be effective in deepening youngsters' grasps of the problem and encouraging them to freely express their feelings toward addiction and its manifestations.

During my years as a teacher, I was amazed by kids who couldn't remember their multiplication tables yet could sing Michael Jackson's song "Beat It" forwards, backwards, and sideways. Music is a universal language that can deeply touch the human soul. An effective way to incorporate music is to take popular rock or rap melodies and have the group re-write the lyrics (over 2 - 3 sessions) to describe their experiences in living with addiction, and/or a variety of ways to positively cope with it. Once youngsters have already learned some basic facts about alcoholism, this powerful activity

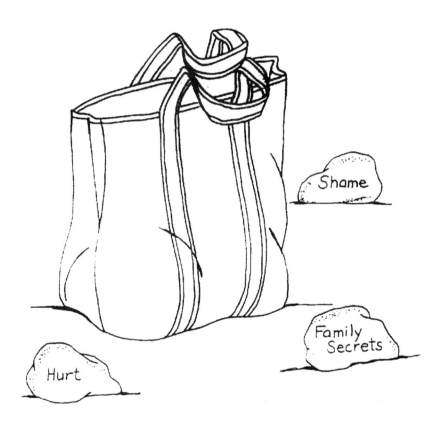

helps them unlock problems and feelings, as well as deepen their understanding about addiction and its impact on them. For example, a group of three twelve- year olds and their facilitator spent time rewriting the lyrics to Elton John's "I Guess That's Why They Call It the Blues". First they listened to the song a few times and studied a copy of the lyrics handed out to each of them. Then through dialogue, debate, and collaboration, "I Guess That's Why I'm Always Confused" was born and became a theme song for the Children's Program (see example). Group members sometimes sing it to newcomers as a way of communicating their common bond and the hope for health and recovery.

Self-Care

Telling young children of addiction to take good care of themselves is largely a futile exercise, like speaking to them in a foreign language. Remember, they live in families without many role models of self-care. Kids need "maps" on this important life skill and lots of practice to integrate it into their daily lives. "Jeopardy, The Self-Care Game", in conjunction with "Self-Care Bags", go a long way in imparting this skill in a fun and balanced manner.

"Jeopardy, The Self-Care Game", is a take-off on the popular television game show, here with an emphasis on taking good care of one's self. (If you don't take good care of yourself, you really are in jeopardy!) With the Jeopardy categories of "Body", "Mind", "Feelings", "Spirit", and "Being a Kid" written on newsprint or a blackboard, the facilitator records the group's brainstormed responses in each important area. For example, "Exercise is a way to take care of your body." The activity continues until there are many useful ideas for all the categories.

After a brief discussion on the importance of self-care, the facilitators pass out lunch bags and instruct the kids to creatively decorate their bags with their name and the words "self-care bag" by using crayons, colored pencils, and magic markers. The group leader then hands each youngster six index cards and tells them to write one self-care strategy on each side of the cards. Children may utilize the results from "Jeopardy, The Self-Care Game", or further brainstorm ideas on taking good care of themselves. They jot down self-care ideas for their bodies, minds, feelings, spirits, and the "little kids" inside. Then everyone puts their cards in their bags, shakes up the contents and pulls out a card. With a suggestion on each side,

I Guess That's Why I'm Always Confused

Just wish it away
Don't look at it
Pretend it's all better
My parents can't stop
I can honestly say they just never get better
Booze and drugs always stay
To cast their demons inside
And it won't be long before Mom and Dad go to
their crazy place
It's time to hide

And I guess that's why I'm always confused
Scared, all alone, and verbally abused
Parents are children
Fighting not hugging
Exploding like thunder
Under their drugging
I guess that's why I'm always confused

Just stare into space
I've been disgraced
Friends just don't understand
Live for each second
With pained reservations and
Never count on parent's plans
It's just no use
Cry in the night if it helps
Yet nothing helps
It seems they love booze
More than they love me or life itself

I guess that's why I'm always confused
Scared, all alone, and verbally abused
Parents are children
Fighting not hugging
Forgetting their loved ones
Under their drugging
and I guess that's why I'm always confused

youngsters quickly learn they have choices about how to take care of themselves. In each subsequent session, the kids practice self-care by pulling a card from their bags and carrying out the suggestion. At the final group, youngsters brainstorm how to use their bags at home—for example, when they're bored or not feeling good about themselves, it is helpful to take a card and follow its instructions. Self-care bags teach and allow children to practice taking good care of the most important people of all—themselves.

Self-Worth

Young children of addiction can get so enmeshed in the negative messages and put-downs of their environments that they believe they have little to celebrate. Some learn to cling to limited self-value based solely on doing, and most sadly, miss out on celebrating their intrinsic beauty and worth. "Living Cards" help children begin to fill this void and touch upon their special and unique gifts.

After participants have creatively written their names in the middle of a piece of paper, they silently reflect upon the special qualities each of the others brings to the group. The facilitators may provide a few examples to initiate the flow of ideas, and then record the group's responses on the board in full view for all participants to see and hopefully use in this exercise. The children then pass their paper to the left, and their neighbors write brief notations describing the special qualities of the person whose name is on the sheet. The process continues until each paper circles the room and comes back to the owner. Then follows a full minute of silence called "finding the buried treasure," as each kid reads and absorbs all the special things written about him or her. Everyone has the opportunity to share his or her Living Card with the group. Amidst clapping and cheering, everybody takes a moment to celebrate their special gifts.

It's important now to celebrate the progress made to help young children of addiction in the past eighteen years. Paying close attention to both the process and content of this work can greatly improve quality services for children. While there's still much to do, there's more hope and help available for children today than in the past. There are highly skilled practitioners, books and age-appropriate games and activities that can deeply touch youngsters. Above all else, it's the relationship you develop with children, not the activities or games, that can make the greatest difference in their lives. One

JEOPARDY

SELF-CARE GAME

BODY
-
-
-

MIND
-
-
-

FEELINGS
-
-
-

SPIRIT
-
-
-

BEING A KID
-
-
-

_____

SHARE FEELINGS

PLAY A GAME

READ

SELF-CARE BAG

TALK TO A FRIEND

EXERCISE

young girl, Jenna, embodies the hope for these children and speaks to the value of early prevention and intervention.

> **Every morning Jenna, age 11, delivers over 200 newspapers. Every cent she earns went to help make ends meet for her family—a little brother and a mom addicted to alcohol and cocaine. After Family Week at Sierra Tucson's Children's Program, Jenna's mom put a portion of Jenna's monthly earnings in a college savings account and let her keep some spending money for herself. All week in the Children's Program, Jenna kept hearing the importance of taking care of yourself first. Her counselor asked her to go out and buy something just for herself when she got home. Three weeks later Jenna called the counselor. She had decided to buy herself ice cream, yet stood frozen outside the store for twenty minutes. "I didn't want to go in because I thought of all the other things I could do with the money—cookies for my brother or a nice card for my mom", she told the counselor. Finally Jenna ordered a double dip, ate one scoop and threw the rest away. "I didn't think I *really* deserved it."**

Jenna took a big step that day. She's since bought many double dip cones and eaten them right down to the final bite.

There is much hope today for young children of addiction. With the love and guidance of skilled facilitators and quality programs the children's small steps become large in changing their own legacies. They can hope for a beautiful today and a brighter tomorrow.

References

Children Are People Support Group Manual. Health Communications, Deerfield Beach, Florida, 1988.

Moe and Pohlman. *Kids' Power: Healing Games for Children of Alcoholics.* Health Communications, Deerfield Beach, Florida, 1989.

Moe and Ways, *Conducting Support Groups for Elementary Children K - 6: A Guide for Educators and Other Professionals.* Johnson Institute, Minneapolis, Minnesota, 1991.

Werner and Smith. *Overcoming the Odds: High Risk Children From Birth to Adulthood.* Cornell University Press, Ithaca, New York, 1992.

Wolin, Bennett, Noonan, et. al., *Disrupted Family Rituals: A Factor in the Intergenerational Transmission of Alcoholism.* Journal of Studies on Alcohol. *41: 199-214, 1980.*

All activities in this paper are taken from

Moe. Discovery . . . *Finding the Buried Treasure: A Prevention / Intervention Program for Youth from High Stress Families.* STEM Publishing, Tucson, Arizona, 1993.

[1]See Kids' Power : Healing Games for Children of Alcoholics, *Health Communications, 1989.*

fun

brave

kind

smiles alot

JOSH

caring

shares feelings

smart

a friend

Matching Services and the Needs of Children of Alcoholic Parents: A Spectrum of Help

Ellen R. Morehouse, ACSW, NCAC II

Introduction

Young and adolescent COAs experience a wide range of effects resulting from a parent's alcoholism. While the vast majority of studies of COAs identify the negative impact of parental alcoholism on children, a growing number of studies have begun to document the factors that contribute to the absence of these negative effects. Clearly, COAs who have been provided with protective factors, appear more resilient, and function well, do not need the same kinds of services as COAs who are experiencing the most negative consequences of a parent's alcoholism. Therefore, services to COAs must be appropriate to the needs of the child, enhance or stimulate protective factors, and reduce the negative consequences when they exist.

This article will examine the range of services for COAs, the settings where they are and can occur, the effectiveness of these services, and the service gaps that exist. Suggested ingredients for services and criteria for matching the needs of the child to the type of service and the setting will be provided. The training, qualifications, and supervision of those who work with COAs will also be discussed.

Historical Perspective

Historically, COAs received services for problems that were caused by a parent's alcoholism in settings that dealt with the child's symptom, such as the school phobia or acting out behavior, rather than the cause of the problem. A 1974 study by Booz Allen Hamilton for NIAAA [1] looked at these services and found that, although these children have access to support systems such as schools, churches, physicians, extended families, social agencies, and specialized services, "there are gaps between the needs of the child and the actual resources available; these involve non-responsiveness, inadequate coverage, ineffectiveness, and failure to identify such children." Some believe that this landmark study combined with the growing popularity of the family therapy and prevention movements in the 1970s stimulated the development of services designed specifically for COAs.

Results of studies on the effects of parental alcoholism on COAs were published throughout the 1970s and services for COAs in schools and in alcoholism treatment programs were being provided in 1974. But by 1979, there was recognition and concern by NIAAA that despite the well documented needs, services were not being provided to meet the demand. [2] As a result, a two day symposium was sponsored by NIAA in September 1979. "The purpose of the symposium was to have a representative sample of professionals providing COA-specific services, share experiences and insights, identify critical policy issues, and assess future needs." [3] The Symposium resulted in a monograph published in 1981 titled Services for Children of Alcoholics. This monograph identified some of the barriers to providing services that still exist today. It also documented how programs were successfully able to overcome these barriers and provide services to COAs.

A 1986 publication of the Children of Alcoholics Foundation, Directory of National Resources for Children of Alcoholics, [4] lists 259 programs that provide direct services specifically designed to serve COAs. Of these programs, 145 serve children under 18. (Programs which treat COAs as part of a larger population but which were not specifically designed for COAS and programs requiring a parent to be in a particular alcoholism treatment program in order for the child to receive services were not included.)

Current Situation

Despite the significant increase in COA-specific services since 1979, it is estimated that only a small percentage of all COAs participate in these services. A 1991 study by Student Assistance Services of the reasons why COAs don't participate in COA services outside the school found that the 10 most common reasons given by adolescent COAs were:

1. "I don't want my parents to know."
2. "I can't get there" (because of transportation or because of location).
3. "I can't afford it."

4. "Trust. I don't want to share my problems with strangers."
5. "It's not that bad" or "I can handle it myself."
6. " I don't have time to go."
7. Embarrassment.
8. Fear of revealing the secret, told not to tell.
9. "I'm not crazy!"   Afraid of stigma.
10. "I don't want my friends to know."

Other reasons cited include: "I tried Alateen and didn't feel comfortable," "I tried counseling and it wasn't helpful," "It's not my problem, Why should I have to go?", "I don't want to lie to my parents" and "It won't help".

These results indicate a need to provide services in different kinds of settings and a need to prepare adolescents for services.

With COAs accounting for approximately 13% of all children and adolescents in this country, an argument can be made to 1) train all professionals who work with youth in the basics of how to help COAs and how to locate more intensive services for them; and to 2) train COA specialists who can provide treatment to COAs and consultation to their professional colleagues or staff in non-COA-specific settings, such as youth centers, mental health clinics, schools; and to 3) establish more COA-specific services in host settings as well as in free standing programs.

Barriers to Service

Parent Consent

Many states have laws requiring parents' consent for medical, mental health, and alcohol and drug treatment for minors. As a result, many organizations that are willing to serve COAs require parent consent.[5] While this is not usually a barrier for COAs with recovering parents, it is often a barrier for COAS with active alcoholic parents for the following reason: First, many active alcoholics deny that they have a problem with alcohol and drugs, and deny that the drinking has negatively affected their children. Some recovering alcoholics also have difficulty acknowledging the negative impact of their drinking on the children because of the high degree of guilt that is generated. The non-using parent may also deny the negative consequences on the children because of guilt. Both parents may deny the negative impact because they may believe that the child doesn't know the parent has a drinking problem. This is illustrated through statements such as "He never drank in the house" or "The children think mom sleeps a lot because she works so hard," etc.

Second, even when denial is not the issue, some parents do not want their children involved in services because of fear that there will be a violation of privacy and the child and family might then be stigmatized and treated differently by others. This is characterized by statements such as "If my child attends that program and someone sees her walk in the door, then everyone in town will know." Despite the increasing acceptance of alcoholism as a disease, there is still a high degree of prejudice. A well known professional in the alcoholism field who is open about her own recovery acknowledges that her 12 year old daughter has a friend who is not allowed to play or sleep at her house yet is regularly invited to the friend's home. The friend told her daughter that this is because "your mom could have a relapse."

The child's and parent's fear of stigmatization has not been given adequate consideration by service providers. This issue can be addressed by providing COA-specific services in non-stigmatizing or generic settings and by instituting internal procedures to protect privacy. For example, a school social worker who learns that the reason a child is having a lot of problems with school is a result of the alcoholic mother's actions, can still give input into a team decision (child study team, Committee on Special Education, etc.) without identifying the alcoholism. This can by done by saying "Lisa" is having a hard time because her mother was absent alot, was having medical problems, provided inconsistent parenting, etc. By describing the actions of the mother and how they affect "Lisa", the team can plan what actions are needed without stigmatizing the mother. Many parents fear that they and their children are gossiped about in the faculty lunch room.

A third reason why parents may not consent is because they need the child to perform parenting tasks that may not be accomplished if the child attends an out-of-school program. Statements such as "You can't go to that program after school because I need you to watch your sister for me, work that part-time job, etc." are examples of this kind of thinking. This thinking would make it difficult to attend any after school or weekend program regardless of the location.

Family Focus

Many programs for children and adolescents insist on parent involvement and don't service youth without parent involvement. While there is general agreement in the youth services field that services to children and youth will be most effective when the parents are involved, parent involvement is not always possible or desirable, especially when providing services to COAs. For example, many children would be punished if they told the parent they wanted help. Others would be forbidden from attending services. Therefore, programs that require parent involvement automatically limit which COAs can attend.

The impact that services without parent participation can have on children should not be underestimated. Services that help COAs develop characteristics that will serve as protective factors for the child are invaluable. Testimonials from adolescents and adults about that person "who made a difference" are well known.

I'm considering the degree of family involvement. It is also important to consider the developmental stage of the child. Specifically with "separation" being one of the primary tasks of adolescent development, it is appropriate that an adolescent may not want any parent involvement in his or her treatment.

It is also important to consider that when a parent is still actively drinking, a child might appropriately not trust that it is safe to share feelings in a family session and fear reprisals from siblings or parents. Similarly, for a young child who has lived with the "don't talk" rule,[6] the child may not understand how, just because dad is in treatment and not drinking, it is now "ok" to talk. The young child may need several to many sessions to develop trust of the counselor/therapist before trusting a conjoint session. Finally, the treatment needs of the child may conflict with the needs of the parent. The most extreme example would be in treating a COA who has been repeatedly sexually abused by an alcoholic parent; no one would argue that the child should only be seen if the parent agrees to be treated.

Settings for Services for COAs

COA-specific services are most commonly provided in the following settings:

Schools

The CASPAR Alcohol Education in Massachusetts was the first documented program to provided COA-specific services in elementary and junior high school. [7] Services were provided through an alcohol education curriculum which included specific material about COAs and training for teachers on how to identify and help COAs. The CASPAR program also provided after-school homogeneous groups for COAs and heterogeneous groups that included COA-specific material. Since CASPAR, a number of other in-school curriculums have been developed that include COA- specific information. Teacher training on COA issues has grown dramatically as has in-school individual and group counseling sessions for COAs.

The Westchester, NY Student Assistance Program was the first documented model for providing professional counselors (called Student Assistance Counselors) in secondary schools for the purpose of working specifically with COAs.[8] In this model assessment, individual and group counseling, and referral of COAs are conducted during school by these specialists.

With the growing knowledge and acceptance of the needs of COAs, schools have provided COA-awareness activities for all students. These include poster contests on how alcoholism affects families, assemblies with skits/plays about alcoholic families, library displays with books about COAs, etc.

These activities are critical because they reduce the isolation felt by many COAs by letting them know that there are many other students with family alcoholism. They also do this without singling anyone out and therefore, reduce or eliminate the barriers discussed earlier. The biggest advantage of in-school programs are accessibility and in many instances, parent notification isn't required.

Alcoholism Treatment Programs

Most alcoholism treatment programs today have a family education component to help the family understand alcoholism and recovery. Many also provide support and counseling for the family members. Programs of this kind fall into two categories. The first includes programs where the children attend only if the parent or parenting figure is receiving treatment. When the parent ends treatment the child(ren) end(s) treatment. These types of programs can be thought of as COA collateral programs because the primary patient is the adult. In these programs, the length of the child's participation can range from one session to an unlimited number of sessions. The parent can be in an in-patient program and the child comes for out-patient visits, or the child may stay over during family week, or both can be outpatients. The biggest advantage of these programs is that the child has the parent's permission to attend and therefore feels less guilt about talking about the situation at home.

The second category of programs for COAs in alcoholism treatment is where the COA is the primary client/patient and is provided services regardless of the parent(s) involvement. For example, in New York State COAs may be treated in alcoholism treatment programs for their COA issues without parental consent if the professional thinks that parent notification would not be in the child's best interest. In programs where the COA is the primary client/patient, services tend to be more tailored to the developmental needs of the individual child. The biggest advantage of these programs is that, like in-school counseling programs, the child's participation is not contingent on the parent.

Free Standing COA Programs

Project Rainbow, started in 1979, was the first free standing program providing COA-specific services. Since then, others have developed around the country. Most of these programs provide services during non-school hours and are offered after school, weekend, and during the summer. Most contain a recreation compo-nent as well and last for several hours. The biggest advantages of these programs are that they offer more opportunities for socializa-tion and fun for the children while providing help, and offer the most opportunity for the child to be out of the dysfunctional family system.

Other COA-specific Services

Other COA-specific services operate in a wide variety of settings. A common setting is the private practice where an individual practitio-ner or group of practitioners offer COA-specific services as part of the private practice. A growing number of child guidance clinics, family agencies and out-patient mental health clinics also provide COA-specific individual and/or group counseling for COAs. These pro-grams offer the advantage of staff with experience in diagnosing and treating the broad range of child and adolescent psychiatric disorders. Therefore, a COA who also has an attention deficit disorder with hyperactivity and is depressed might best be treated in this kind of setting.

Youth programs such as Boys Clubs, "Ys", community centers, sometimes also offer COA-specific services. Perhaps the biggest advantage of these programs is the lack of stigma attached to participation. With these programs, a child can attend to play basketball, do arts and crafts, or talk.

Examples of crisis programs that can provide COA-specific services are programs for runaway and homeless youth, shelters for battered women and children, and rape crisis centers. These programs provide a window of opportunity to address COA issues because of the crisis. An adolescent reluctant to talk about an alcoholic father may be motivated to do so because of the fight he had with his drunken father that resulted in being thrown out of the house or in running away.

Councils on Alcoholism also offer COA-specific services, such as alcohol education programs for children, i.e. the BABES program started by the Detroit affiliate of the National Council on Alcoholism, and COA counseling groups.

Residential Child Care/Juvenile Justice Facilities

Many children under 19 are living in group homes or institutional settings. A large portion of these children are COAs yet rarely are involved in COA-specific services. The Berkshire Farm Center in Canaan, N.Y. was the first program to document COA services in a juvenile justice facility in 1984. [9] Since then Student Assistance Services, through an OSAP High Risk Youth Grant, has built on the Berkshire experience and provides COA-specific services in a variety of residential facilities for youth. Two of the unique problems encountered were the residents' reluctance to disclose the extent of the parental alcoholism, fearing that they would not be allowed to return home if the staff knew "how bad" home was; and second, the reluctance to disclose in a COA group because of fear that a member who lives in the facility with him would bring up what was said outside the group. With these COAs, more individual sessions were needed to establish trust before COAs were willing to join a COA group.

Range of COA-Specific Services

COA-specific services can be viewed on a continuum with awareness raising activities that can benefit everyone on one end to intensive psychotherapy that is only needed by some COAs on the other end of the continuum.

Awareness

Each type of service has different goals. Awareness activities, such as public service announcements (PSAs), print advertisements, posters, book displays, etc., let COAs know they are not alone. They help COAs understand that there are many children with parents who drink too much; that many of these parents do what their parent does, i.e. break promises, or embarrass the child; that many children feel like they do sometimes, i.e. angry, ashamed, scared, etc.; and that there are adults who can help children.

These activities and messages are critical because they break the "don't talk" rule. In most alcoholic families, children are told not to talk about the parents' drinking so they are reluctant to tell outsiders and often other family members about upsetting incidents caused by the alcoholic, or their resulting feelings. As a result, young children especially often believe that what is happening to them is unique. Public awareness activities aimed at youth universalizes their experience and reduces some of the isolation, shame, and confusion.

Education

Education goes a step further by explaining why parents break promises, act differently when drinking, feel and act sick when not drinking, forget things, etc. To be effective, education must fit the cognitive development and learning style of each child. For example, not considering a child's cognitive and emotional development could have a very negative impact when explaining how alcoholism tends to "run in families." Explaining blackouts as a reason for broken promises and forgetfulness would be done very differently for a four year old than for a 14 year old. In providing education, consideration must be given to the fact that some children become highly anxious during this time and may not absorb and integrate the information. Others may have learning disabilities that make it difficult to listen and learn in groups, to read or to write stories, or draw pictures about their feelings or family. In addition, the child's level of moral development (as described by Kolberg[10]) or gender (which affects moral development as described by Gilligan[11]) should also be considered.

Just as awareness can help reduce the isolation, education can help reduce the pain. Understanding that a child is not responsible for the parents' drinking or other activities, that drinking can make it hard for a parent to take care of a child, and that drinking may cause a parent to do things that make a child feel unloved, etc can help a child separate her/himself from the parent's problem. The ability to do this was one of the protective factors identified in Beardslee's study of resilient children of parents with affective disorders.[12] The importance of detaching from the parent's drinking problem has been a long-recognized principle of Alateen. Education is provided in Alateen, and in books, booklets, and movies about COAs. It should be a part of all alcohol education curriculums and COA-specific services.

Education can be provided without identifying or singling out COAs. For example, during COA awareness week, a teacher can assign a book report on one of five articles, books, or booklets on COAs. This allows COAs as well as non-COAs to benefit.

Support for Alcohol Specific Concerns

Giving COAs an opportunity to talk about their situation, listening, and expressing empathy is important because for many COAs, it is not permissible to talk about their situation at home. For those that might try, they often feel no one is listening, or they are told their feelings are wrong. Statements by non-alcoholic spouses such as "You shouldn't feel that way," "Grow up," "You don't know what it means to be upset," "Stop crying or I'll give you something to cry about" are characteristic of parent responses often given to COAs who do express feelings. As a result, many COAs learn it is not safe or wise to express feelings.

Obviously COAs must be identified to receive support for alcohol-specific concerns. The benefits to be gained from receiving support must be compared to the risks of identification in any given setting, and for any COA, in deciding whether or not to participate in this level of services. Support is provided in Alateen and in all individual and group counseling for COAs.

Coping Strategies

The next level of services involves examining how a child is coping with the parent's (s') drinking and resulting behavior, evaluating the efficacy of the strategy, exploring new strategies, and trying them out. The goal of this level of services is behavioral change and/or support for maintaining healthy behaviors. Examples include: learning not to talk back to an intoxicated parent as a way of avoiding punishment; learning that it is normal and healthy to want to go away to college or join the armed services after high school; and learning to draw or call a friend when upset.

While coping strategies are provided in books and booklets, individual and/or group counseling provide a more effective forum.

Often there is resistance from service providers in offering this level of service to COAs because of possible conflicts between what is in the best interests of the child and the parent's wishes. The following case examples illustrate this conflict:

Mrs. Jones and her eight year old son, Tim, were abandoned by Mr. Jones, Tim's father. Mrs. Jones began alcoholism treatment and was lonely and depressed. She looked forward to Tim's arrival after school to keep her company. She let Tim know that he was a great help to her and was now the "man of the house." Tim realized how much his mom depended on him and avoided any out of school activities with peers so he could "help" his mother. Tim was seen individually in the children's program at the clinic his mother was attending. He admitted wanting to attend after school activities with his friends but felt it would hurt his mother if he wasn't with her after school. As a result, he used every opportunity at school to socialize with friends and got into trouble for talking during class, during assemblies, and at other times when he was supposed to be quiet.

When it was suggested to Mrs. Jones that Tim participate in cub scouts and after school activities she was resistant, admitting that she needed Tim's company and help. How hard to push for what was in Tim's interest raised questions between Tim's counselor and Mrs.Jones' counselor. If they pushed for Tim's interests, would Mrs. Jones drop out of treatment and relapse? If this happened, would the benefits of participation in peer activities outweigh the consequences of Mrs. Jones' drinking? Would Tim stay in these activities if his mother returned to drinking?, etc.

The second example is of seventeen year old Carmen who had an alcoholic father.

Carmen's home life was unbearable for her. She hated her verbally abusive father and her mother who made her feel guilty for not helping out more at home. Carmen was an honor student who wanted to get away from her family as quickly as possible. She was able to graduate from high school in three years and was accepted with a full scholarship to a very prestigious university far from her home. Her parents wanted her to attend the local community college so she could live at home and help out. Carmen was furious at her parents for trying to keep her at home. She felt she had the right to go to the university and wasn't going to let her parents stop her. She wanted support from her counselor for her decision and information about how to become an emancipated minor. Her parents saw the counselor as interfering and supporting Carmen's disobedience.

These two examples illustrate the underlying issues in the parent consent and family involvement policies. While states have established limits on parent rights (parents don't have the right to abuse or neglect children), clinical practice often is caught between what is best for the child and the rights of the parents. This dilemma often emerges in helping COAs with coping strategies and especially in providing concrete services.

Therapy

Therapy differs from counseling in intensity and in uncovering blocks to adopt healthy coping strategies. Therapy may be short term or long term and reflect a variety of theoretical orientations, such as family systems, psychoanalytic, behavioral, cognitive, etc. Theoretically, therapy is a treatment for a problem, which implies that the COA involved in therapy is having a problem that needs to be remedied. The problem may be the child's unhappiness or the unhappiness of others that results from the child's behavior, such as stealing, fighting, etc. Therapy for COAs should include each of the other levels of service. As with the other levels, be appropriate for the developmental level of the child. Therapy should also improve functioning in areas where the child is having difficulty, such as social functioning, functioning at school, etc.

Matching Services to COAs

Any COA may need any and all levels of services at any given time. For example, an elementary child may benefit from awareness and education and not want a more intensive level of service because "I'm OK." If the situation at home deteriorates, the child may need additional services. Similarly, the situation may improve, but years later as an adolescent the child may begin experiencing flashbacks of beatings, sexual abuse, or other trauma that occurred and that was repressed. At this time the child may begin to deteriorate and need additional services.

While all young COAs can benefit from the first three levels of service (awareness, education, support), a thorough assessment should be done before providing coping strategies and/or therapy. One of the well meaning mistakes often made in the early days of the COA services movement was to force young and adolescent COAs into treatment so they could avoid the problems of adult COAs. A child who thought "everything is OK" was labeled as in denial. This attitude ignores important concepts. First, parental alcoholism is extremely variable. It can be from short to long duration, mild to severe, and accompanied by an extreme range of behaviors that can affect children. Mitigating factors, such as the child's constitutional factors, and the presence of other caretaking and nurturing adults will greatly influence the child's experience of parental alcoholism. Therefore, when some children say "it's not that bad" or "I can handle it," they may be accurate.

Second, denial is usually viewed as a negative defense in the alcoholism field because it perpetuates the drinking. However, for a child, denial can be a positive defense that provides psychic protection for survival. In this situation, it is important to remember that defenses serve a purpose. Forcing a child to give up a defense before he or she is ready can result in regression to a more primitive defense. In other words, children and adolescents should not be forced to participate in COA-specific treatment. An adolescent who tries Alateen several times and does not want to continue should not be made to do so—just as an adult COA who reads a book for COAs and finds it too painful to continue should not be forced to continue reading.

Ingredients of COA-Specific Services

All COA-specific services should help COAs understand the following four points:

1. You are not alone. There are many other children with alcoholic parents, who experience what you experience, and feel like you do.
2. You are not responsible for your parent's drinking, alcoholism, behavior, or recovery.
3. You can get help for yourself so things will be better.
4. There are people who can help you.

Counseling in general is based on the premise that "For me to help you, you need to <u>trust</u> me and <u>talk</u> about your <u>feelings</u>"—three things that are difficult for COAs to do. Therefore, it is necessary to modify standard counseling techniques. It is suggested that this can be done by having the service provider break the "don't talk" rule first by demonstrating an understanding of how parental alcoholism can affect children.[13] This can be done verbally or with reading materials or visual aids, such as pictures or films. The most common concerns and experiences of COAs should be addressed. These include:

1. Children feel responsible, directly or indirectly, for their parent's drinking.
2. Children equate their parent's drinking with not being loved.
3. Children feel angry with the non-alcoholic parent for not protecting them or for causing the alcoholic's drinking.
4. Children fear that the alcoholic will get hurt, sick or die.
5. Children are embarrassed by the parent's inappropriate behavior which can include criminal or sexual behavior.
6. Children never know what to expect because of the inconsistency.
7. Children are confused by the difference between "dry" behavior and "drunk" behavior.
8. Children sometimes want their parents to drink and then feel guilty.

By stating "Here are some of the concerns of other children who have parents who drink too much sometimes", the counselor demonstrates that many situations or feelings are shared by other children. By recognizing that their situation/feelings are not unique, the COA feels less embarrassed to self disclose and more confident that the counselor will understand.

In describing the common concerns listed above, the counselor should take time to provide concrete examples of each concern. Once this has occurred the counselor can ask, "do you have any of these concerns or do any of these situations occur in your house?"

Next, the child should then be given the opportunity to talk. Some may just nod silently, some may ventilate, some may acknowledge they have some of the concerns, while others may deny those concerns, and some may become so anxious they are unable to sit still. If the child does share, the counselor should listen carefully to what the child is most concerned about and ask questions that determine the extent of the impact of the parent's drinking on the child. It is in this step that the assessment should occur.

The third step in counseling COAs is to provide education. This can be done verbally, but articles, books, booklets, and films should be used as a supplement because the COA's anxiety often prevents absorbing the information.

The fourth step of counseling is to provide coping strategies. This should include the opportunity to role play difficult situations and evaluate the efficacy of different strategies.

The fifth step includes examining the child's adaptation to the parent's drinking, the child's comfort or discomfort with their own behavior, and acknowledging that they have choices in how they react to the parent. Often COAs don't see their "problem behavior" as a reaction to the parent. Once they do, they can begin to choose and then develop alternative healthier ways of coping.

The final step is examining blocks to healthier functioning. Treatment of COAs should help them to understand how their past and current family situation affect them and empower them to make the best of the current situation and positively influence the future. For example, an adolescent, who is always hurt by peer relationships because she/he is looking for nurturing that is not provided by the parent, can understand how she/he has unrealistic expectations of friends, becomes hurt, and then keeps people from getting close. This adolescent can learn to identify what are her/his needs, who can meet different needs, how to get the needs met, and then learn what are realistic expectations in different relationships.

Other Service Issues

When the Parent Becomes Abstinent

Often providers of services to COAs forget that things don't automatically improve for the child, and sometimes get worse when the parent stops drinking. Services for COAs whose parents are abstinent are just as necessary as services to children of actively drinking alcoholic parents. The ingredients of services to children of abstinent/recovering alcoholic parents (CORAs) are similar to those of active alcoholics but in addition they need:

- education about the recovery process
- to re-examine their survival role
- other people to talk with to validate experiences, perceptions, and feelings
- counseling on how to argue with parents and express negative feelings
- to re-examine the impact of the parent on their own behavior

Absent Parents

COAs, whose parents have died or are alive but not living with the child, should also be eligible for COA-specific services because they can still be negatively affected by the parent. Guilt stemming from feeling may be if the child did something different the parent would still be alive or living with the child are common. Anger for being abandoned or guilt that a hated parent is no longer around are also common.

Holidays

Birthdays, religious holidays, and national holidays are supposed to be times for happy celebrations involving the family. Beginning in preschool, children are taught about and celebrate holidays. For many COAs, holidays are the times of great stress and sadness. All services to COAs should be providing holiday specific awareness, education, support, and coping strategies for COAs. This includes acknowledging that holidays aren't always happy and are often disappointing, helping COAs prepare for the disappointment, developing alternative celebrations, and realistic expectations. For example, a COA who anticipates that it will be too painful to stay in the house with the family on Thanksgiving can make plans to volunteer to serve meals to the homeless.

COA Groups

A number of people have documented the positive results experienced by COAs when they participate in groups that focus on being the child of an alcoholic (Miller, 1983;[14] Hawley, 1981;[15] Deckman, 1982; [16] Peitler, 1980; [17] Hughes, 1977; [18] Fairchild, 1974; [19] Weir, 1970 [20]). DiCicco et al. also documented the positive results for adolescent children of alcoholics when they participated in integrated groups that provided general alcohol education. [21]

Groups can be a particularly strong modality for working with COAs. By participating in a group with other COAs, individuals will experience the following benefits:

- Reduced isolation
- New ways of coping
- Positive peer support
- Practice sharing feelings
- Confrontation when needed
- Increased readiness for Alateen [22]

The Goals for COA groups include:

- To reduce isolation
- To practice identifying and expressing feelings
- To increase understanding of the parents
- To learn coping strategies

Regardless of the duration of the group, all groups should include education about parental alcoholism and how it affects children. The group should begin with an educational style since the classroom is often the only group a COA feels safe in because the roles and rules are consistent and clearly defined.

Several manuals for leading COA groups for elementary and middle school aged children are available.

Sexual Abuse and Other Forms of Child Abuse

All COA service providers must report child abuse to the proper authorities. It is critical that COAs understand the limits of confidentiality at the beginning of their participation in programs so they can choose what to self disclose. When a child reports abuse, the service provider should ask the child what he/she wants to happen, and discuss possible ways of stopping the abuse and protecting the child; such as having the family participate in court ordered counseling, having the abusing father removed from the home, having the child leave the home, etc. Ideally, COA service providers, depending how well they know the child, can report the abuse and make suggestions for how it's handled. In most states child protective workers, are overloaded, undertrained, and undersupervised. As a result, many appreciate suggestions and will incorporate them into their handling of the case. Service providers who report child abuse should be prepared for the child's anger and sense of betrayal. They should explain to the child why he or she is making the report and continue to provide ongoing help for the child.

Often COA service providers are reluctant to report some child abuse because the child abuse/protection system in most states is less than ideal and there is a fear that reporting will do more harm then good. While this may be true, all cases must be reported because the consequence of not reporting are serious. It may help to keep in mind that a child abuse report can hurt a child. Hurt children can heal, but dead children cannot.

Service providers to COAs should go out of their way to increase the understanding of COAs by child abuse/protective workers, legal guardians, and judges.

Cultural Issues

All providers of services to COAs should be culturally sensitive. This includes knowing how children of different cultural groups will respond to similar situations and providing culturally appropriate educational materials when they are available. For example, Brisbane and Womble [23] point out that an African American COA may have more difficulty saying negative things about a parent than a Caucasian COA. Professionals should also be aware of how families from different cultural backgrounds define family, view "getting help," and the dynamics that exist when the service provider is of a different cultural background than the child.

Training and Qualifications

The training and qualifications of providers of services to COAs vary depending on the range of services being provided. The person creating a bulletin board display of government posters for COAs obviously does not need the same qualifications as someone who is doing therapy with COAs. However, in viewing the continuum of services for COAs once the service provider goes past awareness, the qualifications necessary include a minimum understanding of child and adolescent development, knowledge of techniques for working with the child at different developmental stages and emotional states, and knowledge of alcoholism and drug abuse.

Until recently, most child specialists did not have alcoholism knowledge and most alcoholism professionals didn't have child development knowledge and skills in working with children of different ages. To understand a "blackout," but not be able to explain it to a child so it can be understood, will not help COAs just as to be an expert in working with children but not know what a blackout is will not be helpful.

The ability to be objective in working with COAs is critical. Adult COAs should be sure to have worked through their own issues and be aware and get help if they re-emerge. For example, an untreated adult COA may try to cap a young COA's expression of angry or hurt feelings because they access feelings and memories of the counselor's childhood that the counselor that have been repressed or sublimated and the counselor doesn't want to deal with them. On the other extreme, a child may begin discussing an experience that was similar to the counselor's childhood experience. The counselor may assume that the child's feelings about the experience are the same as the counselor's past feelings and not give the child the opportunity to discuss it further, and then misread the situation and the child's feelings. Professional supervision is extremely useful in determining if these situations are occurring.

Professional supervision is also useful in determining the appropriateness and timing of self-disclosure. Most professionals working with COAs are asked if they grew up in an alcoholic home. The general rules of professional self disclosure to a client/patient apply. Self disclosure should only occur if it's in the child's best interest. If counselors disclose they are COAs too early in the relationship, the child might assume the counselor automatically understands and not make the effort to organize and express his/her own experience. If counselors who are not COAs share this with the child too early, the child might wonder, "how can she/he possibly understand and help me?". The child might also be too embarrassed about his/her experience and feelings.

On the other hand, self-disclosure can be helpful at the end of the counseling relationship. For example, acknowledging a counselor's own situation as a COA may give a child hope for a healthy future. Acknowledging not being a COA shows COAs that others can understand and help.

Counselors who are recovering alcoholics who drank as parents should be cautioned when considering work with COAs. Hearing the rage and sadness of a young or adolescent COA can ignite feelings of guilt in the counselor who for the first time may be hearing the magnitude of the impact of parental alcoholism on children and then wonder if his/her children also felt like this. Again, having worked through these issues and receiving professional supervision are critical for the counselor.

Adolescent Drinking and Other Drug Use

Treatment

It is estimated that 80-90% of all adolescents in treatment for their own alcoholism or other drug dependency are COAs. Until very recently, their COA issues were not addressed in treatment. (It is the author's view that this was one of the reasons for the high rate of relapse in adolescents.) The COA issues were not addressed because treatment professionals applied the wise practice of not dealing with a chemically dependent adult's COA issues, until a year of sobriety has been achieved, to adolescents. This practice is based on the idea that dealing with COA issues before a year of sobriety will stimulate a high degree of anxiety which could then trigger a relapse.

While this is a wise practice in treating adults, it is an inappropriate practice in treating adolescents who are emotionally dependent, and often financially dependent, on their parents. Many chemically dependent adolescents compare and contrast their chemical use to their parents, may have to attend AA, NA, or CA meetings with their parents, or may live with or return home to active parental alcoholism. They may be using chemicals as a way of coping with the parental alcoholism, and may have parents who sabotage their recovery.[24]

Prevention

While all schools are mandated to provide alcohol and drug education to students, it is ironic that COAs, the group most at risk for becoming alcoholic, may be least affected by the education. There are several explanations for this. First, many COAs do not believe the negative consequences of drinking because of conflicts with the messages at home; such as "people only die if they drink too much. I don't drink that much!" To believe that alcohol is harmful would force them to believe that the parent will die. A young child cannot live with the constant fear of abandonment and maintain emotional health. Therefore, the child decides that "the amount of alcohol my mom drinks is OK."

Second, many COAs become highly anxious during alcohol and drug education and "tune out" or act out, including cutting class. They don't learn the information because they are "not there."

Third, alcohol and drug education has rarely addressed the vulnerability issues. Few COAs understand how they are more vulnerable, such as possibly having a high tolerance to alcohol, and processing alcohol in the body differently.

Alcohol and drug prevention programs must address these issues by providing developmentally appropriate COA-specific material for COAs even if they are not identified. Prevention programs using curriculums should also offer individual attention to COAs, just as schools provide "extra help" for students who have difficulty with other subjects.

Conclusion

Despite the growing number of COA-specific services, a continuum of services in many different settings are still needed. In providing services, the needs of the child should be matched to the level of service needed at that time. To do this, a careful assessment of the child and the impact of the parents' drinking on the child must be done.

Providers of services to COAs must maintain objectivity to be most effective and should use professional supervision to monitor if personal issues are interfering with the delivery of services.

Finally, alcohol and drug education must be more responsive to the learning styles of COAs and adolescent chemical dependency treatment programs must address COA issues if we are going to begin to break the cycle of addiction.

References

[1]   Booz Allen Hamilton, Inc. *An Assessment of the Needs of and Resources for Children of Alcoholic Parents. Prepared for NIAAA 1974.*

[2]   National Institute on Alcohol Abuse and Alcoholism. *Services for Children of Alcoholics Research Monograph No. 4, DHHS Publ. No. ADM 81-1007. Washington, D.C., U.S. Government Printing Office, 1981.*

[3]   *Ibid., p. iii.*

[4]   *Children of Alcoholics Foundation, Directory of National Resources for Children of Alcohlics, New York, 1986.*

[5]   Woodside, M., Henderson, B. and Samuels, P. *Parental Consent: Helping Children of Addicted Parents Get Help. Children of Alcoholics Foundation, Inc., NY, 1991.*

[6]   Black, Claudia. *It Will Never Happen to Me!. Denver, M.A.C., 1981.*

[7]   Deutsch, C., Di Cicco, L., Mills, D. *"Reaching Children From Families wiht Alcoholism." in: Levin, M., ed. Proceedings of the 29th Annual Meeting of the Alcohol and Drug Problems Association of North America, 1978. Washington, D.C.*

[8]   National Institute on Alcohol Abuse and Alcoholism. *Preventing Alcohol Problems Through A Student Assitance Program, DHHS Publ. No. ADM 84-1344, Washington, D.C., U.S. Government Printing Office, 1984.*

[9]   O'Gorman, P. and Ross, R. *"Children of Alcohlics in the Juvenile Justice System." Alcohol Health and Research World, Vol 8, No. 4, 1984.*

[10]   Kohlberg, L. *The Philosophy of Moral Development: Moral Stages and the Idea of Justice. San Francisco: Harper & Row, 1981.*

[11]   Gilligan, C. *In a Differrent Voice: Psychological Theory and Women's Development. Cambridge: Harvard University Press, 1982.*

[12]   Beardslee, W. and Podorefsky, D. *"Resilient Adolescents Whose Parents Have Serious Affective and Other Psychiatric Disorders: Importance of Self-Understanding and Relationships", American Journal of Psychiatry 145:1, January, 1988.*

13 Morehouse, Ellen. "Working in the Schools with Children of Alcoholic Parents." Health and Social Work, Vol. 4, No. 4, 1984.

14 Miller, N. "Group Psychotherapy in a School Setting for Adolescent Children of Alcoholics". Group, Vol. 7, 1983.

15 Hawley, N.P. and Brown, C.L. "Use of Group Treatment with Children of Alcoholics". Social Casework, Vol. 62, No. 1, 1981.

16 Deckman, J. and Downs, B. "A Group Treatment Approach for Adolescent Children of Alcoholic Parents." Social Work Groups Vol. 5, 1982.

17 Peitler, E.J. A Comparison of the effectiveness of group counseling and Alateen on the psychological adjustment of two groups of adolescent sons of alcoholic fathers. Ph.D. dissertation, St. John's University, 1980.

18 Hughes, J.M. "Adolescent Children of Alcoholic Parents and the Relationship of Alateen to These Children." Journal of Consulting and Clinical Psychology, Vol. 49, 1977.

19 Fairchild, D.M. "Teen Group I.: A Pilot Project in Group Therapy with Adolescent CHildren of Alcoholic Patients." Journal of the Ft. Logan Mental Health Center, Vol. 2, 1964.

20 Weir, W.R. "Conseling Youth Whose Parents Are Alcoholic: A Means to an End as well as an End in Itself." Journal of Alcohol Education, 16, 1970.

21 Di Cicco, L. Davis, R., Hogan J., MacLean, A. and Orenstein, A. "Group Experiences for Children of Alcoholics." Alcohol Health and Research World, Vol. 8, No. 4, 1984.

22 Morehouse, E. In: Ackerman, R., ed. Growing in the Shadow, Pompano Beach, Fla. : Health Communications, 1986.

23 Brisbane, F. and Womble, M. A Model for Working with Black Children of Alcoholic and Drug Addicted Parents. The National Black Alcoholism Council, 1987.

24 Morehouse, E. "Working with Alcohol-Abusing Children of Alcoholics". Alcohol Health and Research World, Vol. 8, No. 4, 1984.

The Role of Caring Adults in the Lives of Children of Alcoholics

Emmy E. Werner, Ph.D.
University of California at Davis
Dept. of Psychology
and
Jeannette L. Johnson, Ph.D.
University of Maryland at Baltimore
Dept. of Psychiatry

"Outside of residence in a concentration camp, there are very few sustained human experiences that make one the recipient of as much sadism as does being a close family member of an alcoholic."

George Vaillant, The Natural History of Alcoholism, 1983

Parental alcoholism has been associated with problems among their children, who may show difficulties in school or more severe problems such as psychological dysfunction (West and Prinz, 1987). Increasingly, a substantial segment of research shows that children of alcoholics are at risk for problems which include behavioral, psychological, and neuropsychological deficits (Sher, 1987). These difficulties can place children of alcoholics at risk for future problems in adulthood, especially alcoholism. Much of the research on the behavior and development of children of alcoholics, however, has generally focused on samples drawn from clinical populations. These studies typically include parents whose alcoholism was severe enough, or was comorbid with other problems serious enough to be referred for treatment, and children in treatment themselves. Not surprisingly, most of these studies have found a significant proportion of youths with low self-esteem who developed conduct and learning disorders, and who had records of repeated delinquencies, substance abuse, and suicidal tendencies in adolescence (El-Guebaly and Offord, 1977; Russell et al., 1984).

Longitudinal studies of children of alcoholics in a community context are rare and are of special interest because they provide the opportunity to study families with alcoholic parents who do not reach clinical settings, and with offspring who do not get any professional help. They can inform us not only about the toll that parental alcoholism takes in the lives of the children of problem drinkers, but also about the roots of resilience in youngsters who cope successfully with this family tragedy. Both clinicians and researchers know of youths reared in alcoholic families who are doing remarkably well (Beilin and Davis, 1989; El-Guebaly and Offord, 1977). An evaluation of the sources of inner strength and of the informal supports in their lives should be as important as an enumeration of their handicaps.

Given the financial constraints imposed on human service professionals, it is worthwhile to ask if a community based network of caring adults in the extended family, the neighborhood, and the school, can have beneficial effects on the lives of youth who grow up with an alcoholic. This paper addresses these issues in the context of a prospective longitudinal study of 65 men and women, all offspring of alcoholics. They are a subsample of a cohort of 698 multiracial individuals born in 1955 on the island of Kauai. Their lives were monitored from birth through early and middle childhood, to late adolescence and young adulthood (Werner and Smith, 1977, 1982, 1992).

The Study Population

The 65 offspring of alcoholics who are the focus of this report were chosen from the records of the Kauai Longitudinal Study on the basis of the following criteria: (1) one or both parents had been identified as having serious problems related to alcohol abuse, beginning in the individual's childhood (between ages two and ten). This information was obtained in an interview with the primary caregiver when the youngster was ten years old; (2) problems related to parental alcohol abuse (for example, domestic, financial, legal, medical, psychological, or social) were reported as major sources of stress by the individuals themselves in interviews at ages 17 or 18 and 31 or 32; (3) references to parental alcoholism were noted in the social service records available on their families in the community (Criminal and Civil Court; Family Court; Department of Health; Department of Housing and Social Services). Seventy-five percent of the youths in this group had fathers who were alcoholic; 12.5% had mothers with serious drinking problems, and another 12.5% had parents who were both problem drinkers.

Data Collection

The data on which these analyses are based are quite extensive and have been described in detail elsewhere (Werner and Smith, 1977, 1982). Here we very briefly describe the data collection methods. Social workers and public health nurses observed the interactions between the parents and the children at ages one, two, and ten, and noted the caregivers' perceptions of the children's temperamental characteristics, as well as any behavior problems they displayed in the home. Teachers evaluated the classroom behavior and problem-solving skills of the youngsters in grades four and five. Scholastic aptitude and achievement tests were administered to them in grades 8, 10, and 12. Their scores on the California Psychological Inventory and the Nowicki Locus of Control Scale were available as well.

Interviews with the parents when the youngsters were ten years old yielded information about the adults within the family and outside of the family whom provided emotional support and served as positive role models.

When the individuals were 18 years old, we interviewed them personally with a number of questions that dealt with the quality of family life they had experienced in adolescence. They were asked about their attitudes toward their family, the neighborhood, the school and church; their feelings of security within the extended household they lived in; and the degree of identification with their parents or other caring elders. They evaluated the help they had received from both formal and informal sources of support, such as older siblings, grandparents, aunts, uncles, cousins, neighbors, peer friends, teachers, youth workers, mental health professionals, and ministers.

During the follow-up on the individuals who were aged 31 and 32, a structured interview assessed the individuals' perception of the major stressors and supports they had encountered while growing up in an alcoholic family: at school, work, and in their relationships with adults inside and outside of the home. It included a number of questions about the persons who had helped them most in dealing with the difficulties and stresses in their lives and the kind of help that had proven to be beneficial.

In addition, the adult children of alcoholics completed Rotter's Locus of Control Scale (1966) which assesses the degree to which a person believes that he or she is in control of his or her own life (internal) and the degree to which events are perceived to be a result of fate, luck, or other factors beyond personal control (external). At age 18, such a locus of control measure had differentiated significantly between offspring of alcoholics who did and those who did not develop serious delinquencies, mental health problems, or teenage pregnancies (Werner and Smith, 1992).

Each of the participants in the 31 and 32 year follow-up completed the EAS Temperament Survey for Adults (Buss and Plomin, 1984) which assesses dimensions of temperament (activity, excitability, sociability); temperament has shown a fair degree of stability at different stages of the life cycle. In infancy and early childhood, these temperamental characteristics had differentiated significantly between offspring of alcoholics who later developed serious coping problems in their teens and those who did not (Werner, 1986).

An independent perspective on the quality of adaptation of the adult children of alcoholics was gleaned from their records in the community. From the courts on Kauai and the other islands (Oahu, Hawaii, Maui) information was obtained on members of this cohort who were convicted of a crime or involved as defendants in a civil suit, or whose marriages had ended in a divorce. The files of the criminal, civil, and family courts (which are open to the public) not only contained records of major violations of the law, but also information on domestic problems, such as delinquent child support payments, and child and/or spouse abuse. From the State Department of Mental Health, information was ascertained on every member of this cohort who had received in- or out-patient treatment for mental health problems, or whose parents had received such treatment. Information on special services rendered to cohort members who had disabilities was obtained from the State Department of Social Rehabilitation, and information about the causes of death for members who were deceased was obtained from the State Department of Health.

The status of the adult children of alcoholics at the age of 30 can be seen in Table 1. Table 1 shows that there were some differences between male and female adult children of alcoholics. More male children of alcoholics had come from divorced parents and had criminal records. When compared to the offspring whose parents were not problem drinkers, again, male children of alcoholics came from divorced parents more so than male children of non-alcoholics. Both male and female children of alcoholics had more health problems compared to their peers of the same age and sex whose parents were not problem drinkers. Finally, female children of alcoholics had more frequent indications of family court records compared to female children of non-alcoholics.

Table 1: Status of Adult Children of Alcoholics by Age 30

Outcome Variables	Males	Females
	n=27	n=38
Has some coping problems	45.5	54.8
Divorced	25.9*	10.5
Has record in family court	14.8	13.2*
Has criminal record	11.1	0
Has sought state funded mental health care	3.7	2.6
Reports chronic health problems	38.9*	45.2*
Died in young adulthood	3.7	0

Numbers reported in terms of percentages.
*=Proportion of problems significantly higher for offspring of alcoholics than for peers of same age and sex whose parents were not problem drinkers.

Criteria for Adult Adaptation

Ratings of the quality of adult adaptation were based on both the individuals' self-evaluations (in the clinical interviews and biographical questionnaires), and on their record in the community at age 31 or 32. The ratings were made independently from any knowledge of the information on stressful life events that had been obtained at previous follow-up stages in childhood and adolescence. A developmental psychologist and a graduate student in child development independently read transcripts of the adult interviews and the questionnaire data and agency records that contained information on the current status of the men and women who participated in the 31 and 32 year follow-up. The following criteria were used to define 'successful coping' in early adulthood:

- School/Work: is employed and/or is enrolled in school. Is very satisfied with work and/or school achievement;

- Relationship with spouse/mate: is married or in long-term committed relationship; is satisfied with partner and reports little or no conflict; no record of desertion, divorce, or spouse abuse in court files;

- Relationship with children: evaluates children (very) positively; is (very) satisfied with parental role; no record of child abuse or delinquent child support payments in court files;

- Relationship with reports parents and siblings: evaluates father, mother, and siblings positively; little or no conflict with them;

- Relationships with peers: has several close friends who provide emotional support when needed; is (very) satisfied with their relationship of no assualt, battery, rape or other criminal offenses in court files;

- Self-assessment: is (very) happy or mostly satisfied with present state of life; reports no dependency on alcohol or drugs; no psychosomatic illnesses; no record of psychiatric disorders in Mental Health Register.

Status of COAs at ages 31 and 32

Follow-up data in adulthood on 55 of the 67 COAs in the cohort was obtained comprising 82% of the original sample. Two individuals had died by the age of 32. One was a male who died from complications associated with AIDS, the other was a female who died from heart failure. The twelve individuals that were unable to be contacted in adulthood did not differ significantly in mean PMA IQ from the follow-up sample. The proportion with coping problems by age 18 in that group was the same as well. On the whole, sample attrition did not appear to introduce any selective bias in the results.

Some 51% of the offspring of alcoholics satisfied the criteria for 'successful adult adaptation.' Some 28% had developed minor coping problems in the transition to adulthood and some 21% had developed major coping problems that included at least two of the following conditions: a marriage irrevocably broken, a record of serious mental health problems, a criminal record, and/or a poor self-evaluation. Offspring of alcoholic mothers had a higher proportion of coping problems at age 32 than did the offspring of alcoholic fathers; in each group, more males than females had developed major problems (see Table 2).

Table 2: Adult children of alcoholics with coping problems at age 30 by gender of alcoholic parent and gender of offspring

	Gender of Offspring	
Gender of Alcoholic Parent	Male	Female
Alcoholic Mother	83.3%	60%
Alcoholic Father	43.8%	42.3%

The majority (71.5%) of the offspring of alcoholics with coping problems had remained on their native island; the majority (60%) of those without coping problems had moved elsewhere, either to Honolulu, or the west coast of the US mainland (California, Oregon, Washington, Alaska), seeking and finding opportunities thousands of miles away from their parental home. Among the most peripatetic were a nurse, employed at a state hospital at Yap, in the Carolinas, and the wife of a serviceman, stationed in Maryland.

Protective Factors in the Caregiving Environment

There were no significant differences in social class between the offspring of alcoholics who did and those who did not develop serious coping problems in later life. The overwhelming majority of youngsters in both groups had grown up in chronic poverty. How then did they manage these children born to alcoholic parents? Tables 3 and 4 give a summary of the varied sources of informal support that buffered the impact of parental drinking problems in the lives of the sons and daughters of alcoholics.

Individuals who coped effectively with the trauma of growing up in an alcoholic family and who became competent, confident, and caring adults relied on a significantly larger number of sources of support in their childhood and youth than did offspring of alcoholics with coping problems by age 32. Daughters of alcoholics tended to turn to a significantly larger number of caring adults in their childhood and youth than did sons. Let us now examine the contributions of individual

Table 3: Differences in availability of informal support systems between sons of alcoholics <u>with</u> and without coping problems at age 32

| | Sons of alcoholics | |
	with problems n=12	without problems n=10
Adults living with family (not parent) by age 10	33.3%	0
Living with both natural parents by age 17	16.7%	100%
High social support by peers*	40%	100%
High social support by extended family*	40%	100%
Divorced by age 30	58.3%	0
Sources of support in times of stress: (18-30)		
Siblings	0	20%
Minister	0	10%
Mental Health Professionals	0	20%
Faith, prayer	12.5%	10%
Active involvement		
with religious community	0	10%
with social concerns	0	20%

* in adolescence

Emmy E. Werner and Jeannette L. Johnson

Table 4: Differences in availability of informal support systems between daughters of alcoholics <u>with</u> and without coping problems at age 32

	Daughters of alcoholics with problems	without problems
	n=14	n=17
Adults outside family child likes to be With (by age 10)	64.3%	70%
Adults living with family (not parents)	42.9%	17.6%
Living with both natural parents (by age 17) 55.6%	75%	
High social support by extended family*	0	33.3%
High marital satisfaction	30.0%	94.1%
Divorced by age 30	28.6%	0
Sources of support in times of stress: (18-30)		
Teacher, mentor	0	5.9%
Minister	0	11.8%
Mental Health Professionals	21.4%	0
Faith, prayer	28.6%	58.8%
Active involvement		
with religious community	0	11.8%
with social concerns	0	11.8%

* in adolescence

127

members of the network of caring adults in the home, neighborhood, and school, who, from the vantage point of the youths, made a significant difference in their lives.

The non-alcoholic parent

In a review of the literature on protective factors in the lives of children of alcoholics, Berlin and Davis (1989) find that the supportiveness of the non-alcoholic spouse is a crucial variable in the degree of impact of alcoholism on the family. The more supportive the non-alcoholic parent, the more likely there is available the nurturance, protection, and guidance which children need for optimal development. A supportive non-alcoholic spouse also can create a positive family atmosphere where members of the extended family can provide supplementary parenting and positive role models for the children and youth.

This experience was born out in the reports by the offspring of alcoholics in our sample—especially among those who developed into adults who worked well, loved well, and had a positive outlook. In most cases (among 94% of the successful daughters and among 80% of the successful sons of alcoholics), the mainstay of the family was a non-alcoholic mother. In two cases, a stepmother was perceived as the main support of the family. Among offspring of alcoholics who later developed coping problems, the mother was less frequently perceived as a protective buffer in a traumatic family situation (females=60% and males =33.3%) and was more often a problem drinker herself.

A higher proportion of the resilient offspring of alcoholics had received a great deal of attention from their mothers during the first year of life than those who later developed serious coping problems. Significantly fewer resilient offspring of alcoholics had mothers who became pregnant again or gave birth to another sibling before the index child was 20 months old.

The supportive mothers in our sample had no access to self-help organizations for families of alcoholics, such as Al-Anon. They tended to rely on their own competence and determination and the assistance of the extended family and church groups. Three out of four mothers were steadily and gainfully employed when their offspring were in early and middle childhood.

Siblings

Among the offspring of alcoholic parents who made a successful adult adaptation, a supportive non-alcoholic mother was frequently backed up by siblings who were able and willing to look out for one another. Positive support by an older brother or sister seemed especially important for male youths. Four out of five among the sons of alcoholics who developed into competent and confident adults reported that an older sibling was an important buffer in their lives, in contrast to only one of three among the men who developed coping problems in adulthood. Among the women, sibling support was common in both the positive and negative outcome groups.

Berlin and Davis (1989) have argued that the oldest child in an alcoholic family is more vulnerable to the expectations and needs of the parents when the going gets tough. Our data indicate that it was more often the oldest girl rather than the oldest boy who had to assume many parental responsibilities, and put aside individual pursuits or preferences for the sake of maintaining stability and order. This experience affected their choice of adult vocations as well: A high proportion of the women who were sibling-caretakers in our sample entered the helping professions in young adulthood and became nursery school or elementary school teachers, nurses, social workers, and parent facilitators.

While most of the resilient offspring of alcoholics acknowledged that they now led separate lives from their siblings who have grown up, married, and have children of their own, they still felt that they could count on them in an emergency. The exceptions were those who had left behind brothers or sisters who were mired in multiple problems, similar to those with which their parents had to contend: alcoholism, financial problems, marital problems, divorce, and mental illness. Most of the resilient men and women refused to get en-meshed in these problems. They tended to avoid disapproval, and they eventually detached themselves and withdrew, just as they did when they encountered similar problems with their alcoholic parents. But often a resilient adult sibling continued to play the role of the comforter, counselor, or protector which he or she had assumed in late childhood or adolescence.

The resilient men and women who went to college often credited a sibling for counsel and support while away from home. The strong ties among siblings who experienced a traumatic childhood together continued, even when the resilient sibling moved far away. Some of the resilient women were so closely identified with the role of sibling caretaker that they had a hard time letting go when they reached adulthood. A positive relationship among step siblings and foster children also increased the likelihood of a successful adaptation among the youths in our sample whose parental drinking problems led to the break-up of their family. Even a foster home could occasionally sustain lasting positive relationships among unrelated children.

The majority of the youths in our study grew up in large families, with four or more children, creating a number of potential sibling caretakers than are accessible to a child in the average American family with two closely spaced children. It also allowed for a great variety of role allocations in the ongoing family drama. Sibling care among offspring of alcoholics tended to be more effective if it constituted supplementary rather than substitute parenting. This is true for other high risk youth as well, notably handicapped children and children of divorce (Wallerstein and Blakeslee, 1989; Werner, 1984).

The availability of supplemental adult resources for organizing sibling care seems to be an important element in determining whether the sibling caregiver helps or hurts herself or the sibling entrusted in her care in the long run. Among the vulnerable but invincible children of Kauai, we noted that when an alcoholic parent was debilitated or absent, other concerned adults in the extended family, such as grandparents, aunts or uncles, acted as parent substitutes and shared the burden of care with the older siblings in the family (Werner and Smith, 1982).

Grandparents

Foremost among relatives was the positive role played by grandparents, especially a maternal grandmother, in the lives of the children of alcoholics. Daughters of alcoholics with positive adult adaptation had a higher proportion of grandmothers as supplementary parents than daughters of problem drinkers with coping problems in adulthood (47.1% vs. 33.3%). Among the sons of alcoholics, however, there was a higher proportion with negative outcomes among those reared by grandparents who acted as parent substitutes in the case of the break up of the family.

Grandparents provided a wide range of caregiving activities. A number of the adult children of alcoholics remembered fondly the grandparents with whom they lived during their childhood or teen years. A married housewife with two children of her own had lived with her maternal grandparents since her birth, and considered them to be her major source of emotional support. She was most influenced by her grandmother who helped her with her school work and praised her when she was doing well. The resilient sons of alcoholics tended to stress the companionship and financial support they received from their grandparents, especially their grandfathers.

The experience of the children of alcoholics in our sample dovetails with reports from other research, notably the studies reviewed by Werner in 1991 in The Psychology of Grandparenthood: An International Perspective. American grandparents in all ethnic and socioeconomic groups tend to play the role of "family watchdog". While the majority prefer compassionate relationships, an increasing number are significantly involved in the lives of their grandchildren. Positive effects of grandparents on their grandchildren's behavior have been repeatedly demonstrated-not only among the offspring of alcoholic and abusive parents, but also among children of divorce and children of teenage mothers, especially in the context of poverty.

Aunts and Uncles

Nearly half of the daughters of alcoholics and a third of the sons of problem drinkers also had a favorite aunt or uncle who helped buffer the trauma of their family life. Most of these were older teenagers or young adults who lived in the same neighborhood or community. The resilient daughters of alcoholics usually mentioned a favorite aunt who was available to talk things over with them. Some of these aunties took the place of an older sister who had left the home, and were appreciated for their caring qualities and the physical affection they showed. Other aunts became mentors and role models; they read to them or gave them advice about school and life.

The resilient sons of alcoholics tended to single out a favorite uncle for whom they had high respect and who took a special interest in them. Often times this was a younger brother of their mother. This uncle might help them with their school, play cards with them, take them to Scouts activities, and generally do things together with the boy—a treasured member of the family. Older teenage boys, like the girls, appreciated the fact they could talk to their uncle about their plans and ask him for the kind of advice (educational, vocational) that would usually be given by a father to his son.

Teachers and Elder Mentors

Most of the offspring of alcoholics who grew into competent and confident adults enjoyed school. Even if they were not unusually gifted, those who ultimately showed the greatest resilience tended to put whatever abilities they had to good use. In many cases, they made school into a home away from home, a refuge from a troubled and disordered household. None of the men and only one woman among the offspring of alcoholics with coping problems in adulthood recalled receiving some support from a teacher. But about half of those who grew into competent and confident adults encountered at least one teacher who became a positive role model in their lives. For these youths, a special teacher was not just an instructor who taught them academic skills, but someone who raised their self-esteem who became a counselor and confidante, and who opened doors for them that changed their lives in a positive way. Some youths had also sought out elder mentors who were not part of the school system, but who played the same roles as a supportive teacher. A florist who now owns her own shop gave credit for her success to a classmate's mother who became a mentor to her during her teenage years. Another daughter of an alcoholic befriended an elderly woman in her neighborhood.

Friends and Parents of Friends

Even though they came from poor, chaotic, and discordant homes, the resilient children of alcoholics tended to be well liked by their classmates, and had one or more close same sex friends. They tended to keep their childhood friends for long periods of time, and relied on them for ongoing emotional support. This was more often true for the females (94%) than the males (70%). Association with friends and the parents of friends who came from stable, non-alcoholic families helped these youngsters to gain a perspective and to maintain a constructive distance between themselves and their own chaotic household.

A high proportion of the offspring of alcoholics who developed into responsible and caring adults married spouses whom they had known as long-term friends (females=88.2% and males=70%). A high proportion of the resilient offspring of alcoholics who married long-term friends also had good relationships with their future in-laws. This was especially true for the daughters of alcoholics. These women had recruited substitute parents among their in-laws, just as they had sought counsel and comfort from the parents of their boyfriends during their teenage years. The majority of the resilient offspring of alcoholics valued the emotional support given by their parents-in-law, especially by the mother-in-law.

Some one out of five among the offspring of alcoholics with coping problems in adulthood had married into a family where the in-laws had drinking problems themselves. Very few (7.4%) of the resilient sons and daughters of problem drinkers reported alcoholism or marital discord among their in-laws. However, when difficulties with parents-in-law arose, the resilient men and women employed the same defense mechanism they used with their own alcoholic parents. They detached themselves emotionally and avoided getting enmeshed in their troubles.

Links Between Protective Factors within the Individual and Outside Sources of Support

When we examined the links between protective factors within the individual and outside sources of support, we noted a certain continuity that appeared in the life course of the high risk men and women who successfully overcame a variety of childhood adversities. Their individual dispositions led them to select or construct environments that, in turn, reinforced and sustained their active, outgoing dispositions, and rewarded their competencies. In spite of occasional deviations during transitional periods, such as adolescence, their life trajectories revealed cumulative 'interactional continuity.' These continuities have also been demonstrated in other cohorts of high risk individuals followed into adulthood; for instance, in the life course of shy and ill-tempered Caucasian children in the Berkeley Guidance Study (Caspi, Elder, and Bem, 1988).

There was, for example, a significant positive link between an 'easy' infant temperament and the sources of support available to the individual in early and middle childhood. Active and sociable babies, without distressing sleeping and feeding habits, tended to elicit more positive responses from their mothers at age one and from alternate caregivers by age two. In middle childhood, such children tended to elicit more positive responses from their mothers at age one and from alternate caregivers by age two. In middle childhood, such children tended to rely on a wider network of caring adults both within and outside the family circle.

Positive parental interactions with the infant and toddler were, in turn, associated with greater autonomy and social maturity at age two, and with greater scholastic competence at age ten. 'Difficult' temperament traits in infancy, in contrast, were moderately linked with behavior problems in the classroom and at home at age ten, which in turn, generated fewer sources of emotional support during adolescence.

Scholastic competence at ten was positively linked with the number of sources of help that the teenager attracted, including support from teachers and peers, as well as from family members. Scholastic competence at ten was also positively linked with a sense of self-efficacy (self-esteem, internal locus of control) at age 18. A greater sense of self-efficacy at age 18 was, in turn, linked to less distress and emotionality for the sons of alcoholic parents at age 32, and generated a greater number of sources of emotional support for daughters of problem drinkers in early adulthood, including support from a spouse or mate.

For the women, a sociable temperament in infancy and young adulthood showed a stronger link with positive outcomes by age 32 than for the men. Mothers who had graduated from high school, and who were steadily employed by the time their children were two years old appeared to be more powerful positive buffers in adversity for their daughters than for their sons. The absence of behavior problems in middle childhood, and high self-esteem and an internal locus of control at age 18, also were more strongly linked to successful adult adaptation for the women than for the men.

For the men, scholastic competence at ten, including at least average intelligence, problem-solving, and reading skills, were more strongly associated with a successful transition into adult responsibilities than for the women. The strongest positive buffer for the men, however, were the sources of emotional support upon which they could rely after they left home, including the support of a spouse or mate, siblings and elders, as well as faith and prayer.

Parental competence, as manifested in educational level achieved, also proved to be a significant protective factor in the lives of the men and women on Kauai who grew up in alcoholic families. A higher parental educational level was linked to more positive parent-child interactions in the first and second year of life, and to more emotional support provided for the offspring during early and middle childhood. Parental education was also positively linked to the infants' health and physical status by age two. There were also significant positive links between parental educational level and the child's scholastic competence at ten; one path was direct, the other was mediated through the infant's health and physical status. Better educated parents had children with better problem-solving and reading skills, but they also had healthier children with fewer handicaps and absences from school, due to repeated serious illnesses.

While parental competence and the sources of support available in the childhood home were modestly linked to the quality of the adult adaptation, they made less of a direct impact in adulthood than the individuals' competencies, degree of self-esteem and self-efficacy, and temperamental dispositions. Many youths who had grown up in alcoholic families left the adverse conditions of their childhood homes (and their island community) after high school, and sought environments they found more compatible.

As they moved into adulthood, they encountered opportunities that turned the life trajectories of significant proportion of these high risk men and women, who had struggled with personal and family problems in their teens—on the path to recovery and maturity. Among the life events that were considered critical turning points by these men and women were: marriage or entry into a long-term committed relationship; the birth of their first child; joining the work force and establishing themselves in a career or job; seeking additional education in a (community) college; and becoming an active member of a church or religious community.

Implications

What lessons have we learned from following the lives of the children of alcoholics on Kauai that might be of relevance to those who care for other children, of other races, in difference places, at different times? The most precious lesson that we choose to learn from this study is Hope: a hope reinforced by reports from a handful of other long-term studies into adulthood which have identified some of the protective buffers and mechanisms that operated in the lives of vulnerable children and youths who succeeded 'against the odds'. In a variety of risk conditions studied—economic hardships, parental psychopathology, foster home placement (Anthony, 1987; Bleuler, 1978; Vaillant, 1983; Rutter and Quinton, 1984)—there appeared a common core of individual dispositions, sources of support, and pathways that led to positive outcomes in adulthood.

Our findings and those by other American and European investigators using a life-span perspective suggest that these 'buffers' make a more profound impact on the life course of children who grow up under adverse conditions than specific risk factors or stressful life events. They appear to transcend ethnic, social class, geographical, and historical boundaries. Most of all, they offer us a more optimistic outlook than the perspective that can be gleaned from the literature on the negative consequences of growing up in an alcoholic family. They provide us with a corrective lens—an awareness of self-righting tendencies that move children toward normal adult development under all but the most persistent adverse circumstances.

Implications for Social Action

Rutter (1987) reminds us that if we want to help vulnerable youngsters, we need to focus on the protective processes that bring about changes in life trajectories from risk to adaptation. He includes among them (1) those that reduce the risk impact; (2) those that reduce the likelihood of negative chain reactions; (3) those that promote self-esteem and self-efficacy; and (4) those that open up opportunities. We have seen these processes at work among resilient offspring of alcoholics in our study and among their peers who recovered from serious coping problems in young adulthood. They represent the essence of any effective intervention program, whether by professionals or volunteers.

We noted, for example, that children of parents with chronic alcoholism could detach themselves from the discord in their household by spending time with caring adults outside the family circle. This process altered their exposure to the potent risk condition in their homes. In other cases, the negative chain reactions following the intermittent hospitalizations of alcoholic parents were buffered by the presence of grandparents or older siblings who acted as substitute parents and provided continuity in care.

The promotion of self-esteem and self-efficacy in a young person is probably the key ingredient in any effective intervention process. Most of the resilient children in our high risk sample were not unusually talented, but they took great pleasure in interests and hobbies that brought them solace when things fell apart in their home lives. They also engaged in activities that allowed them to be part of a cooperative enterprise in 4-H or the Scouts, in a high school choir or orchestra, or in a church youth group.

Self-esteem and self-efficacy also grew when youngsters took on a responsible position commensurate with their ability, whether it was part-time paid work, or managing the household when the alcoholic parent was incapacitated; or most often, caring for younger siblings. As some point in their young lives, usually in middle childhood and adolescence, the offspring of alcoholics who grew into resilient adults were required to carry out some socially desirable task to prevent others in their family from experiencing distress or discomfort. Such acts of required helpfulness (Rachman, 1979) can also become a crucial element of intervention programs that involve such high risk youths in part-time community service; either paid, or for academic credit.

Most of all, self-esteem and self-efficacy was promoted through supportive relationships. The resilient offspring of alcoholics in our study all had at least one person in their lives who accepted them unconditionally, regardless of temperamental idiosyncrasies, physical attractiveness, or intelligence. Most established such a close bond early in their lives, if not with the non-alcoholic parent, then with another family member—a grandparent, older sibling, or favorite aunt or uncle. Some of the high risk youths who had problems in their teens, but staged a recovery in young adulthood, gained a more positive self-concept in the context of an intimate relationship with a spouse or in-laws. The experiences from intergenerational mentoring programs also suggest that a close one-to-one relationship with an unrelated elder (teacher or mentor) can foster self-esteem in a troubled child or youth. An essential aspect of the encounter is that the youth feels that s/he is special to the other person (Freedman, 1989).

One of the most important lessons we learned from our adult follow-up was the opening up of opportunities that led to major turning points in the lives of these sons and daughters of alcoholics as they entered their twenties and early thirties. Our findings at ages 31 and 32 indicate that earlier events in the lives of these high risk children and youths were not the only ones to affect their later adjustment to the world of work, marriage, and parenthood. Among the most potent forces for positive change in this group were education at (community) colleges, active involvement in a church or religious communities, and meeting a supportive mate or friend. Attendance at community colleges was also associated with geographical moves for many children of alcoholics. It provided them with an opportunity to obtain educational and vocational skills that were instrumental in moving them out of a context of poverty into skilled trades and middle class status.

Involvement in church activities and a strong faith provided meaning for their adult lives. Such a faith was tied to identification with fundamentalist religious groups for a significant minority who had been troubled by mental health problems in their teens. Participation in their communal activities provided structure for their lives, and assured them salvation, security, and a sense of mission in an alien world. However, for the majority of the sons and daughters of problem drinkers in this cohort, faith was not tied to a specific formal religious affiliation, but rather to confidence in some center of value. Their faith enabled them to perceive the traumatic experiences of their childhood youth constructively, even if they caused pain and suffering. It did not seem to matter, whether they were nominally Buddhist, Catholic, mainstream Protestant, or members of a minority religious group, such as the Latter-Day Saints—the resilient individuals used their faith in order to maintain a positive vision of a meaningful life, and to negotiate successfully an abundance of emotionally hazardous experiences.

The central component in the lives of the resilient individuals in this study that contributed to their effective coping in adulthood appeared to be a feeling of confidence that the odds can be surmounted. Some of the luckier ones developed such hopefulness early in their lives, in contact with caring adults. Many of their troubled peers had a second chance at developing a sense of self-esteem and self-efficacy in adolescence sometimes even by virtue of apparent chance encounters with a person who opened up opportunities and gave meaning to their lives.

This research shows that if a parent is incapacitated or unavailable, other persons in a youngster's life can play such an enabling role, whether they are grandparents, older siblings, caring neighbors, peer friends, teachers, ministers, youth workers in the Scouts, 4-H, or the YMCA/YWCA, Big Sisters, and elder mentors. Such informal and personal ties to kith, kin, and community are preferred by most children of alcoholics to impersonal contacts with formal bureaucracies. These ties need to be encouraged and strengthened.

A cooperative effort by concerned volunteers and competent professionals could generate a continuum of care and caring for such youth that cuts across narrow disciplinary boundaries. It would involve peer tutors for children who have learning and/or behavior problems in the primary grades, counselors who assist high school youths with realistic educational and vocational plans, retired individuals who become mentors for potential school drop-outs or jail-bound juvenile offenders, foster grandparents who work with teenage mothers and their infants, community college instructors who encourage young adults motivated to return to school to upgrade their skills, and civic and religious leaders who provide a sense of moral values. Such intergenerational community-based programs involve no great expenditures of money, but a commitment in time and caring. If these programs are to multiply across the country, we need a change in America's individualistic 'habits of the heart' (Bellah et al., 1985).

References

Anthony, E.J. (1987). Children at high risk for psychosis growing up successfully. In E.J. Anthony and B.J. Cohler, (Eds.), The Invulnerable Child. New York: Guilford

Bellah. R.N., Madson, R., Sullivan, W.M., Swidler, A., and Tipton, S.M. (1985). Habits of the Heart: Individualism and Commitment in American Life. Berkeley: University of California Press.

Berlin, R. and Davis, R.B. (1989). Children from Alcoholic Families: Vulnerability and resilience. In T.F. Dugan and R. Coles (Eds.), The Child in our Times. New York: Brunner/Mazel.

Bleuler, M. (1978). The Schizophrenic Disorders: Long-term Patient and Family Studies. New Haven: Yale University Press.

Buss, A.H., and Plomin, R. (1984). Temperament: Early Developing Personality Traits. Hillsdale, NJ: Erlbaum.

Caspi, A., Elder, G.H., and Bem, D.J. (1988). Moving away from the world: Life course patterns of shy children. Developmental Psychology, 24, 824-831.

El-Guebaly, N., Offord, D.R. (1977). The offspring of alcoholics: A critical review. American Journal of Psychiatry, 134, 357-366.

Freedman, M. (1989, March-April). Fostering intergenerational relationships for at-risk youth. Children Today, 10-15.

Rachman, S. (1979). The concept of required helpfulness. Behavior Research and Therapy, 17, 1-6.

Rotter, J. (1966). General expectancies for internal or external reinforcement. Psychological Monographs, 80(1), Whole No. 609.

Russell, M. Henderson, C., and Blume, S.B. (1984). Children of Alcoholics: A Review of the Literature. New York: Children of Alcoholics Foundation.

Rutter, M. (1987). Psychosocial resilience and protective mechanisms. American Journal of Orthopsychiatry, 57, 316-331.

Rutter, M., Quinton, D. (1984). Long-term follow-up of women institutionalized in childhood: Factors promoting good functioning in adult life. British Journal of Developmental Psychology, 18, 225-234.

Sher, K. (1991). Children of Alcoholics: A Critical Appraisal of Theory and Research. Chicago: University of Chicago Press.

Vaillant, G.E. (1983). The Natural History of Alcoholism. Cambridge, MA: Harvard University Press.

Wallerstein, J., Blakeslee, S. (1989). Second Chances: Men, Women, and Children a Decade After Divorce. New York: Ticknor and Fields.

Werner, E.E. (1984). Child Care: Kith, Kin, and Hired Hands. Baltimore: University Press.

Werner, E.E. (1986). Resilient offspring of alcoholics: A longitudinal study from birth to age 18. Journal of Studies on Alcohol, (47)1, 34-40.

Werner, E.E. (1990). Protective factors and individual resiliency. In S. Meisel and J. Shonkoff (Eds.), Handbook of Early Intervention. Cambridge: Cambridge University Press.

Werner, E.E. (1991). Grandparent-grandchild relations among U.S. ethnic groups. In P.K. Smith (Ed.), The Psychology of Grandparenthood: An International Perspective. London: Routledge.

Werner, E.E. and Smith, R.S. (1977). Kauai's Children Come of Age. Honolulu: University of Hawaii Press.

Werner, E.E. and Smith, R.S. (1982). Vulnerable but Invincible: A Longitudinal Study of Resilient Children and Youth. New York: McGraw Hill.

Werner, E.E. and Smith, R.S. (1992). Overcoming the Odds: High Risk Children from Birth to Adulthood. Ithaca and London: Cornell University Press.

West, M.O., and Prinz, R.J. (1987). Parental alcoholism and childhood psychopathology. Psychological Bulletin, 9, 207.

The Secret Everyone Knows
Help for You If Alcohol Is a Problem in Your Home

Cathleen Brooks

What This Is All About

This booklet is for, and about, children whose parents have drinking problems. But there are no age limits set by the word "children." I am one of those children and I am 26. Other children may be middle-aged and have children of their own! We all share some common feelings and problems. We can help ourselves and each other by talking about them.

This booklet has been written—with a lot of love—especially for kids who are living right now in that frightening and confusing world created when a parent drinks too much. About 20 million children and teenagers in the United States today are suffering the pain of feeling alone, feeling to blame and feeling helpless and hopeless about their parents' drinking.

Are you one of them? The answer to that question does not depend on whether your mother or father thinks that she or he has a drinking problem. That's not the point. The important thing is HOW YOU FEEL and what you can do about that.

So first, check to see whether any of these feelings sound familiar:

1. Do you worry about your mom's or dad's drinking?
2. Do you sometimes feel that you are the reason your parent drinks so much?
3. Are you ashamed to have your friends come to your house and are you finding more and more excuses to stay away from home?
4. Do you sometimes feel that you hate your parents when they are drinking and then feel guilty for hating them?
5. Have you been watching how much your parents drink?

6. Do you try to make your parents happy so they won't get upset and drink more?
7. Do you feel you can't talk about the drinking in your home—or even how you feel inside?
8. Do you sometimes drink or take drugs to forget about things at home?
9. Do you feel if your parents really loved you they wouldn't drink so much?
10. Do you sometimes wish you had never been born?

No matter how many of your answers were "yes," there's really just one more, very important question you need to ask yourself: Do you want to start feeling better? If so, reading this booklet will help. I have written it because, at one time, I would have answered "yes" to every one of those questions. Yet, today I am a happy person. And I am certainly glad that I was born. It can happen to you, too. Let me tell you how it happened to me.

Secrets

I want to tell you a secret. It's something I tried to hide—even from myself—for many years because I thought it was so awful and dirty. I decided that no one should ever find out about it.

But when I look back at it now, I realize that it was never much of a secret. Lots of people must have known all along. It's the type of thing people know without you telling them. It just wasn't such a big deal to anybody else. It's such a common thing and it happens in so many families. Probably for every four or five kids I knew, there was one who had the same problem I had. But I didn't know that then.

Now I see the only real secret was how I felt inside: scared and miserable and a little sick all the time. I am writing this booklet because you might have the same secret. If so, it will help to learn that you're not alone—and that your secret is not really dirty at all. You can stop being so scared and miserable if you do a very simple thing: share your secret. Let me tell you mine.

My mother is an alcoholic. So is my father. Today I can say that word without feeling sick to my stomach. It was not always that way. When I was eight, a girl friend told me her mother said my parents were alcoholics. I hated that word. It was filthy and disgusting. It was for old men curled up on sidewalks and women who hung around sleazy bars. My parents were not like that! I never spoke to that girl friend again. I did not want to know anything about alcoholism and tried my best to put the word out of my mind.

But I could not deny that something was terribly wrong in our house. It was a nice house and my dad had a good job. But there was horrible yelling late at night in my parents' bedroom. Sometimes my parents acted very strangely and embarrassed us kids in public. There were nights when they forgot about dinner until it was too late to eat.

We had to be really quiet around the house, especially in the afternoons when Mom was in bed with some illness that never seemed to go away. I told my friends they couldn't come play at my house because my mom was dying. Actually I was just ashamed of what went on there. As I got older, my lies became more outrageous. I said I was an orphan. Or with other kids, I'd make up fabulous stories about how rich and famous my father was. I guess I lied because I hated the truth about my life.

I didn't make many friends in elementary school. I felt ugly and unlikable and so I was terribly shy. When I went to other kids' houses I was jealous of their nice, "normal" parents.

I had the strange feeling that somehow it was my fault that my parents seemed so unhappy. I tried to please then by bringing home good report cards. They didn't seem to notice. I felt frightened a lot because I never knew whether my parents would be in a good mood or a bad one. Sometimes, everything would be fine and then suddenly one of them would blow up for no reason. It was so confusing. But I thought that if I worked harder around the house and was careful not to upset them, things would get better.

Well, nothing got better. Gradually, I began to admit to myself— and only to myself—that all the sadness and yelling and sick feelings I had inside were somehow connected to the fact that my parents drank so much. I didn't realize this until I was in junior high school. I wasn't stupid. I just really didn't want to believe that there was something seriously wrong with my parents. I loved them and wanted to believe that one day we could be the nice family I had created in my lies and dreams.

But I had started to feel that I hated them sometimes. I was sick of being punished when I hadn't done anything wrong. I began to resent them for not doing their share of work around the house. I got grumpy about all the responsibilities I had when other kids had more time to play. My mom and dad forgot promises. They sometimes said things that weren't true—including some really rotten things about me. I wondered why they lied like that. I wondered if maybe I was crazy. Most of all, I wondered why my parents were never there when I needed them. They were always busy, sick or asleep.

My mom and I started arguing constantly. She just didn't make any sense, but she was my mother so I had to obey her. That seemed so unfair. I tried to get back at her by being as mean as I could be. I tried to see how much I could get away with when she was too drunk to notice. I hated myself for being so nasty, but I couldn't seem to stop.

I felt so alone, but I thought no one could understand. I still didn't like the idea of talking behind my parents' backs. I had been taught to respect adults, especially my parents. And I thought it would be wrong to mention their drinking outside the family. The strange thing is that my brothers and sisters and I never talked about it among ourselves either. We always said Daddy was "tired" when he passed out in the living room and Mommy was "sick" when she didn't get out of bed for days.

Once, though, I remember one of my sisters was having a terrible fight with my parents and she called them "alcoholics." My father slapped her and said, "Don't ever use that word again in this house." I remember I agreed with him silently. After all, it was a dirty word.

When I was 15, my mother was sent to a mental hospital. By then, I knew what was happening and why. But no one in the family mentioned alcoholism when they talked about what was wrong with my mother. They called it "exhaustion" or a "nervous breakdown." It was as if there were some crazy, unspoken rule against discussing the thing that was making all of us so miserable. The craziest thing is, we all obeyed the rule.

When Mom came home from the hospital, she was different. She told me she had decided to quit drinking and she was going to attend Alcoholics Anonymous (A.A.) meetings. For the first time in my life, I could talk to one of my parents. It was fantastic.

By this time, the older kids had gone off to college or to get married, leaving just my little brother and me at home. I wanted to be with my mother every second. We talked a lot about my dad. He was still drinking and resented my mother being involved with A.A.

Six months after my mom quit drinking, our family moved across the country. Both my mom and I were lonely in our new town. I thought she was my only real friend. One day I came home upset about my new school and walked in to talk to her. We kids of alcoholics usually know instantly if our parents have been drinking. And I knew—just by the expression on her face, the silly half-smile, the shaky way she said hello—I knew the stuff in her glass was booze, not soda. I grabbed it from her and threw it out.

I had never been so angry in my life. I wanted to hit her, but all I could do was scream and cry. I felt that my last hope had just disappeared. I knew enough about alcoholism by then to know that first drink would be the beginning of more hell...and the end of the closeness she and I had found.

When my father came home that night, my mother drunkenly told him how "disrespectful" I had been. My father stormed into my room. I'll never forget his words. "You are a child," he said. "We are adults. Don't you ever try to tell us how to run our lives again."

That night my brother and I sat in my room. It was the first time we had ever talked to each other like friends. I told him what had happened that day and I said, "From now on, we have to stick together because we're all we've got." At least we were sharing our sadness with each other and that felt better.

But I was wrong about one thing. We weren't really alone at all. There were plenty of people who could have helped—if we had only asked. We didn't know then that we had no reason to feel ashamed or guilty about our parents' alcoholism. It wasn't our fault that they drank... and it really wasn't their fault either. They were sick with the disease of alcoholism. They did not mean to hurt us.

Despite everything, I still loved my parents very much. If I hadn't, the whole thing would not have hurt so much. When I went away to college, I worried about them all the time. I was constantly afraid they would die.

Just before I graduated from college, I got bad news from home. My dad had lost his job. Next I heard that he had gone into a severe depression, then gotten terribly sick and nearly died in the hospital.

The only thing that wasn't mentioned was the cause of his depression and his sickness: advanced alcoholism. It was still a dirty, unspoken word in our family!

To get another job, my dad and mom had to move back across the country again. I had my own job by then and I only saw them once or twice a year. Each time they were drunk and sicker than the time before. I still did not like to bring my friends to their home, but on one trip, I brought my boyfriend to meet my parents. I was so humiliated and horrified at what he saw during that visit! I made the decision that I would never allow myself to be hurt that way again.

Without knowing it, I was probably doing the best thing I could have done. I was beginning to "let go" of my parents emotionally. I stopped thinking and worrying about them all the time. I was finally giving up on the idea that I could save them, control them or make them quit drinking.

At the age of 22, I had finally decided to stop letting my parents' alcoholism—my "dirty secret"—ruin my life.

Unfortunately, by then, I had another problem that was about to ruin my life: my **own** alcoholism.

More Surprises

How did you react when you read that last sentence? Did you think I had to be stupid to become an alcoholic after watching my parents drink all those years? Did you wonder how somebody could be an alcoholic at 22? Or maybe you're just confused about why—and how —I'm writing this booklet if I'm just another drunk.

Maybe this would be a good time to clear up some misunderstandings about this thing called alcoholism. It is not a dirty secret. It is a very common disease, like diabetes. It can affect people of all ages, but it does get worse the longer you have it, if you keep drinking. There is no cure for it, but you can recover from it by not drinking anymore. That sounds simple, but for an alcoholic it is the hardest thing in the world to do.

Alcoholics drink too much—not because they are bad people or because they hate their children or because they are stupid. They drink because they have an illness that makes their bodies and minds crave alcohol. The strange thing about alcoholism is that people who have it desperately want to believe that there is nothing wrong with their drinking. That is why parents will sometimes become furious if their children mention alcoholism or ask them why they drink too much. DENIAL—refusing to admit that there is anything wrong—is a major symptom of alcoholism.

And now I'm going to say something that might sound strange to you. Every person in an alcoholic's family suffers from the disease, even without ever taking a drink. Just living in an alcoholic's home— the type of home where fear and anger and shame are everyday facts of life—this alone can make a person feel sick. Your emotions and feelings can get so confused and miserable that you can develop unhealthy ways of thinking and acting. Sometimes these feelings can make your body feel sick, too, with stomachaches, headaches or other physical troubles. Most of all, living with an alcoholic parent can cause you to feel lousy about YOURSELF and this can lead to serious trouble.

For me, it led to becoming an alcoholic. But that didn't happen overnight. The trouble started inside of me when I was very young— long before I admitted anything was wrong.

Remember how I said I hated even the word alcoholism and never wanted to talk to anyone about my parents' drinking or my own feelings? Well, I was doing the same thing my parents were doing: I was playing the game of DENIAL.

Even as a little kid, I wanted to believe I had everything under control. I even thought I could control my parents' drinking by watching how much they drank. I tried to make everything run smoothly in the house so they wouldn't **have** to drink. I didn't know then that NO ONE can control an alcoholic's drinking—including the alcoholic. I thought my parents needed me to take care of them and make sure they didn't hurt themselves. I was trying to be my parents' parent! But I was still a kid and I needed someone to take care of me. I needed someone to hold me when I felt hurt.

IF ONLY I HAD KNOWN MY PARENTS NEVER MEANT TO HURT ME. THEY HAD NEVER STOPPED LOVING ME. THEY WERE JUST UNABLE TO SHOW IT. It wasn't anyone's fault. We were all suffering from alcoholism.

Maybe if I had understood that, I wouldn't have felt so lonely and unloved. Maybe I wouldn't have tried so many dumb things to make people like me.

When I was still in grade school, I tried to impress my friends by shoplifting. I stole a lot of little, stupid things that I didn't even want. I would feel really ashamed but then I'd do it again. I stole from my parents, too. Maybe I was trying to get them to "give" me something (like love and attention) and since booze made them unable to do that, I decided to take things from them!

I also stole sleeping pills and tranquilizers from the medicine cabinet. Like a lot of alcoholics, my mom was hooked on those, too. She never seemed to miss them so I stole enough for me and my friends. I thought getting high on pills made me look cool. Actually, they made me awfully sick and I felt guilty and dumb for doing it.

When I was 11, I tried drinking. The stuff tasted terrible and burned my throat. But I liked the feeling it gave me. It made me feel giddy and grown-up. I thought I was more popular with the other kids when I drank. I certainly never imagined that I could become an alcoholic. I had sworn never to be like my parents. I didn't think my drinking was anything like my parents' drinking. They seemed miserable when they drank. I thought I was having fun.

I didn't know then that most alcoholics start drinking because it makes them feel good. And for people like me, who had been holding a lot of hurt and fears and anger for a long time, it was a way to blot out those feelings for a while. Booze was my ticket to a little bit of happiness, even if it only lasted a few hours.

My parents never knew I was drinking or stealing. To them and to my teachers, I looked like a happy, well-behaved kid who got good grades and never caused much trouble. I was even a class officer and editor of my high school newspaper. My parents said they were proud of me. No one knew what was going on inside of me. I kept my secrets hidden well.

In college, I did notice that I was drinking more than other people. But my friends congratulated me on how well I could hold it. I graduated from college and got a really good job. My drinking got heavier as I had more money to spend and more excuses to drink. But I certainly never looked like a drunk—just a pretty young woman partying and having a good time.

Inside, though, I had that old familiar feeling that something was terribly wrong. Although I had moved out of my parents' home, I was still carrying around all those terrible feelings I had growing up. I had never talked about them, so they stayed buried deep inside. They had just gotten more complicated and harder to identify. I was still ashamed of the hatred and anger I felt for my parents. I was still longing for their love and approval. I was terrified of not being liked by other people. I had painted on a pretty face for the outside world, but inside I felt scared and ugly.

I had never learned to reach out for help with my problems. So I did what came naturally … what I had seen my parents do. I reached out for a drink. It was the only way I knew to feel better. Soon, I was drinking even when I tried not to. I was getting sick all the time. I tried to control my drinking but I couldn't. It was awful. It hadn't taken very long. I had become an alcoholic.

Lots of people—most in fact—are able to drink and it never becomes a problem

But we who have lived with alcoholism in our families know that for people who drink to "feel better" or to try to solve problems, alcohol **becomes** the problem. It is never more than a temporary solution.

Yet, despite what we know, an awful lot of children of alcoholics try to find comfort in booze. Experts say kids with family histories of alcoholism have a much higher risk of eventually becoming alcoholics themselves.

This booklet is not intended to preach against drinking. And there is no reason to think you will become an alcoholic just because your parent is one. But there **is** reason to think that children who grow up in alcoholic homes often become very unhappy adults if they do not learn how to recognize and talk about their feelings. Whether or not we decide to drink, we kids of alcoholics need to take a good look at what is going on around and inside us and ask for help when we need it. The next section will talk about how to do that.

Towards New Beginnings

I don't know about you, but I never believed in stories with happy endings. I spent my whole childhood waiting for "things" to get better in my family and they never did. I never realized that the only person I had any control over was myself and the only thing I could try to make better was me!

I'm not going to write a happy ending to my story. Not yet. In fact, in many ways, I feel like my life has just begun. So let's talk about new beginnings instead.

A few years ago, my dad got so sick that he decided to quit drinking and give A.A. a try. None of us in the family really thought it would work, but after a year we saw that he had stayed sober and seemed like a different person. My mom and I started going to A.A. meetings with him.

Alcoholics Anonymous is a group of people who have decided to quit drinking and are trying to live better, happier lives without booze. At meetings, they talk about their experiences and offer to help new people who are trying to stay sober.

Well, eventually both my mom and I realized that we wanted to quit drinking, too. It wasn't easy for any of us, but we had a lot of help from new friends in A.A. At the meetings, I finally learned to talk about my feelings. At long last I was sharing my secrets. I was no longer alone.

You can make a new beginning too. But you don't have to become an alcoholic to do it, or wait until you're 24 or even until your mom or dad quits drinking. That may never happen and there's nothing you can do to make it happen. But you can learn to cope with the problems in your home and make some really good changes happen inside YOURSELF.

How do you start? Well, just reading this booklet is a big first step. You have taken the time to learn more about alcoholism and the trouble it caused in my family. You know now that you are not responsible for your parents' drinking. You cannot do anything to make them drink or make them stop. You have no reason to feel guilty or ashamed of their drinking—or your feelings.

And maybe you have seen yourself a little in parts of my story. No two alcoholic families are alike, of course, and there may be big differences between your life and mine. But many of the FEELINGS experienced by children of alcoholics are similar and very under-standable. When you see these similarities, you may feel better just knowing you are not alone—or crazy—just because you have those feelings. This is a way of sharing.

You might remember in section two I said: You can stop being so scared and miserable if you do a very simple thing—share your secret.

That is the next step in your new beginning. Find someone to talk to.

Maybe you have a teacher you really like, or you get along well with your guidance counselor at school. Perhaps you feel very close to a particular aunt or uncle or one of your grandparents. Maybe you've always liked one of your friends' mothers or fathers and wished you could talk to him or her alone sometime. Well, just ask! Your team coach or scout troop leader—or a minister, priest or rabbi—might be the person you could ask. Or pick a neighbor you really like or trust.

If you think about it, there are probably a lot of people who would like to help you. Find someone you feel you can trust to be a good friend. Tell this person that you need to share some of the feelings you're having because you think there is a drinking problem in your home. You need to talk—as honestly as you can—about what has been happening at home and inside you.

Once you have started talking to this person, it is important that he or she understands that alcoholism is an illness that affects the entire family. Maybe you could lend your friend this booklet. Unfortunately, many people—even doctors, ministers and teachers—may have big problems understanding alcoholism. If you don't feel you are getting the understanding you need, choose someone else to talk to.

There is one place where you are most likely to get understanding and that is with other children of alcoholics. There is a special organization called Alateen that holds meetings in places all over the country and even in other parts of the world. It is for teenagers with a parent, relative or close friend who is an alcoholic. The purpose of Alateen is to give you a place to share your feelings with other teenagers who have lived through the same things. The idea behind Alateen is that you can't change your parent but you can change yourself.

You might be too young for Alateen right now. The age limits are different in various parts of the country. So the thing to do, no matter how old you are, is look up Alateen in your phone book and call and ask. If you don't find Alateen listed, call the local office of Alcoholics Anonymous or Al-Anon, an organization like Alateen but for adults.

If you are talking to the people at A.A. or Al-Anon, you might want to ask them if they could send you pamphlets that could help you understand your parent's alcoholism better. The more you know about this subject, the more you will be able to understand your alcoholic parent—and your own feelings.

The public library also has books on alcoholism, including Alateen's own books called *Alateen—Hope for Children of Alcoholics* and *Courage To Be Me*. You can also write for more information on Alateen to Al-Anon, 1600 Corporate Landing Parkway, Virginia Beach, VA 23454-5617, or call them at (757) 563-1600. You can also learn more about Alateen online at *http://www.alateen.org*

OK, now that you've made your new beginning, how do you handle the problems at home? They won't just disappear by magic. You have to face them honestly. That means no more denial games. You are doing nothing wrong by seeking help for yourself, so there is no need to hide it from your parents.

If you go to Alateen, you may want to, very calmly, tell your parents that you believe you need help to deal with the alcohol problem and how it is affecting you. Try not to lecture or criticize your parents. Who knows? Maybe one of both of your parents will follow your example and get help too! On the other hand, your parents may become very angry and even forbid you to go to Alateen meetings. It will be tough, but only you can decide what you need to do.

You may not want to mention this subject at all to your parents. That, too, is your choice. You are the one who has to live in your home. If you decide to talk to your parents, perhaps you could lend them this booklet first to help explain how you feel. The last section is written especially for them, but it would be good for you to read it, too.

Whatever you decide, try to talk this whole thing over with the person you have chosen to help you.

If you have any brothers or sisters, maybe this would be a good time to start really talking to them too. They might like to read this booklet or, if they are too young for that, you could try to explain some of these ideas to them. You might find, as I did that night my brother and I sat in my room, that you can find new and special friends right in your own family.

Remember, alcoholism is a disease that affects the entire family. And so even if one of your parents doesn't drink too much, he or she can be troubled too and might be relieved to talk things over with you. On the other hand, your non-alcoholic parent might be playing the old denial game or trying to "protect" you by not telling you the truth. So instead of agreeing with you that there is something wrong, your mom or dad could react with anger. Be prepared for that and try to understand.

Some of us keep our secret feelings hidden for years. Others of us have ways of acting to make people notice how unhappy we are—like skipping school, taking drugs, getting drunk, stealing, fighting and running away from home. None of these things ever solved anything. And if someone **does** notice, we rarely get the type of loving attention we're looking for. Juvenile Hall is not a great place to go looking for love.

Remember, there is nothing shameful or weak about asking for help. In fact, it takes a lot of courage! But aren't you worth it? Maybe you don't think so right now. But take it from me, you are.

In almost every town and city, there are special hot line or crisis line numbers for kids and other people with problems. You might also want to consider talking to a trained, professional counselor at one of the youth centers or family service agencies in your town. You can find them listed in the yellow pages of the phone book under headings like "Alcoholism Information," "Social Service and Welfare Organizations" or "Youth Organizations." Or you can ask your school counselor or your special friend to help you find the right agency.

Most of all, remember that no matter how bad things look to you right now, there's always a chance for a happy ending as long as you're willing to make some new beginnings. The sadness you may be feeling today does not have to last forever.

In the meantime—and that means right now—you can begin to discover a "new you." After awhile, you might take another look at the questions at the beginning of this booklet and find some very different answers—especially to the last one. Because I'll bet that "new you" will be mighty glad to have been born.

For Parents

In this booklet, I have shared with your child what it was like for me to grow up with alcoholic parents. I have also told your child that despite all the misery alcohol caused me as a child, I became an alcoholic myself.

If your child has asked you to read this book—or if you have found it by accident among your child's things—you might feel angry or threatened. You might feel someone is pointing an accusing finger at you and labeling you or your spouse as an alcoholic.

That is not at all the intention of this booklet. My only purpose here is to encourage children who are troubled by situations in their homes to talk about their feelings and get the help they need. If your child feels that there is a drinking problem in your home, then there **is** a problem—of some sort—and it is worth thinking about. Children rarely fabricate problems. They are much keener observers of us than we like to think.

Why not take a few minutes and read through this booklet. If nothing else, it might give you a chance to see things through your child's eyes. If you think you or your spouse might have an alcohol problem, contact a counseling or referral agency that deals with alcohol and family problems. Or call your local chapter of Alcoholics Anonymous or Al-Anon, the self-help group for the relatives of alcoholics. Go to a few meetings and see if you might belong there. Neither organization expects you to make any commitment and what you say is held in complete confidence.

Even if you decide you don't want—or need—help yourself, try to understand if your child decides that he or she does. Your child does not want to hurt, embarrass or anger you. Your child is just looking for a way to stop hurting and needs your love and understanding.

This booklet, originally published by the Joan B. Kroc Foundation in 1981, has been reprinted with permission of the author.

SECTION III: THE ADULT CHILD

Adult Children of Alcoholics: An Expanded Framework for Assessment and Diagnosis

Stephanie Brown

I. Introduction: The Birth of a Concept

The field of alcoholism, or chemical dependence, has undergone tremendous change over the last 15 years. Today, it is hard to conceive of a time when the concepts "adult children of alcoholics" or "codependence" didn't exist. These terms have been established quickly in popular and clinical language, labeling a particular kind of patient and treatment for at least ten years.

The popular movement (including the mass media, lay confer-ences, and trade books) named and described a phenomenon never before legitimized. Academic theoreticians and clinicians of all disciplines simply had never considered the impact of one individual's alcoholism on another, which is precisely what the popular movement accomplished. This shift in perspective—from a singular focus on the alcoholic as identified patient to a broader interactive systems focus on the family and other individuals within the family—has dramatically affected popular and professional thinking about health and illness. At this point, nothing is clear, and our understanding of chemical dependence, though no longer hidden and denied, is muddy, vague, and full of serious problems. Just what is a codependent? An ACA? What do these terms mean and how can we best use them to clarify our thinking and our treatments? In this paper, we will examine the origin and evolutionary development of these terms, outlining problems with both and radical suggestions for improvement.

Next, we will leave "codependence" behind and focus on ACAs, arguing that the term ACA be used descriptively and not as a singu-lar diagnostic entity. We will look at the commonalities of ACA themes in treatment, which mistakenly have been generalized to an ACA diagnosis. I will propose that the ACA label, and our new understanding of the impact of trauma and systems dynamics on individual development, demand an expansion in our thinking to include multi-level developmental diagnostic tracks.

We can identify three separate assessment tracks illuminated by the concept ACA: 1) the childhood alcoholic family environment, including the reality of trauma; 2) the family system, organized to both deny and maintain the reality of parental alcoholism; and 3) the nature of attachment within this environment and system and its impact on individual development. Taken together, this expanded framework constitutes a much fuller, deeper understanding of child and adult development and adaptation.

Surprisingly, multi-track theory is a revolutionary idea, both in popular thinking and in academic circles. We simply have no means to integrate multiple theories because we have been so committed to an individual diagnostic framework. The drive to define codependence and ACA as individual diagnostic entities reinforces this narrow, reductionistic bias. It is time to challenge this favored view and expand our thinking, even though it means giving up simple cookbook formulas for change.

Popular, revolutionary concepts that literally blew the lid off of denial at a national level are already limited and restrictive. It is up to academia and clinicians to make sense of these ideas by tackling their inherent complexity rather than succumbing to an equally global, vague and ultimately meaningless singular diagnosis.

II. What is Codependence?

Origins of the Term

The origin of the idea "codependence" goes back to the 1950s when Al-Anon, the autonomous arm of Alcoholics Anonymous (AA) designed for the spouse of an alcoholic was born (Al-Anon, 1984). Al-Anon provided the first official recognition that alcoholism has an impact on others. Until this time, all attention had been on the drinking alcoholic, as if that individual and the alcoholism existed in a vacuum.

Like AA, the focus of Al-Anon was on the individual, but it was clearly the individual in an interpersonal, familial context. In a similar program to the twelve steps of AA, Al-Anon provides instruction in how to detach and disengage from maladaptive and unhealthy reactions to the alcoholic in the same way that the drinker relin-quishes alcohol.

At the same time Al-Anon was developing, Joan Jackson (1954; 1962) outlined stages in a developmental process of alcoholism for the spouse, similar to the stages of the disease process defined for the alcoholic by E.M. Jellinek (1960). Prior to Jackson's work, research on the family focused only on personality traits or the role of the wife, who was thought to cause, perpetuate, or reinforce the alcoholism of her mate (at this time thought to be almost entirely men). Jackson reversed cause and effect, as did Vaillant much later (1982). Instead of starting out with problems that caused her husband's drinking, the wife's difficulties were now recognized to be a consequence of or a response to his drinking.

A Family Disease

The disease concept, just gaining acceptance in the 50s and 60s for the alcoholic, now translated into "family disease." The term "co-alcoholic" was coined to describe the partner and the focus broadened to include the interactions, adjustment and development of the family with an alcoholic member. Co-alcoholics learned that they were part of a disease process bigger than any one individual. While they were now relieved of the responsibility for causing the alcoholism of their mates, they were learning instead that their reactive response (which was co-alcoholism) was unhealthy for them and ineffective in changing the drinker.

The Alcoholic Family: Systems Theory

Peter Steinglass (1980; 1987) shifted the emphasis from a disease model to exploration of interactional systems dynamics in developing the concept of the alcoholic family. He and Brown (1977; 1985; 1988; 1991) described the alcoholism of a parent as a "central organizing principle" determining interactional patterns within the family. They suggested that parental alcoholism be viewed as a governing agent affecting the development of the family as a whole and individuals within. Until now, co-alcoholism applied only to the alcoholic's mate. The systems concept of an alcoholic family paved the way for including children.

The Value of Co-Alcoholism

As a systems term, specific to alcoholism and the response to it, co-alcoholism was extremely useful. Appropriately negative, the term described the mutual reinforcement of pathological systems dynamics. When limited to interactional alcoholic dynamics, the implicit dichotomous all-or-none frame was also appropriate. In any dyad governed by one partner's alcoholism, there was an alcoholic — who was dominant — and a co-alcoholic, who was submissive and reactive to the dominance of the drinker. Family systems dynamics, including the maintenance of family homeostasis, evolved around the pathology of active alcoholism and the couple's or family's efforts to sustain it. In family systems theory, this dominant-submissive system was analogous to polarized, highly skewed, schismatic families, or enmeshed or hostile dependent systems (Framo, 1965; Minuchin, 1974; Bader & Pearson, 1988).

From an individual perspective, the co-alcoholic was someone who subordinated or literally forfeited an independent self—feelings, perceptions, beliefs, and explanations of reality—in favor of the alcoholic and the larger pathological alcoholic system (Brown 1988).

Codependence

With the birth of the COA movement and the application of family systems theory to alcoholism, the term co-alcoholism was broadened to codependence, referring now to any reactive, submissive response to the dominance of another (Brown, 1988). Implicit in this generalized view was the loss of self to another's control. Why would anyone go along with such a sacrifice? We will see later that the human need for attachment is so powerful and so basic as to make this kind of accommodation to another quite common and part of normal behavior.

That is why this terminology is so problematic. Like co-alcoholism, codependence is an exclusively negative term which turns much of normal human behavior into pathology.

The reactive codependent stance defines the individual as a passive victim, while its opposite—the dependent—is ironically seen to be the aggressor. In fact, both terms deal with dependence and need in humans. The dependent person is seen to be overtly needy and demanding, while the codependent is seen to sacrifice all claim to personal need. From an interactional perspective, the codependent satisfies dependency needs just like the dependent individual. It is simply more disguised.

This framework misses entirely the long-accepted developmental and psychodynamic view (Rolf et al, 1990) that all human beings are engaged in dynamic interaction with others and their environment. Individuals are not passive recipients as the dichotomous dependent-codependent frame suggests.

The fact that all individuals are actively engaged does not mean they are to blame, a faulty conclusion unfortunately drawn by many when the passive "victim" status of codependence is challenged. In fact, to counter this faulty trap of blaming the victim, popular thinking simply reverses it, now holding abusive parents or partners responsible for all disappointments in childhood or adult relationships. Neither "solution" helps anybody out of the dichotomous trap.

In the current frame, the dependent-codependent system is pathological, making both partners victims to a system they actively participate in maintaining. Why and how they do this is related to attachment and issues of normal human development which we will look at later.

Negative Bias

The terms dependence and codependence are exclusively negative, reflecting our cultural preference for "self-sufficiency" and our distaste for need in any form. Thus, we have totally eliminated the option for healthy, positive dependency or caretaking reactivity. With this restrictive, negative terminology, we have further eliminated the possibility of healthy interdependence, a fluid and flexible interactional system in which both partners are capable of "give and take" and both roles are valued.

The unhealthy dependent-codependent framework makes our human values of kindness, altruism and self-sacrifice totally suspect. By offering no positive options and equating dependence with failure and unhealthy need, we have successfully pathologized the entire human race.

Elsewhere (Brown 1991), I have proposed a solution to this dilemma, if we must keep the basic terminology. In essence, we could add a modifier, distinguishing between healthy and unhealthy dependence and healthy and unhealthy codependence. It is a simple solution, but difficult to implement because it requires a capacity to recognize and tolerate "shades of gray" or ambiguity, a cognitive and emotional flexibility that is missing or restricted in many people. Thus, the all or none polarity of the dependent-codependent frame appeals to the need for rigid, air-tight right and wrong classifications. Unfortunately, both options in this dichotomy are "wrong" and there is no way to get it "right."

Other Problems: Over-Generalization and Over-Simplification

Ideally, clinical terminology should clarify distinctions or diagnostic entities. The term codependence does the opposite, virtually obliterating differences. It crosses theoretical frames, defining systems dynamics as individual pathology. It also moves from psychology to sociology. Epstein and Epstein (1990) argue that codependence is "social narrative," a comment on the values and mores of the culture. They suggest that traditional masculine and feminine roles of dominance and submission are being challenged by pathologizing them to aggressor and victim.

The term crosses turf in other ways. Codependence can now be applied as a noun, an adjective or a verb. People can be codependents, they can behave in a "codependent manner," or they can "co" another individual, all of which are negative.

Perhaps the worst over-generalization is the crossover that equates codependents and ACAs on the basis of the shared reactive position in relation to a dominant other. An early paper by Greenleaf (1981) suggests the folly of this condensation in understanding the interpersonal dynamics within the alcoholic family. Greenleaf suggests distinguishing between the co-alcoholic and "para"-alcoholic to underscore the different origins and functions of a reactive stance in adults and children.

The terms codependent and ACA are simply not interchangeable. Codependence refers to adult status, a submissive "partner," while para-alcoholism, or ACA, refers back to childhood to the impact and consequences of growing up with parental alcoholism. It is essential to make distinctions between adult and child status.

What to do?

Although I have suggested the possibility of an expanded framework to include healthy and unhealthy codependence (Brown, 1991), I will advocate an extreme position for purposes of this paper, to underscore the enormous problems we have created and continue to reinforce. As lay and professional, we are caught in a thinking disorder similar to the pathology of the alcoholic family. We are over-generalizing and over-simplifying in order to make sense of cherished terms. By attempting to create a singular individual diagnosis of codependence or ACA, we are blurring, denying and rationalizing away vast significant differences between individuals and between experiences.

I recommend limiting the use of the term codependence to the interactional systems dynamics of alcoholism and chemical dependence. I recommend abandoning the use of the term to describe interactional patterns and systems dynamics not related to chemical addiction. By taking such a strong stance, we force ourselves to acknowledge the problems with our terminology and to start over. Such a position requires us to expand our thinking, to add a systems track and a separate, environmental, trauma track and to move away from a condensed individual diagnosis.

We are in danger of turning systems dynamics into individual pathology. If we continue with our faulty terminology and faulty logical premises, we will take the next "logical" but faulty step of equating the now global, vague, almost meaningless term of codependence with "relationship disorder."

In the next section, I will follow through on my own recommendation. Leaving codependence behind, I will outline a multi-level diagnostic framework for understanding ACAs. I will then illustrate how the multi-level and complex experiences of living with parental alcoholism affect the individual interpersonally. I will argue that the ACA experience requires massive defensive accommodation, the impact of which is felt most severely and acutely in interpersonal relationships.

III. What is an ACA? Common Themes

The term ACA started simultaneously in different parts of the country in the late seventies, predominantly in clinical settings. Brown and Cermak reported their initial findings of ACAs in interactional group therapy in 1979 (Brown and Cermak).

Others were also describing shared family experiences. Claudia Black focused on young children living with an alcoholic parent

(Black, 1980). Newsweek magazine (1979) announced this new "idea" in its Lifestyle section, describing common experiences, as did charter statements of ACA lay associations (NACOA, 1983).

At this point, ACA had become an important description of a certain kind of family history characterized by common themes (Cermak and Brown, 1982) including chaos, uncertainty, and a changing reality. In interactional group therapy, ACAs demonstrated an overwhelming emphasis on issues of interpersonal safety, including long-standing serious problems with trust, guardedness, hyper-vigilance, a need for control and the fear of the loss of control, cognitive and affective denial, all-or-none thinking, and an overriding, inappropriate assumption of responsibility for others (Brown, 1986; 1988; 1991; Cermak and Brown, 1982), which Cermak (1986) later linked to post-traumatic stress disorder.

These clinical descriptions painted a portrait of alcoholic family life never previously acknowledged or legitimized. They established the "what-it-was-like" reality of parental alcoholism, literally describing what happens to children living in such an environment — that is, the kinds of experiences, sights and sounds that accompany parental alcoholism.

Black (1981) and Wegsheider (1981) added systems theory to the base of environmental description, outlining various role assignments children assume as a systemic accommodation to parental alcoholism.

The popular movement next made an inappropriate leap, going from common themes of childhood family history to individual adult diagnosis, based on a classification of shared personality traits (Woititz, 1983). Though well received at the public level, these characteristics reflected the over-simplification and over-generalization now characterizing the popular field. The shared personality traits, thought to differentiate ACAs from others, are actually part of all normal development and human behavior. Like the terms codependence and dependence, these traits are also exclusively negative when referring to the ACA experience.

The ACA movement got off track at this point, moving in the wrong direction toward individual diagnosis as the simplest way of fitting in with current accepted diagnostic standards. It did so understandably because DSM (1987), the official standard of practice, does not separate out or recognize environmental or systems pathology, either in etiology or consequence. But environmental and systems pathology were reflected in the themes. Nor does DSM have any mechanism to link childhood experiences with adult disturbance — a cause and effect connection implicit in the label "adult child."

In reducing ACA to an individual diagnosis, the popular movement missed its most important unforeseen impact: to lay bare the absence of any multi-level, integrated theory of child and adult development.

The early descriptions and identified treatment themes, plus the multi-level label "adult child" provide the guidelines for an expanded theory. In the remainder of this paper, I will outline three distinct assessment tracks suggested by these early themes: the environmental context, the system, and individual developmental perspectives. At this stage of theory development, these domains may be viewed loosely as "assessment tracks", each exerting separate and interactional influences on the child. We will then examine the experiences and the consequences of living with parental alcoholism for the child and adult within each domain. Finally, we will look at interpersonal problems for ACAs in close couple relationships.

IV. Three Assessment Tracks

Environment

The term ACA, in its broadest form, refers to the experience of growing up with an alcoholic parent(s). The environment refers to "what it was like": the experiences of daily, routine family life outlined by the popular press.

The alcoholic family has been described as chaotic, unpredictable, inconsistent, with arbitrary, repetitious and illogical thinking, and not infrequently violence and incest (Brown, 1988; 1991). There is an atmosphere of tension, fear and often pervasive shame (Brown, 1988). This is a family that is out of control, overtly or covertly, with no means to regain it.

Adjusting to the uncertainty of this kind of environment or "family context" requires enormous energy and attention. Children are forced to assume a reactive, defensive posture to accommodate to the reality of the drinking and the defensive maneuvers necessary to sustain it within the family.

In dealing with constantly changing standards of parental behavior and logic, chronic tension, and the unremitting potential for disaster, ACAs share a sense of being "on guard" as a lifestyle.

> *"The chaos was the only thing I knew for sure. I always could rely on the unexpected and the knowledge that I'd have to quickly adjust—turn my attention to the crisis at hand and get into gear. I always grew up on guard. It was the only way to survive."*

> *"My mother's unpredictability was so distressing. I was always on guard and shielded from her violence and rage. I insulated myself emotionally and physically by just checking out. I don't know where I went mentally, but I sure left. Now I don't feel anything and I can't even remember much of what happened."*

This guarded stance is described as a constant watchfulness, hyper-vigilance, and a defensive attitude of mistrust toward others. Because of the lack of basic environmental safety, children cannot feel secure and therefore free to focus their attention on their own internal development. Attention turns outward and self-development becomes dominated by the need for accommodation and defense. Several patients illustrate:

> *"I always expect a hostile environment. I see people as fierce, dangerous animals. I approach the world with suspicion and a belief that I will be betrayed and hurt."*

> *"Being on guard is what life is all about. I am always assessing the world around me—will I be trapped, make a mistake, break a rule and humiliate myself? Surviving means always staying one step ahead."*

Trauma

Within the last few years, it has been widely accepted that the alcoholic home environment is "traumatic" (Cermak, 1986; Brown, 1988). Defined by psychiatrist, Henry Krystal (1978), trauma is the "overwhelming of the self's normal preservative function in the face of inevitable danger."

The "everyday" alcoholic environment or "life context" is likely to be characterized by what is called chronic or "strain" trauma, the chaos or inconsistency we've just seen in examples. Thus, what many kids experience as routine and normal, is also by definition traumatic. These same kids may also experience episodes of "acute" trauma that punctuate the "normal" atmosphere. Acute trauma might include a single experience, or many episodes of violence, incest, or a terrible fear coming home to an empty house. A child might also experience trauma through witnessing violence or abuse to others (Eth & Pynoos, 1985; van der Kolk, 1987). Many ACAs must struggle with survivor guilt because they escaped direct brutality when someone else did not.

The child's normal, natural mechanisms of defense and adaptation will be stretched to the limit. Eventually, children omit, redefine or distort information and affect in order to cope (Guidano & Liotti, 1983; Bowlby, 1988; Brown, 1988; 1991).

Reality can't be known. With this dominant emphasis on trauma and the constant need for defense, the child's basic sense of security is thwarted. Attention must go outward, with internal development impaired, arrested, or influenced and shaped by the dominance of environmental danger. The base of an "other-directed," reactive position in relation to others is firmly planted. So are the seeds for a fundamental mistrusting, guarded, insecure attitude toward others that will influence the subsequent development of the self and all interpersonal relationships.

The System

In shifting from the environment to systems theory, we move from what actually happened, what can be seen or not seen, and the way it feels, to a focus on how the family works, the mechanisms or structure that allow the alcoholic household to function.

Family systems theory explains how interactional patterns of relationship and behavior maintain a family's sense of balance, what is called technically, homeostasis or equilibrium (Bowen, 1974; Watzlavich, Weakland & Fisch, 1974; Satir, 1964). Homeostasis is a point of balance, not a judgment of health or well being. All groups, organizations, or families naturally strive toward achieving and maintaining a sense of internal stability.

The alcoholic family is a system dominated by alcohol, alcoholism, or the alcoholic as the central organizing principle, governing family dynamics and systems balance (Steinglass, 1980; Brown, 1977; 1985; 1988). The alcoholic family, contrary to popular belief (and

Individual Development

In addition to environmental and systems experiences, the term ACA also refers to individual development, the third assessment track. Clinical theory remains poorly articulated or understood in this domain with several exceptions (Wood, 1987; Beletsis and Brown, 1981; Brown, 1988; Brown, 1991). These authors have examined the developmental impact of parental alcoholism emphasizing the dominance of defense and necessity for accommodation to the demands of the environment, system and parental need. Attachment theory serves as an organizing construct that links these tracks and explains how individual development in an alcoholic family is grounded and organized around defense.

Attachment

Major developmental theorists including Jerome Kagan (1984), Margaret Mahler (1975), Eric Erickson (1963), Peter Blos (1962) and John Bowlby (1980; 1985; 1988) agree on the critical and fundamental importance of attachment to human development. Bowlby defines attachment as a very close tie with a care-giving or parental figure, usually the mother. No human being can survive without this kind of bond, the base on which all processes of normal childhood and adult development take place. This bond is so important that many difficulties and unhealthy adaptations in development can be traced to problems between parent and child or other significant figures such as siblings, grandparents, or other primary caretakers. Healthy development can also be explained on the basis of a strong, positive core attachment in infancy and the early childhood years.

There is virtually no argument that humans are social animals who develop and survive in relation to others. These core bonds are established and maintained throughout life by what Bowlby refers to as "attachment behavior," "any form of behavior that results in a person obtaining or maintaining proximity to some other clearly identified individual who is conceived as better able to cope with the world (Bowlby, 1988, p. 27)."

Bowlby suggests that attachment behavior is most obvious in early childhood, or when a person is frightened, fatigued or sick. An attachment figure provides comfort and care, giving the individual a strong feeling of security and therefore encouragement to value and continue the relationship (p. 27).

The origins of attachment theory lie with the neo-Freudians and later with the object-relations schools of individual development. The neo-Freudians, including Sullivan (1953), Horney (1937) and Fromm (1947), veered from the Freudian emphasis on intrapsychic drive, adding the critical shaping influence of interpersonal experiences in individual development. The object-relations school, represented by such early theorists as Winnicott (1953; 1960), Fairbairn (1952), and Guntrip (1969) elaborated the significance of interpersonal relationship to the development of the self. Most recently, the self-psychologists represented by Kohut (1971) and others also emphasized the significance of core relationships to all individual development. The newest schools of cognitive-constructivism (Mahoney, 1977; Guidano and Liotti, 1983), control-mastery theory (Weiss and Sampson, 1986) and developmental psychopathology (Rolf et al, 1990) also stress the importance of the interpersonal bond and relationship patterns as developmental influences. These theorists accent the importance of deep beliefs a child develops about self and others in direct response to interactions with significant figures. These deep beliefs are often unconscious and enduring, serving as the organizing structure for perceiving and interpreting self and world. In this view, individuals develop certain core beliefs about themselves and the world based on early interactions. They then interpret self and world from a view that repeatedly reconfirms these basic beliefs regardless of their validity.

Attachment theory posits that the origins of the self—one's affective experience, identity, deepest beliefs, and patterns of relationship -- reside within the relationship of the child to its mother (or parent figure (Bowlby, 1980; 1988.) The child develops and internalizes core beliefs about the self and a persistent kind of relationship pattern that then serves as a model or template for all succeeding relationships.

Patterns of Attachment

Bowlby, in close collaboration with Ainsworth (Karen, 1990), defined three major patterns of attachment, each persistent over time between child and parent and later replicated with others in adult life. The first is a pattern of "secure" attachment in which the infant is confident that the parent (or parental figure) will be available, responsive, and helpful should painful or frightening situations arise. With assurance, the child feels confident in exploring the world. This pattern results when a mother is readily available, sensitive to the child's signals and responsive to the child's request for comfort and protection (Bowlby, 1988, p. 24). This pattern lays the groundwork for healthy development beginning with a close dependent bond that facilitates later emotional separation and autonomy.

The second pattern is "anxious resistant," in which the child is uncertain about the parent's availability or responsiveness. This uncertainty leads to separation anxiety and a tendency to be clinging and anxious about exploration. There is conflict in this pattern, reinforced by the uncertainty of the response and by threats of abandonment used as a method of control.

The third pattern is "anxious avoidant," in which the individual expects to be rebuffed when seeking care. Such individuals may attempt to become emotionally self-sufficient, living without the support and love of others. The traumatic alcoholic environment and pathogenic systems dynamics may both cause and/or reinforce anxious resistant or anxious avoidant patterns.

These patterns of attachment incorporate behavioral, cognitive and affective elements, and, like genetic coding, hold within them the most rudimentary early experiences with significant others and the most important feelings and beliefs about other people and the world.

Other theorists stress the importance of attachment and the problems in development related to the nature or pattern of this bond. Mahler (1975) suggested that the road to mature development starts with a very close dependent relationship, a "symbiotic" bond, in which parent and child are like one. This merged relationship and period of time in infancy correspond to what Erikson calls the first developmental stage of "basic trust." It is the infant's first experience with communication, the time when the child learns, through close contact with the mother or other primary care-giving figure, that he or she will be understood and responded to.

Or, as Alice Miller (1981; 1984) and others (Lidz, 1973; Winnicott, 1953;1965) suggest, the child learns the opposite: that parents cannot hear or respond because they are so dominated by their own problems, conflicts and needs. Miller describes a common but very unhealthy parent-child bond in which the child exists to reconfirm the parent's value or point of view and thus becomes an extension or tool of the parent. This is an insidious, often subtle kind of role reversal, in which the primary parent-child bond is structured to meet the needs and particularly the defenses of the parent rather than the child. This relationship structure leads to a loss of self, or the development of a "false self" (Winnicott, 1953; 1965) or a "defended self," in service to the parents, rather than healthy development and ultimate separation. This pattern also leads to an "anxious resistant" or "anxious avoidant" attachment pattern.

The alcoholic family is organized around the dominance and centrality of the traumatic, out-of-control environment, the rigid, defended system and the parents' predominant need for defense, which leads to a pattern of "reverse attachment" or role reversal as the predominant structure of the child-parent bond. A patient illustrates:

> "I was my mother's confidante from as early as I can remember. I had to listen, sympathize and offer suggestions that would somehow make everything O.K. But nothing ever changed. She was the child and I was the ineffective, helpless parent."

Most recently, developmental psychopathologists (Rolf et al, 1990) add to this picture, suggesting that children who must accommodate to parental need and defense as the context and structure for self development, may be characterized as "hard growing" or "straight jacket" survivors rather than resilient or "invulnerable" as previously believed. These theorists now suggest that the child's development is based on defensive adaptation, in response to the external demands of the environment, system and parental needs as a patient demonstrates:

> "Adjustment probably says it right, but I never knew that's what I was doing. I might have been mad if I'd have known. No, that's all there was. You just waited and watched, ready to swing this way or that to hold it all together."

Defensive Development

Bowlby and his colleagues accent the importance of open communication and accessibility between infant and mother. He, like classical theorists, and much like the interpersonal theorist, Harry Stack Sullivan, sees much of pathology as an over-emphasis on defensive processes. Sullivan believed that the core of unhealthy individual development rests on the assumption and solidification of a "fundamental malevolent attitude" (1953). The child experiences others and the world as anxiety-provoking and begins to enlist massive defensive operations to ward off the negative influence of others. As one patient told another:

> "You are your defenses! We see, feel, and hear your barriers to the world, your rational processes, the way you keep people out, the way you explain, the way you defend yourself against enemies that aren't there now but certainly were there in your childhood."

The patient responded:

> "I feel like a deck of cards: if you pull one out, the whole deck will collapse. I only exist as I am defending myself. Then I know that I am."

Bowlby (1980; 1985) and Sullivan (1953) suggest that a child shuts out, closes down, or otherwise does not see or take in information about others or the self that might threaten the parent or the all-important bond to the parent. Similarly, the child develops behaviors and affects consistent with the perceived needs of the parent and the overwhelming need to preserve the dynamics of the alcoholic family system.

Earlier (Brown, 1988) I spelled out an integrated theory based on the relationship between the central organizing influence of alcoholism in the environment, the family system and attachment. In that theory, I suggested that:

> "Attachment—early and ongoing—is based on denial of perception which results in denial of affect which together result in developmental arrests or difficulties. The core beliefs and patterns of behavior formed to sustain attachment and denial within the family then structure subsequent development of the self including behavioral, cognitive, and affective development." (Brown, 1988)

In outlining the three assessment tracks, two factors stand out: first, the importance of the interpersonal perspective, organized by attachment theory, and second, the dominance of defense in accommodating to parental alcoholism. The environment is unsafe, the system is restrictive and pathological, and individual development is characterized by unhealthy attachment patterns. Let us now move from the child to the adult and examine the impact of defensive development on interpersonal relationships. We will explore the dominance of defense within each assessment track and the fundamental interpersonal attitude, "relationship structure" or attachment pattern that results.

V. Interpersonal Relations

"Once upon a time everything was lovely, but that was before I had to deal with people." Harry Stack Sullivan (1953, p. 216.)

The Defensive Self in Adult Relationships

What do children of alcoholics bring to adult relationship? Adults born and raised in the environment, system and attachment patterns designed to sustain pathology experience the normal tasks and stages of close interpersonal development as threatening. They have internalized a sense of confusion, a requirement to "not know," the anxiety of the attachment bond and anxiety and fear about what relationship means. Physical and emotional safety and integrity are vested in the self. For many, being involved in a close, intimate relationship requires <u>more</u> defense, not less.

> "My whole sense of self is related to my ability to be self-sufficient, to defend against needing others or having others need me too much. You know what nurturance is? Nurturance is taking care of all of my own needs. Nurturance is successfully defending <u>against</u> closeness. Closeness means the loss of myself and destruction."

Another agreed:

> "A successful interaction means surviving without being humiliated, exposed, or revealing myself as bungling, starving, angry or overbearing. I end up in the delicate position of trying to balance superficial interactions to protect myself."

Nurturance—loosely, the feeling of being taken care of—is equated with surviving. It's a sense of relief, a feeling that one's defenses worked.

> "Nurturance means I win. I kept myself in control, intact, and didn't let others in. This is the only idea I have of being cared for. It comes only from me."

For these ACAs, relationship is toxic. For others, relationship holds a magical potential for fusion or rescue. These individuals maintain a hope of finding the idealized perfect mate, the one who will be the good parent, the adult needed early on. These ACAs feel lost, abandoned and orphaned as they suffer repeated disappointments in relationship. With either stance, intimate bonds are bound to bring up the need for defense so characteristic of childhood at all three levels.

The Environment

As we have seen, safety is chronically threatened for many children in alcoholic families. For others, safety is uncertain, regulated by parental drinking, inconsistency, unpredictability, and out-of control parental behavior. One's sense of self, view of others and basic framework of relationship are all structured by the level of physical and emotional safety and the need for defense. In emphasizing the interpersonal aspects of trauma, Krugman (1987) suggests that "avoidance of intimacy" or "relationship distortions" are also consequences. He emphasizes that "traumatic experience is central in organizing, structuring and reproducing the emotional, interpersonal, and systemic features common to abusive and intrusive families." (page 129.) He outlines specific consequences, accenting the dominance of defense, to avoid the recurrence of traumatic memory or experience. Unresolved, acute and chronic trauma "effects cognitive function, object relations, and interpersonal skills, leaving the victim with maladaptive first-order defenses, constricted ego function, and distorted role relationships." (p. 131.)

When trauma is chronic, it becomes normalized, more predictable, and easier to defend against. Yet the need for defense dominates; more and more of the self is organized to ward off vulnerability (p. 131).

Krugman further suggests that the defenses adapted by previously traumatized adults shape and limit the relationship structure of the couple and family they will form. He suggests that "trauma-driven deficits in cognitive, emotional, and interpersonal skills limit frustration tolerance, problem solving and conflict resolution." He adds that these families lack basic social skills, avoid anxiety-arousing situations, and often rely on drugs and alcohol. With poor boundaries and difficulties separating, they are likely to be socially isolated, psychologically impoverished, and vulnerable to stress of all kinds (p. 131).

Krugman also looks to Bowlby, suggesting that traumatized children will develop insecure attachments which then structure family relationships. The inconsistency of the parent-child relationship leads to anxiety over separation and abandonment alternating with avoidance of closeness and outright rejection. This anxiety regarding interpersonal closeness and distance matches what many describe as a central "co-dependence" problem, or disorder of relationship with ACAs—the inability to find, create, or experience the "right amount" of intimacy with a partner.

> *"I'm always looking for the perfect person. I have this idea that if we're really a good match, really in love and in tune with each other, we should always know just what the other needs. But it doesn't happen. I'm always disappointed."*

The anxiety of the attachment bond also reduces the depth and breadth of the child's affective experience. In essence, children cannot have feelings about a reality that does not exist. They also cannot have perceptions that counter the explanations constructed by parents to protect themselves and the preservation of the drinking privilege.

Krugman (1987) describes several unhealthy patterns of trauma-driven relationship structures formed by adults who experienced childhood trauma and the anxious attachment believed to accompany it, including: 1) symbiotic fusion, the inability to experience or tolerate a sense of separate self; 2) re-enactment, replaying roles and relationship patterns from earlier experiences; or 3) disengagement, a distanced, controlled and often hostile relationship dominated by defense.

Trauma distorts internal models of object relationship. Parental relationships are often structured along dominant-submissive extremes. Models for identification are equally polarized. The child can identify with the aggressor, denying vulnerability, or with the victim, needing protection, but too frightened and untrusting to seek it or let it in.

Some individuals exposed to chronic trauma in the environment will develop an internal schema of chaos with trouble or crisis normative. These individuals may require constant stimulation to feel attached, "connected" or alive, at the same time they suffer continually from the pain of the trauma they now must create. Others may experience a different kind and level of trauma, living in an "anxious environment" characterized by fear and the constant potential for harm. These individuals may be more influenced by anxiety as an inherent feature of the interpersonal bond.

In this environment, the need to keep a secret and the ongoing threat of discovery mobilize defenses. Ultimately, the child shuts out, distorts and reinterprets reality. This massive closing down leads to chronic distrust of others, inhibition of curiosity, a distrust of one's own senses and a feeling that everything is unreal. A patient who grew up in an atmosphere of tension with frequent violence and chronic criticism describes his sense of awareness as an adult.

> "I look at the world, people, events, and feelings through a filter. It's like a haze, a cheesecloth, that mutes the intensity of what's out there—and what's coming in. I couldn't tolerate my feelings without this filter."

ACAs may feel out of control in relationship. Polarized models ensure an unequal relationship structure. Mutuality, reciprocity, and flexibility in role—characteristics of mature relationship—are ruled out.

Close intimate adult bonds, organized by defensive needs and pathogenic internal models, often replicate the very childhood experiences or feelings they were designed to avoid.

The System

Alcoholic family systems dynamics are also predominantly defensive and reinforce unhealthy patterns of relationship. Interactional patterns, roles, beliefs, and behaviors are all structured to preserve the core pathology of the system.

The rigid, tightly regulated and increasingly defended alcoholic system (Steinglass et al, 1987) is characterized by disorders of hierarchy and boundaries (Krugman, 1987) and extremes of dominance and submission, a relationship structure necessary to sustain the pathology and a consequence of it. ACAs in treatment frequently recall the dictatorial nature of family relationships and family life.

> "There was one ruler, one king, and the rest of us were slaves. My father was the only one entitled to hold an opinion about anything."

Unhealthy systems dynamics are often reflected in role inconsistency and confusion between parents and in role reversal and triangulation between parents and children. Individual development is sacrificed to preserve the rigid, inflexible and increasingly threatened system.

ACAs experience great anxiety about all aspects of development, but it is particularly acute when it comes time to form their own intimate couple or family system. The paradigm for intimate relationship or family life dictates a loss of self to the preservation of a destructive, unhealthy "we." Many ACAs establish a comfortable adult life by ruling out close intimate bonds. As one patient put it:

"The only relationship is to be alone."

In the polarized system, there is a winner and a loser. This structure often guarantees an arrest in the developing couple relationship (Bader and Pearson, 1988). The couple cannot progress because one or both partners is bound to the unhealthy polarized structure of the first family. Loss of self, boundary diffusion and intrusion, fusion or disengagement are seen as normal. Within a structure that values the preservation of the system, or "we," autonomy within a close relationship will be viewed as selfish or rejecting.

Healthy relationship requires the ability to hold a strong "I" and a "we." With the polarized relationship structure of the alcoholic system, the flexibility required to maintain both perspectives is not possible. Individuals are stuck preserving a pathological "we," or defending an isolated, endangered "I."

The dominating power of unhealthy systems dynamics is reflected early in treatment as ACAs struggle with issues of guilt, betrayal and disloyalty implicit in accepting the label ACA and the need for help. For many, the very idea of autonomy or an identity separate from the family, is fraught with anxiety. As Shirley put it:

"If I even think about growing up, leaving home, and creating a family of my own, I'm overcome with guilt. Nobody ever leaves my family. We learned one thing—the family is sacred. Nobody gets out and nobody gets in."

Individual Development

Given the dominance of trauma, systems pathology and parental need in structuring the attachment bond, children develop a sense of self dominated by a malevolent interpersonal attitude (Sullivan, 1953) and a strong need for defense. In essence, the "self"—that identity connected with "me" or "I"—is equated with the ability to successfully defend oneself.

"I have a deep sense of myself as needy and vulnerable, but I have an entirely different face I present to the world. The mask of competence, strength and defiance isn't real but I rely on it anyway. The facade is my bricks and mortar, my support of myself."

Close adult partnerships will be formed from this base of a deeply vulnerable, needy, but "non-existent" or chronically endangered self, a self dominated by defense.

Another individual illustrates:

"I know at a deep level that I am needy, vulnerable, empty and sometimes non-existent. If I wasn't fending off, manipulating and constantly observing and taking in what's out there from a framework of danger and the need for protection, I wouldn't exist."

From this deep view of the world and people as dangerous, the individual develops a constellation of defensive traits or maneuvers (Brown, 1988; 1991) that dominate all aspects of interpersonal relationship. These traits are designed to keep the enemy out, to minimize anxiety, fear and the threat of humiliation, experiences that characterize the anxious attachment with parents and the anxious, or angry, parental relationship pattern observed repeatedly by the child. These interpersonal defensive maneuvers include denial or perceptual and cognitive distortion, a need for control, all-or-none thinking and an overriding assumption of responsibility for others (Brown, 1988; 1991).

Denial

The child learns that denial preserves bonds, that reality is bound to and regulated by defensive need. The child's view of self and world is literally defined by the parents' needs at any given time. The child tacitly agrees to shut out, or redefine anything that might threaten the all-important bond to parents. In adult relationships, the individual shields out any threatening information and constructs a version of reality in response to the perceived dictates of the partner. This reinforces the submissive position, with all authority for the relationship vested in the other.

Alternatively, the individual denies and distorts by rejecting all perceived "demands" of the other. This more aggressive, often overtly hostile stance, declares the partner to be dangerous and the source of potential harm. This stance reproduces the anxious resistant or avoidant pattern often dominated by intense conflict in relationship.

Control

The dominance of defense also leads to an emphasis on control. The child experiences the absence of control in the environment and in the changing nature of reality. Basic survival becomes equated with the need for control of self and other. An adult patient illustrates:

> "Everything is control. That's all there is. I need to be in control of myself, my perceptions, my feelings. I need to be in charge of my definition of reality. I need to control the distance between us, what and how much you say, feel or think. Close relationship means danger."

The dominant need to ward off anxiety and the chronic danger of calamity in relationship also result in an inordinate emphasis on control. It is sometimes experienced as a drive for perfection oneself, or a demand for rigid, strict "perfection" from others, which leads to chronic tension and anxiety (exactly what was to be avoided) in the relationship. The atmosphere is often one of "pins and needles." A patient illustrates:

> "I can't do anything right. Anything out of place, any change in routine, any uncertainty about who does what leads to an outburst or outright tantrum."

This couple eventually could see that anything out of place instantly reminded Todd of his alcoholic home, particularly the chronic disarray, arguments and abuse that organized family life. Todd's tantrums recreated the exact scenario modeled repeatedly by his parents—his mother could do no right and his father blew up.

All-or-None Thinking

Linked to control is the dominant cognitive-perceptual filter of all-or-none thinking, a concrete dichotomous frame that reduces all perception, cognitions and feelings to right or wrong, good or bad.

The defensive emphasis on all three tracks restricts open, fluid, flexible thinking, while reinforcing rigid, rule-bound cognition, virtually eliminating tolerance for ambiguity, a hallmark of mature development and relationship.

In the all-or-none frame, individuals cannot hold conflicting thoughts or feelings at the same time. This set reinforces a re-stricted range of perception, cognition and affect in relationship and sustains the polarized, dominant-submissive, or victim-aggressor relationship structure.

This primitive thinking also characterizes the popular movement. Individuals who now identify with the "codependent" position in relationship may equate change or improvement with reversal — for example, "I used to be bad, but now it's you." In essence, the partners change position within the relationship structure but main-tain the pathology.

Responsibility

Finally, defensive development is often structured by the assump-tion of responsibility. The child copes with the pathology of the environment, system and structure of relationship by developing a view of self as bad, responsible for all that goes wrong. In Sullivan's view, the child takes on a "bad me" identity, versus the "good me" that stems from healthier interpersonal experiences or the "secure" attachment pattern of Bowlby. The "bad me" or "responsible me" is the natural result of role reversal, an attachment pattern that assigns responsibility for all aspects of parental welfare to the child.

The assumption of responsibility is also tied to omnipotence, a great protection for children who feel helpless, vulnerable and perhaps out of control themselves. Children who assume the identity of "bad me" maintain an idealized image of the parents instead of recognizing their incompetence and unavailability. All the problems then lie with the children whose task it is to fix themselves.

> "I always knew deeply that I had caused all the pain. It had to be my fault. In a way, that was reassuring: if I caused the mess, then surely I could fix it too."

With an emphasis on defense and a deep, basic mistrust of others, the ACA is set to have troubles in a close couple relationship.

The ACA Couple

Recent theoretical advances in couple and family theory (Bader and Pearson, 1988; Steinglass, et al, 1987) emphasize development — the couple and family are not seen as static, but rather constantly in process, negotiating normal developmental tasks and stages leading to mature interpersonal relationships. Pathology results from arrest, restriction, or a dominance of defensive adaptation, the kind of defensive adjustment that characterizes adult children of alcoholics.

In Bader and Pearson's (1988) developmental model, the couple progresses normally through stages similar to those outlined by Mahler and others (1975) for the developing infant. The first stage is symbiosis, a healthy experience of close, fused bonding. In normal couple development, this intensity and merger do not last, although many couples see this fused partnership as ideal. Normal couple development moves toward differentiation as the partners begin to move away from the symbiotic fusion of their early bond. At this stage, they must learn to tolerate separateness and the emergence of a strong, healthy "I" in the relationship, while not losing the foundation of the "we."

The inability to tolerate differentiation leads to what is being called "codependence." Autonomy is sacrificed to preserve the system which then itself becomes unhealthy because it cannot grow.

The healthy couple moves on toward practicing, a time of greater distance and emphasis on individuation. Successful separation allows the couple to come back together in rapprochement. Here, there is flexibility, fluidity, and movement back and forth between the "I" and the "we."

The healthy couple in rapprochement, and the next and final stage of interdependence, has open access to all stages, tolerating the "regression" to the fused state and the moving away that naturally follows in the rhythm of healthy interdependence.

The couple in which one or both partners is ACA has trouble with close relationship to begin with. If the ACA can form a bond, the couple frequently gets stuck in the earliest stage, developing a closed, rigid and unhealthy symbiotic alliance. This partnership values merger, the avoidance of conflict and minimization of differences (Bader, 1990).

Alternatively, the ACA couple may form a "hostile-dependent" bond dominated by anger and conflict, in which the "I" is constantly endangered and therefore defended.

These relationship structures recreate the anxiety and chronic danger of the traumatic environment, the enmeshed or disengaged, polarized systems dynamics and the anxious attachment patterns of the earliest relationships.

The ACA suffers fears of abandonment and loss, while feeling chronic mistrust. Inconsistency and unpredictability may be recreated or warded off by rigid restrictions and limits. Any normal "coming and going" will be experienced as traumatic.

The ACA couple often gets stuck because differentiation, or the normal moving away process, is viewed as negative. A partner's need to separate within the relationship will be experienced as an abandonment, loss or betrayal. The move away automatically means "I did something wrong."

Or, the ACA feels needy and seeks close companionship, but mistrusts the other and expects to be disappointed, swallowed up or abused. The individual may challenge the partner constantly or move away sharply, denying any need. The couple develops a hostile-dependent bond in which the need is great but the anxiety more overwhelming.

The ACA cannot get out or get in — any move represents annihilation and loss, regardless of whether the individual is identified with the aggressor or victim. The ACA grew up with poor boundaries, difficulties separating from disturbed parents, social isolation, emotional impoverishment, and great vulnerability to stress. Forming a close relationship activates all of these problems.

ACAs may also have difficulties when their needs within the relationship differ. One partner may desire more autonomy than the other wants, or what the couple can accommodate. In this scenario, one partner is always feeling trapped and trying to "get more space" while the other just "wants to be close." Many couples never move beyond this stuck position of regulated distance based on apparently different needs.

Many ACA couples seek treatment because they are baffled and upset by their inability to create anything but a very troubled, defended or tightly restricted relationship. They have no internal schema for a healthy relationship.

Although their concept of relationship is based on survival and defense, they cannot comprehend why they keep repeating negative, defensive interaction patterns, or why they keep choosing the "wrong" partner, one who will only disappoint.

These ACAs enter relationships with a hope it will be different. But they also enter defended and proceed to recreate the trauma of the early family, the pathological systems dynamics and the anxiety of the early bond.

Or, they enter defended and closed, unconsciously frightened that intimate bonds will bring up a flood of intense feelings and memories from the past. They need and want a close partner, but are emotionally lifeless or inaccessible themselves. Many ACAs have cast off the capacity to feel as a protection and cannot reclaim it in the couple relationship. Or, they feel everything for everyone and are dominated by the need for control and over responsibility.

A patient in a long-term interactional therapy group for ACAs illustrates these numerous dilemmas for the defended ACA.

> "Toni is feeling anxious as she deepens her relationship. She can maintain a separate sense of herself and clear boundaries about what she sees, feels, and believes, but the clarity is brief. Then she feels herself sucked back into her old family system, now recreated with Jim. She wants to run away or she has to shut down emotionally to feel safe."

As Toni allows herself to feel close, she experiences painful and uncomfortable feelings that actually belong to childhood. Ironically, the closer she gets to Jim, the more defended she becomes. She sees that being close meant disaster in her family. Toni sees that the feelings of helplessness and fear, the "walking on eggs" with Jim, are feelings she must have experienced as a child. But the connection is still mystifying.

"Toni feels a tremendous sense of guilt about becoming healthy herself and moving away from her early family. To move toward health means abandoning her family which will lead to their destruction."

Toni chuckled ironically: "The more progress I make, the more guilt I feel and the more defended I become."

VI. Conclusion: ACA: A Relationship Disorder or Diagnosis?

We began by challenging the concept of "codependence" and the move toward viewing ACA as an individual diagnosis. I proposed three major assessment tracks instead -- the environment, the system, and individual development perspectives -- to better deal with the complexity and the <u>differences</u> between ACAs. I proposed that the ACA develops a reactive, defended self which then influences the person's entire view of self, other and world. This dominance of defense has a particularly negative impact on the ACA's capacity and ability to form and sustain close intimate interpersonal relationships.

Are all ACAs disturbed? We do not know yet, and it certainly is too soon to draw such a conclusion. It may be true that all ACAs make defensive accommodations to parental alcoholism, but some also go on to form relationships in which their defenses work well or are complementary with those of a partner, just like non-ACA individuals. We may see that ACAs in treatment are the one's whose childhood accommodations and adult defenses are more restrictive than they are useful, also just like non-ACA individuals in treatment.

We might stretch, however, and say that the ACA develops an increasing vulnerability to anxiety in forming close bonds, based on the pathology of the early relationship structure on all three levels -- environmental, systems, and individual development. It may also be useful to speculate that the ACA develops a "state" disorder, similar to the "fundamental malevolent attitude" of Sullivan. The notion of "state" suggests a readiness or particular vulnerability to the defensive stance in relationship.

We should go no further. It is too soon to reduce the ACA "disturbance" to a "relationship disorder" or a diagnosis within the current DSM. With the multiple axes and multiple variables within each track, it is impossible and still undesirable to reduce the ACA experience to any single category or disorder.

This brings us full circle. The task for understanding the ACA is one of expansion. We need to add assessment tracks and all the infinite variety of variables necessary to improve our understanding of the commonalities of the ACA experience and the unique individual differences.

ACA References

1. Al-Anon Faces Alcoholism. New York, Al-Anon Family Groups., 1984.

2. Bader, E. Personal Communication, 1990.

3. Bader, E. and Pearson, P. In Quest of the Mythical Mate: A Developmental Model of the Couple Relationship. New York, Brunner/ Mazel, 1988.

4. Beletsis, S. and Brown, S. A developmental framework for understanding adult children of alcoholics. Focus on Women: Journal of the Addictions and Health, 1981. Reprinted in: Brown, S., Beletsis, S. and Cermak, T. Adult Children of Alcoholics in Treatment. Orlando, Health Communications, 1989.

5. Black, C. My Dad Loves Me, My Dad Has a Disease. Denver, MAC, 1980.

6. Black, C. It Will Never Happen to Me. Denver, MAC. 1981.

7. Blos, P. On Adolescence: A Psychoanalytic Interpretation. New York, Free Press, 1962.

8. Bowen, M. Alcoholism as viewed through family systems theory and psychotherapy. Annals of the New York Academy of Science, 233, 115-122.

9. Bowlby, J. Attachment and Loss. Vol. 3. New York, Basic Books, 1980.

10. Bowlby, J. The role of childhood experience in cognitive disturbance. In: M. Mahoney and A. Freeman (Eds.), Cognition and Psychotherapy. New York, Plenum Press, 1985.

11. Bowlby, J. A Secure Base. New York, Basic Books, 1988.

12. Brown, S. Defining a Continuum of Recovery in Alcoholism. Doctoral Dissertation, California School of Professional Psychology, San Francisco, 1977.

13. Brown, S. Treating the Alcoholic: A Developmental Model of Recovery. New York, John Wiley and Sons, 1985.

14. Brown, S. Children with an alcoholic parent. In: N.J. Estes and M.E. Heinemann (Eds.), Alcoholism: Development, Consequences and Interventions. St. Louis, C.V. Mosby, 1986.

15. Brown, S. Treating Adult Children of Alcoholics: A Developmental Perspective. New York, John Wiley and Sons, 1988.

16. Brown, S. Safe Passage: Recovery for Adult Children of Alcoholics. New York, John Wiley and Sons, 1991.

17. Brown, S., Beletsis, S. and Cermak, T. Adult Children of Alcoholics in Treatment. Orlando, Health Communications, 1989.

18. Brown, S. and Beletsis, S. The Development of Family Transference in Groups for Adult Children of Alcoholics. International Journal of Group Psychotherapy, 97-114. Reprinted in: Brown, S., Beletsis, S. and Cermak, T. Adult Children of Alcoholics in Treatment. Orlando, Health Communications, 1989.

19. Brown, S. and Cermak, T. Group therapy with adult children of alcoholics. California Society for the Treatment of Alcoholism and Other Chemical Dependencies Newsletter. 7(7), 1979, 1-6.

20. Cermak, T. Children of alcoholics and the case for a new diagnosis of co-dependency. Alcohol, Health and Research World, 8, 38-42, 1984.

21. Cermak, T. Diagnosing and Treating Co-Dependence. Minneapolis, Johnson Institute, 1986.

22. Cermak, T. and Brown, S. Interactional group psychotherapy with the adult children of alcoholics. International Journal of Group Psychotherapy, 32, 375-389, 1982. Reprinted in: Brown, S., Beletsis, S. and Cermak, T. Adult Children of Alcoholics in Treatment. Orlando, Health Communications, 1989.

23. Diagnostic Criteria from DSM III-R. Washington D.C., American Psychiatric Association, 1987.

24. Erikson, E. Childhood and Society. New York, Norton. 1963.

25. Eth, S., and Pynoos, R. Post-Traumatic Stress Disorder in Children. Washington, D.C., American Psychiatric Press, 1985.

26. Fairbairn, W.R.D., Psychoanalytic Studies of the Personality. London, Tavistock Publications, 1952.

27. Fromm, E. Escape from Freedom. New York and Toronto, Farrar and Rinehart, 1947.

28. Guidano, V.F., and Liotti, G. Cognitive Processes and Emotional Disorders. New York, Guilford Press, 1983.

29. Guntrip, H. Schizoid Phenomena, Object Relations and the Self. New York, International Universities Press, 1969.

30. Horney, K. The Neurotic Personality of Our Time. New York, W.W. Norton, 1937.

31. Kagan, J. *The Nature of the Child.* New York, Basic Books, 1984.

32. Karen, R. Becoming attached. *Atlantic*, Feb. 1990, 35-70.

33. Kohut, H. *Analysis of the Self.* New York, International Universities Press, 1971.

34. Krugman, S. Trauma in the family: Perspectives on the intergenerational transmission of violence. In: B. van der Kolk, (Ed.), *Psychological Trauma.* Washington, D.C., 1987, 127-152.

35. Krystal, H. Trauma and affects. *Psychoanalytic Study of the Child*, 33, 81-116, 1978.

36. Lidz, T. *The Origins and Treatment of Schizophrenic Disorders.* New York, Basic Books, 1973.

37. Mahler, M., Pine, F., and Bergman, H. *The Psychological Birth of the Human Infant.* New York, Basic Books, 1975.

38. Mahoney, M. Reflections on the cognitive learning trend in psychotherapy. *American Psychologist*, 32(1), 5-13, 1977.

39. Miller, A. *The Drama of the Gifted Child.* New York, Basic Books, 1981.

40. Miller, A. *Thou Shalt Not Be Aware.* New York, Farrar, Straus, Giroux, 1984.

41. *Newsweek*, May, 1979, p. 79.

42. O'Neill, E. *Long Day's Journey Into Night.* New Haven, Yale University Press, 1955.

43. Satir, V. *Conjoint Family Therapy.* Palo Alto, Science and Behavior Books, 1964.

44. Steinglass, P. A life history model of the alcoholic family. *Family Process*, 19(3), 211-226, 1980.

45. Steinglass, P., Bennett, L., Wolin, S., and Reiss, D. *The Alcoholic Family.* Basic Books, 1987

46. Stern, D. *The Interpersonal World of the Infant*, New York, Basic Books, 1985.

47. Sullivan, H.S. *The Interpersonal Theory of Psychiatry.* New York, Norton, 1953.

48. Vaillant, G. and Milofsky, E. Natural history of male alcoholism, IV. Paths to recovery. Archives of General Psychiatry, 39(2), 127-133, 1982.

49. van der Kolk, B. Psychological Trauma. Washington D.C., American Psychiatric Press, 1987.

50. Vanicelli, M. Group Psychotherapy with ACOA's. New York, Guilford Press, 1989.

51. Watzlawick, P., Weakland, J., and Fisch, R. Change. Palo Alto, Science and Behavior Books, 1974.

52. Weiss, J. and Sampson, H. The Psychoanalytic Process: Theory, Clinical Observation and Empirical Research. New York, Guilford Press, 1986.

53. Wegsheider, S. Another Chance: Hope and Health for the Alcoholic Family. Palo Alto, Science and Behavior Books, 1981.

54. Winnicott, D.W., Transitional objects and transitional phenomena. International Journal of Psychoanalysis, 34, 89-97, 1953.

55. Winnicott, D.W., The theory of the parent-infant relationship. International Journal of Psychoanalysis, 41, 585-595, 1960.

56. Woititz, J. Adult Children of Alcoholics. Orlando, Health Communications, 1983.

57. Wood, B. Children of Alcoholism: The Struggle for Self and Intimacy in Adult Life. New York, New York University Press, 1987.

This paper was originally entitled "Codependence and ACAs: Theoretical expansion from an Interpersonal Perspective." It was presented at the National Consensus Symposium, Washington, D.C., October, 1991. Portions of this paper were used in an expanded article entitled "Alcoholism and Trauma: A Theoretical Overview and Comparison," published in the Journal of Psychoactive Drugs, 26(4), 1994. Portions of that paper appear in this monograph. Thay are reprinted with permission of the Journal of Psychoactive Drugs. All rights reserved.

You Can't Go Forward
Without Finishing the Past
Healing the Pain of Abandonment, Fear, and Shame

Claudia Black

"In this dream I was stationed underground, in the grave....This was my company, my life, my mission—to watch over the bones. And then slowly...I walked away and climbed out of the grave, into the sun and the wide expanse of the world....I turned one last time to say good-bye. The vigil was over."

—*John, Adult Child of an Alcoholic*
Quoted by Stephanie Brown, Safe Passages

"To free yourself from the past you must break the rules of silence and compliance."

—*Claudia Black,* It's Never Too Late to Have a Happy Childhood

When children are raised with chronic loss, without the psychological or physical protection they need and certainly deserve, it is most natural for them to internalize incredible fear. Not receiving the necessary psychological or physical protection equals abandonment. And, living with repeated abandonment experiences creates shame. Shame arises from the painful message implied in abandonment: "You are not important. You are not of value." Unresolved pain of the past and pain in the present created by past-driven behaviors fuel our fear of abandonment and shame. This is the pain from which we need to heal.

PAIN FROM THE PAST
Physical Abandonment

For some children abandonment is primarily physical. Physical abandonment occurs when the physical conditions necessary for thriving have been replaced by:

- lack of appropriate supervision.
- inadequate provision of nutrition and meals. There was a book titled *Potato Chips for Breakfast*, and a talk by educator and lecturer Dan Barmettle called *Macaroni at Midnight*; these titles poignantly reflect

the poor eating habits of children in some families.
- inadequate clothing, housing, heat, or shelter.
- physical and/or sexual abuse.

As children, we are totally dependent on our caretakers to provide safety in our environment. When they do not, we grow up believing that the world is an unsafe place, that people are not to be trusted, and that we do not deserve positive attention and adequate care.

Emotional Abandonment

Emotional abandonment occurs when parents do not provide the emotional conditions and emotional environment necessary for healthy development.

Because more people experience emotional abandonment than physical abandonment, and because it is a more subtle dynamic, the following abandonment experiences may be helpful to understanding emotional abandonment. Two frameworks for abandonment that can simplify the term are:

1. Abandonment is experienced by parental indifference to a child's needs and wants, or the parents (or other primary caregivers) are emotionally unavailable on an ongoing basis. They do not offer the support and nurturance a child needs. Therefore the child can neither experience nor express his or her feelings appropriately.
2. Abandonment occurs when a child has to hide a part of who he or she is in order to be accepted, while others do this to avoid rejection. Having to hide a part of yourself means:
- when it is not proper in your family to make a mistake.
- when it is not okay in your family to show feelings, being told the way you feel is not true or okay. "You have nothing to cry about and if you don't stop crying I will really give you something to cry about." "That really didn't hurt." "You have nothing to be angry about." When in the child's experience they are feeling great fear, sadness, pain or anger. We are not talking about the occasional time a parent becomes frustrated with a child and makes such a comment, but a family situation where there is continual discounting of a child's emotions.
- when it is not okay in your family to have needs. Everyone else's needs appear to be more important than yours, and the only way you even get attention is by attending to the needs of others.
- when it is not okay to have successes. Accomplishments are not acknowledged, are many times discounted, or even used as ammunition to shame a child.

Other acts of abandonment occur when:

- Children cannot live up to the expectations of their parents. These expectations are often unrealistic and not age-appropriate, such as expecting the eight-year-old to remember her dental appointment or the twelve-year-old to be able to manage his younger siblings for hours at a time.
- Children are held responsible for other people's behavior. They may be consistently blamed for the actions and feelings of their parents.
- Disapproval is shown toward children that is aimed at their entire beings or identity rather than a particular behavior, such as telling a child he is worthless when he does not do his homework or she is never going to be a good athlete because she missed the final catch of the game. Who the child is, is not separated out from what the child does.

Abandonment and Boundaries

Many times our abandonment issues are fused with distorted, confused, or undefined personal boundaries. We experience abandonment when parents have a distorted sense of boundaries, their boundaries and ours.

When parents do not view us as separate beings with distinct boundaries—we will experience abandonment.

They want us to like what they like, dress like they dress, and feel as they do. This is particularly painful during our teenage years when, as part of discovering our own self, we seek out behaviors different from our parents'. This teenage/parent struggle is common to many. Some parents cannot recognize this as part of the adolescent stage, but see it as a personal affront to their image and their own sense of worth. If we in any way express differences from our parents, or make different choices than they would, we know we run the risk of rejection.

When parents expect us to be extensions of themselves, fulfilling their dreams—we will feel abandoned.

How many of us went to the school of our father's choosing because he had wanted to attend but had been unable to? How many entered into careers that our parents chose for us? How many of us married who we did or when we did because that was expected or desired by our parents? I offer a caution in that having done what our parents expected, wanted, or demanded does not mean that it was the wrong thing to do. It just so often means that the decision was never totally ours. It is the process that is more painful or possibly wrong, not necessarily the outcome.

Judy told how her mother spoke as if it were simply fact that neither of her daughters were to have children due to the possibility of transmitting a terminal genetic disease. "My mom made it clear that it was not an option for me. Because that decision seemed based in her wanting to protect us from pain, and to protect a child from a premature death, it was hard to want to question this dictate. Mom's motivation was sincere. But I was twenty-nine years old when I realized I had never made my own decision about this. Until then it had been my mother's dictate. I realized I had to sit down and separate my life choices from my mother's pain in having a child who died young. I wrestled with the decision for a few years and ultimately made the decision to not have a child. Today, the decision is mine, not my mother's."

Certainly, many people do exactly what their parents *don't* want them to do. Often this is a part of their attempt to be a separate person. We don't marry the person our father liked so much. We don't go to the college our mother aspired to attend. Often we choose to marry the person they would like the least or simply choose to not attend college at all. Again, it is not the outcome that is the issue as much as it is the decision-making process. Instead of choosing freely, we make a reactive decision based in anger.

> *When parents are not willing to take responsibility for their feelings, thoughts, and behaviors, but expect us to take responsibility for them—we will experience abandonment.*

When parents hold children responsible for what should be their responsibility, such as telling the child it is their behavior that has caused the break up of the parents' marriage, or it is the child's behavior that creates the stress that results in the parent's need to drink or use drugs, they are expecting something impossible of a child. In effect, they are telling children that they have more power than they truly have, setting them up to experience futility and inadequacy.

> **When parents' self-esteem is derived through our behavior, when their needs override ours—we feel abandoned.**

Henri still feels pain when he talks about how his father publicly gloated over Henri's accomplishments. "Some people told me I should be grateful that my dad even noticed what I was involved in. But there was always something missing about his being proud of me. When I was growing up, I did well in school; I was a very good athlete. I was a student leader and often had my picture in the local paper. My dad came to my events, boasting about me in a way that never seemed real. His boasting was so grand and his need for people to know I was his son was so strong. Yet there was this total lack of interest in me when I was home. When I got home from the ball games, he would already be in bed. He never boasted to me. He never once congratulated me or patted me on the back."

What is important to note is that Henri did not get the validation he needed to feel special, important, or of value to his father. What he believed was that his value to his father was in how he could make his father look to his father's peers.

When children are treated as peers with no parent/child distinction—they are abandoned by their parents.

Many times parents develop relationships with their children in which they are their friends, their peers, their equals. In doing so, they share information that is not age-appropriate for a child. Inappropriate information often creates a sense of burden, or even guilt, for children; that is not fair. To tell a ten-year-old daughter that her father has had an affair cannot offer the daughter any security. The mother may need to talk about it, but that needs to be with someone who has the adult resources to be able to offer appropriate support or feedback. To share with an eight-year-old son the fears related to a situation at work only makes the child feel that his parent is too vulnerable to be available as a source of protection.

Abandonment plus distorted boundaries, at a time when children are developing their sense of worth, is the foundation for the belief in their own inadequacy and the central cause of their shame.

When parents are disrespectful of their children's boundaries and violate them, the message given is that they don't value the child as a person. That message becomes internalized as "I am not of value. I am not worthy." When parents don't acknowledge children's boundaries, the message they give is "You are here to meet my needs," and/or "I am more important than you," and/or "It is not okay to be your own person with individual feelings, desires, or needs." The message also implies that the children have to give up themselves to be available to another. This internalizes to the belief, "I am bad for having different or separate needs, wants, and feelings." "I, in my uniqueness, am not of value." When children experience chronic abandonment with distorted boundaries, they live in fear and doubt about their worth. The greater the clarity a child has around boundaries, understanding who is responsible for what, and the greater a child's self-esteem, the more likely a child will be able to reject, rather than internalize, shameful behaviors and messages.

The following is an example of a young person, Sandi, who, in spite of the fact that she was raised in an alcoholic family, experienced some stability in her early years. As a result, she developed a sense of autonomy and self-esteem, which helped her ward off shame. "Up until I was about eight, home seemed okay. I felt valued, life was fun. Then as if it was overnight, my dad was always angry. My mom was preoccupied and distant or very sad. It was as if neither our parents had any time for us. Looking back now I realized that something was happening. I just couldn't figure it out. No one was talking about what was wrong. Life just became more and more frightening. I tried to not get in the way. I took care of my brother and sister. I tried to do things to make my dad and mom happy. Nothing I did really made a difference."

One night when she was sixteen and cheerleading at a basketball game, her father showed up so drunk he could hardly walk on his own and created a scene that nearly incited a racial riot. With his arms thrown over her shoulders and her pom poms tucked under her arms, Sandi was leading her drunk father out of the gym when he began to scream racial slurs at a group of African-American teenagers. "He said things I never heard him or any one else say," Sandi said. "He said things I never knew he thought. Thank heaven this group of kids couldn't reach us. It was all I could do to get him out of the gym. Everyone was screaming and jeering. Well, I got him into his friend's car and off they went. I didn't know why my dad acted like he did—I was so angry at him."

Sandi had the ability to be angry because she had not previously internalized shame and therefore could clearly differentiate who was responsible for what. She had healthy boundary distinction. She knew what took place in the gym was about her father, not her. Because she did not take this incident as a statement about her worth or value, she was also able to access other feelings. With shame we lose the ability to identify our feelings and are more likely to reinstate the Don't Talk rule. Sandi said she was angry, and then became sad. She could talk about her fear. While this scene was certainly an act of abandonment by her father, she nonetheless had an emotional boundary that protected her self-worth and her autonomy. Sandi's ability to maintain a healthy emotional boundary ("My father's behavior does not determine who I am") prevented her from feeling shamed and personally diminished by her father's behavior.

Linda was born into an already hectic, frightened family. Her first memories were of hiding behind a table in the kitchen, trying not to be noticed, while listening to her parents arguing and thinking to herself, "Just don't let them see me." She spent most of her life trying to be invisible. "In my family there was a lot of arguing, unhappiness, and a lot of moving from place to place. I was the youngest of four and an unplanned pregnancy. My mother let me know right away that she was content with three babies, not four. I felt I came out of the chute needing a protective shield, trying to ward off the hurtful words, the painful glares. I was always in their way, yet I worked so hard not to be. My very existence seemed like such a thorn." When childhood is spent on survival, such as Linda's was, there is little energy left to develop an autonomous or separate sense of self. Linda was chronically abandoned, subject to emotional boundary abuse; as a result she experienced and internalized shame.

When we are abandoned by our caretakers we do not perceive that they were bad people or what they did to us was bad. As children we cannot reject parents, because they are so desperately needed. Instead, we take the burden of being wrong or bad onto ourselves. In doing this, we purge the caretakers of being wrong or hurtful, which reinforces a sense of security. In essence, outer safety is purchased at the price of inner security.

> Abandonment, plus distorted or undefined boundaries as you are developing your worth and identity, creates shame and fear.

This truth bears repeating because it defines the root of our pain. What we must understand now is that our abandonment experiences and boundary violations were in no way indictments of our innate goodness and value. Instead, they revealed the flawed thinking, false beliefs, and impaired behaviors of those who hurt us. Still, the wounds were struck deep in our young hearts and minds, and the very real pain can still be felt today. The causes of our emotional injury need to be understood and accepted so we can heal. Until we do, the pain will stay with us, becoming a driving force in our adult lives.

 Describe the ways you experienced physical and/or emotional abandonment in your growing up years.

Past-Driven Present Pain

In recovery we seek to change the course in our present lives by healing the pain of our past. As a result of our experiences,

- We adopted false beliefs; i.e., "I can't make a mistake or I will be worthless," or "I have to produce to be of value."
- We learned defense skills; i.e., to blame others before they blame us.
- We developed cognitive defense mechanisms; i.e., to deny, mini-mize, or rationalize. We developed mechanisms to distract us from our pain; i.e., excessive behaviors such as overeating, drinking or drug use. All of these are strategies for the preservation of ourselves when our Self is threatened.

Jan said, "I knew my parents loved me. They provided for me. They came to my school events. They told me they loved me. They would hug me. Yet, they would blatantly reject me if I showed feelings of sadness or anger. There was clearly a Don't Talk rule around being emotional unless the feelings were positive. My shame was for having feelings. So while I knew I was valued in one way, I felt very rejected and abandoned in other ways. There was a lot of loss in my family. My dad lost his job and did not find one for four years. My mother had to be hospitalized for unknown reasons twice when I was between nine and eleven. My sister went to live with my grandmother during those times. And we weren't to talk about any of this. I was angry. I was very frightened. I was sad. I wanted to scream so I could be heard, and yet knew I would not be heard and only banished further."

Jan did what most of us do when feeling abandonment and fear—she did her best to be "lovable" so her family would be there for her. Being lovable would be defined by others. For Jan, it meant discounting her own feelings and needs and putting those of others ahead of hers, which in turn meant disconnecting from her own feelings and needs. Jan learned these defenses and skills as a young girl; now these are the only defenses and skills she knows for protecting herself and relating to others. Paradoxically, in adulthood, Jan's beliefs and behaviors no longer protect her, but actually cause her more pain. Unfortunately, this pattern will continue throughout her adult life until the painful weight of chronically discounting her needs and feelings is so great that she is no longer able to continue as she has. Then she will seek new, often harmful protectors, such as alcohol, prescription pills, or food. These present-day defenses will only perpetuate, and probably escalate, her pain until she turns from the course of protection to the path of healing.

Most people develop protective strategies when they are young, carrying them into adulthood, often generalizing the impact into other areas of life. For example, as a child you may have used food to medicate your pain, and continue to use food this way as an adult, but now you have also added alcohol as a medication. Or, as a child, if you used people-pleasing behaviors to get attention from parents, you may also employ this strategy to get attention in the work place; it may also fuel an addictive relationship pattern.

The mechanisms we develop to reduce our anxiety and fears are defensive protectors. *In no way should we ever be critical of what we needed to do to protect ourselves while growing up.* Today, we need to recognize when these defenses and protectors are intrusive in our lives or when they create harm and pain. The purpose or theme of these strategies has been to lessen the pain of abandonment; also to compartmentalize or distance ourselves from the incredible fear and sense of powerlessness. The basis for all these attempts is to control or compensate for the pain.

The burden of pain we presently carry and try so hard to control is the combination of unresolved pain from the past *plus* pain from the present. As we know, events and family conditions that caused our past pain cannot be changed. Our response to pain is a choice we are making in the present. How we choose to respond can change the course of our lives. In the next few pages, we'll discuss how people respond to pain so we will be able to understand the choices we can make.

Attempts to Control Our Pain

Whether or not we understood the source of our pain in our early lives, we felt it. We were anxious, fearful, saddened, or angry. To live with a high degree of emotional pain was so unbearable for most of us that we sought ways to control the pain to defend against it. Ironically and unfortunately, as we have now seen, those ways of compensating created their own pain.

As adults still trying to control our pain, we have sought ways to create a sense of control or power to compensate for the overwhelming experience of powerlessness. We have attempted to control the pain and/or to control the sources of pain. We have tried to be in control to protect ourselves from further exposure so that our vulnerability would not be visible. We have tried to be in control so that no one would ever shame us again and so that we would not have to feel our pain.

We feel our pain. We medicate our pain. We rationalize our pain. These are all responses to the pain we have felt for so long. We first respond to pain on an emotional level, most commonly in terms of victimization, rage, and depression. Then, in an attempt to control the pain, we may respond with behaviors that try to medicate it such as alcohol, food and drug abuse, or compulsive behaviors related to sex, money, or relationships. Last, we may respond on a rational level, thinking we can avoid the pain if we don't do anything to cause it. Perfectionism and procrastination are two cognitive attempts to control pain by avoiding it.

Emotional Responses to Pain

Victimization As a Response to Pain

Chronic victimization is the result of when we accept and operate on the shameful messages that we internalized as a result of the abandonment. It is a combination of not believing in our own worth and not developing the skills that go with a belief in our worthiness. Setting limits is one such skill. When we have internalized beliefs, such as "I am not worthy," "I am not of value," "Other people are more important than me," or "Other people are more worthy," then it is difficult to set limits. We don't believe we have the right to set limits. We do not know how to say no. Those of us who are victims struggle with appropriate boundaries. We are most apt not to have boundaries or have boundaries that are easily permeable.

Victims have learned not to trust their own perceptions, believing that another person's perception is more accurate than their own. They always give others the benefit of the doubt and are willing to respond to the structure others set. Victims are not apt to question. In addition to the family rules Don't Talk, Don't Feel, Don't Trust, they have learned the rules Don't Question and Don't Think.

Not believing in their own worth, victims often fail to realize they even have needs and, as a result, do not take care of themselves. They operate from a position of fear, unable to access any anger or indignation that comes with being hurt, disappointed, or even abused. When asked what they need or want, victims often literally do not know.

While the development of the victim response is the result of the belief in personal powerlessness, it is clearly a response to the intense emotional pain in one's life. It not only is an outcome of helplessness, it is also a kind of defense in that victims believe they may not have as much pain if they give in and relinquish their autonomy to someone else.

Victims have developed a high tolerance for pain and for inappropriate behavior. They have become emotionally separated from themselves by becoming highly skilled at rationalizing, minimizing, and often flatly denying the events and emotions in their lives. They are not as readily able to identify others' behavior that has hurt them because that would, in their perception, create a greater feeling of helplessness or invite more trouble.

Some victims stay in isolation. Those who choose to stay more visible often play a victim/martyr situation: "Look at how I am victimized. Aren't they terrible for doing this to me! I will just have to endure." Being the victim becomes part of a cycle. Victims already feel bad about themselves as a result of being abandoned and/or used and abused. They don't act in a way that provides safety and security for themselves, leading to greater abandonment or abuse.

Typically, the greater a person's shame, the more likely he or she will invite someone else with shame into their lives. Very often, for the victim, this other person is someone who appears to have the ability to take charge, make things happen, someone who feels strengthened by association with the victim's vulnerability. Depending on the specific history of the two people involved, that attraction often leads to the dominant one battering the victim, either emotionally or physically.

Almost inevitably, victims have great difficulty protecting themselves in the context of intimate relationships. For example, a woman may have such a desperate longing for nurturance and care that it makes it difficult for her to establish safe and appropriate boundaries with others. Her tendency to denigrate herself and to idealize those to whom she becomes attached further clouds her judgment. Typically, her empathic attunement to the wishes of others and her automatic, often unconscious habits of obedience also tend to make her vulnerable to anyone in a position of power or authority. Her defensive style makes it difficult for her to form conscious and accurate assessments of danger.

For all of the reasons noted above, whether male or female, the shameful person is at great risk of repeated victimization.

Rage As Response to Pain

Rage is the holding tank for accumulated fears, angers, humiliations, and shame. It is for many a response of no longer wanting to endure the pain. Emotionally, rage is an attempt to be heard, seen, and valued when people are most desperate and lacking in other resources. For some people rage becomes an integral part of their lifestyle. Growing up, they found anger to be the one safe feeling for them to express, so all their other vulnerabilities were masked with anger. Many people who are rageful don't show any sign of emotions; they keep a tight lid on all of their feelings until something triggers an eruption. There may not be signs of any feeling, and suddenly their rage is in someone else's face. Perhaps it is a scathing memo at work or an outburst of criticism toward a waiter or gas station attendant, etc. It could be a lack of tolerance for any disagreement in a discussion, followed by a theatrical exit, or it may take the form of physical or verbal abuse.

People with chronic rage do exist but they are not tolerated in most neighborhoods or communities. They usually live in isolation, often with someone who is the chronic victim of their rage; or they move around a lot, wearing out their welcome after relatively short periods of time in one place. While we may view others' rage as being out of control, those who are ragers feel very much in control and powerful. In their rage they no longer feel inadequate and defective.

Rage is intended to protect against further experiences of pain. Rage is a way of actively compensating for powerlessness and feelings of shame by offering a false but attractive (to the rager) sense of power. When rage is the only way people know to protect against their emptiness, powerlessness, and pain, their choice is a quick one. Rageful behavior also offers protection by keeping people at a distance. As a result, other people cannot see into the raging person's inner self that he or she believes to be so ugly.

Rage as a defense also offers protection by transferring the shame to others. The outwardly rageful person chooses a victim-like person who, consciously or not, is willing to take the abuse and take on or assume the shame.

Rage can be accumulated anger that has never seemed safe to expose. When anger is held back, it becomes internalized. With time it grows, festering into chronic bitterness or, even more likely, chronic depression. When there has been no outlet for rage, it is more apt to explode suddenly as a significant single hostile act such as physical abuse or even murder. Such an act is the consequence of the accumulation of feelings combined with the inability to tolerate painful feelings, to resolve conflict, or to perceive options and choices.

Depression As a Response to Pain

Unfortunately, a depressed person is typically pictured as one who sleeps excessively, is unable to eat, and is suicidal. While that picture represents the severe end of the depression continuum, many depressed adults are able to function daily and meet most of their responsibilities. After all, that has been their survival mode. In *It Will Never Happen To Me*, "looking good" children are described as those raised in a troubled family who maintain the outward appearance of "doing just fine while dying on the inside." They present a false self to the world that may not have the look of depression, but their true self, their emotional and spiritual self, is experiencing great despair. When this is practiced day in and out, week after week, month after month, and year after year, it can easily translate to being "closeted depressed."

To keep depression hidden, those of us who are depressed avoid getting close enough or spending enough time around others who may recognize our true feelings and the pervasive emptiness our depression is masking. We don't develop close friendships where others are invested enough to "pull our covers." We appear very capable and seem to put out an impenetrable force field that says, "Don't ask me about myself. Don't push me." It is difficult enough being depressed. It is even more difficult when we have shame around it—shame as one cause of depression and added shame because we are depressed.

There are many different theories about the cause of depression. Some clinicians and researchers believe it to be a biochemical imbalance, a disordered neurochemistry, best treated with antidepressants. It is commonly accepted among professionals that depression tends to run in families, suggesting there may be a physiological predisposition towards depression. Other theories support the belief that depression is a consequence of a habitually pessimistic and disordered way of viewing the world. It can also be a consequence of loss and the inability to do the griefwork necessary to bring completion to the feelings of sorrow. [Note: All depression needs to be assessed by a qualified physician.]

There is tremendous loss associated with being raised in a shame-based family. With the family being denial-centered, as it often is, and it not being okay to talk honestly, the sense of loss is amplified because there is no way to work through the pain. The hurt, the disappointment, the fears, and the angers associated with life events, as well as with abandonment experiences, are all swirled together and internalized. When you add to this a personal belief that says you are at fault, it is easy to see why you came to believe in your unworthiness, and so try to hide your real self from others. Eventually, whether you are thirty-five or fifty-five, you suddenly hit a wall. The burden of hiding eventually becomes too heavy and all of those protecting, controlling mechanisms that kept you going for so long just stop working. Depression sets in.

Most people who experience depression related to loss are extremely frightened of their feelings. And they have so much to feel about. When it is not safe to speak these feelings, they become directed inward against the self. This becomes another means of perpetuating shame, which then further protracts the depressive mood.

There are necessary and unnecessary losses in life. Because it was not safe to acknowledge them, we didn't learn coping skills for the loss that would occur in our adult years. So, when loss occurs and/or accumulates in adulthood, we resort to the same defenses we learned in childhood to deny what we are feeling.

When we have had chronic loss in our lives, many of us develop thought processes wherein we catastrophize and exaggerate fear to such a point that we feel hopeless and in despair. For example, when your husband is twenty minutes late for an important appointment, you think he must have been in a terrible car accident. When your boss forgot to say hello, you feel certain that she is angry with you and is going to let you go. Armed with some small bit of knowledge, we presume the worst will happen.

Over the years, given our experiences, we have developed a committee of internal voices that have become our Inner Critic, telling ourselves we are stupid, not wanted, ugly, and unimportant; this is in response to any slight or perceived loss, or when we feel slighted by someone we value.

Most adults from troubled families experience a combination of both unresolved loss and a pessimistic view of life. When we feel our powerlessness, our despair, and our fear, we send ourselves into a downhill spiral so quickly anybody's head would be spinning.

Acute Episodes of Depression

Many adults make their way through life cut off from their internal pain, until they experience a significant present-day loss—the last child leaving home, a significant health problem, the death of a close friend or family member, the loss of job or career opportunity. As great numbers of women enter peri-menopausal and menopausal stages, the combination of physical changes and the symbolism around such changes can create an incredible sense of loss. For men and women both, one significant present-day loss can be the straw that breaks the camel's back. In other words, the new loss can trigger the beginning of a downward emotional spiral in which the adult becomes overwhelmed in despair, shame, powerlessness, and depression.

Sally, who was raised in a physically abusive family, was a department manager in an engineering firm. She had tucked away the pain of her childhood history into a corner of her heart and put a lock on it. She was involved in raising her own family, and kept a distant relationship with her sister and parents. All aspects of her life were compartmentalized. Then one day, she lost her oldest daughter in an accident.

Six months after that, her father died. Three weeks later, Sally made her first suicide attempt. To lose a child is one of life's greatest tragedies for anybody. Further, Sally had no skills, no internal supports to deal with the intense pain when her daughter died. While she did not feel close to her father, his death unleashed all of the childhood pain she had so neatly and quietly tucked away. When present-day loss occurs, we may not be aware of remembering our growing up years, but we are certainly feeling the accumulated pain.

Tom, who was raised in an extremely critical home and felt his loss through chronic rejection, quickly separated from his parents and all his siblings after high school. Then, at the age of twenty-eight when his fiancee broke up with him, his exaggerated and catastrophic thinking led into incredible despair. He had talked himself into seeing himself as totally unworthy. He envisioned that his fiancee would marry someone much more financially stable than he was and certainly a lot more fun and exciting. She would have children with someone else. He would be alone all of his life. He was convinced he would never find happiness and he would never be able to offer anything to anyone else. On and on and on Tom's incredibly painful thinking continued. Soon, he was sleeping twelve to fourteen hours a day, missing days at work, and no longer exercising or eating properly.

Losing a relationship, particularly in young adulthood, happens to many of us. However, because of chronic losses in his childhood, Tom had not learned the skills needed to grieve through the loss of his fiancee. He was not able to understand the experience in any way except as further evidence of his inadequacy and worthlessness. This loss was simply one more that added fuel to his already existing fire of shame.

Like victimization, depression is a consequence of the inability to defend and protect ourselves against the pain of loss.

Suicide: The Most Severe Response to Pain

"I am hopeless. I am unworthy and I don't deserve to live. Life won't get any better and I can't stand this pain." Suicidal thoughts, attempts, and completions speak of many issues. They are often a reflection of anger, rage turned inward, and depression. For some people, the act of suicide seems to grant power that compensates for the powerlessness in their life. For others, death is perceived to be a better option than living with certain memories and shame. The pain is too overwhelming and, out of despair and hopelessness, people become their own victims. Thoughts of taking our own lives are much more prevalent than people realize. While pain creates such thoughts, we also experience shame for having the thoughts. My message to you is, *Please don't feel ashamed. But, please do speak up and let someone know how frightened, angry, or hopeless you are feeling.*

In recovery, you can speak about those issues that have created the pain. You can say no to your shame. You can learn to find ways to express your anger without hurting yourself. You can develop new beliefs and behaviors that support you in the way you deserve to be supported. You can learn how to access the power within you that does exist. You deserve to be able to live without pain. But when you are considering suicide as a way out of your pain, you must reach out and get assistance from a helping professional.

Behavioral Responses to Pain

"Medicating" Pain

Whether our emotional response to pain is one of victimization, rage, or depression, we may also try different behaviors to control our pain, hoping to lessen the hurt. Unfortunately, our efforts to control the pain don't remove the cause or source of our feeling. One way people try to control and regulate their pain is by "medicating" it through addiction to substances or compulsive behaviors.

Substance Addictions

Types of addictions may include dependency on food, caffeine, nicotine, sugar, alcohol, and other drugs. Many of the substances people become addicted to are socially sanctioned and supported, making it very difficult for the abuser to see how they are using them in unhealthy ways.

In addition to temporarily controlling our pain, the substances we use and abuse very often provide something for us we do not know how to seek naturally. As an example, alcohol may give a sense of power to someone who has only known powerlessness. It may give access to a sense of courage and confidence to someone who feels lacking. This is certainly drug-induced, temporary and false, but for many people, false is better than none. For someone who is isolated and feels alienated from others, alcohol makes it easier to reach out to people. "Give me a little bit to drink and I become alive. I pull myself away from the wall and I find myself talking, laughing, listening. I see people responding to me and I like it." This kind of thinking doesn't mean that a person is addicted, but it does mean he or she is thirsty for connection with others. In this case alcohol becomes the reinforcement in order to feel whole and complete.

For people who have never taken time for play or laughter because life has been so serious and "I have to get things done," alcohol gives them the opportunity to relax. Alice identified, "My entire life has been spent taking care of other people. I am always busy. I make these lists daily, thinking the world will stop if I don't get the job done. I don't think about missing out on fun—it has never been a part of my life.

I was a teetotaler. I never drank until I was twenty-six. I don't even know why I started. But those first few times I remember thinking that I was being silly, hearing myself laugh with other people. It actually scared me. Yet at the same time there was this attraction. It was as if there was this whole other part of me I didn't know and maybe was okay to know.

"The attraction to relaxing with alcohol kept getting stronger. I can actually remember thinking, 'I don't have to make this decision tonight,' or 'I don't have to do this by myself.' Pretty soon it was, 'I don't have to do this at all.' I was having fun. I was relaxing." Alice's new ways of letting go and becoming less rigid were not harmful, but because she did not know how to relax without alcohol she ultimately became dependent on it. Alice, like so many others, was seeking wholeness. But the only glimpse she had of it was "under the influence."

Variations of this scenario fit for other addictions. Our relationship to certain foods or the intake, lack of intake, and/or purging of food may be about an internal struggle with power and control. We may be attempting to access power that we don't have the skills or confidence to access more naturally. Starving ourselves, purging, and compulsive overeating may be anger turned toward ourselves. Possibly we are punishing ourselves for being bad. The anorexic may be literally starving herself to become invisible in response to shame; the anorexic and bulimic may be seeking perfection—which is based in shame.

When we come from a pain-based family, it is common to go outside of ourselves for a quick answer to relieve our suffering. It doesn't seem possible that we have any way to help ourselves. Yet, ultimately, we can keep our pain under control only so long before it starts to leak out. Frightened, we feel out of control and we seek a medicator. Sometimes that medicator is a person or possibly an activity; many times it is a substance. Often it is a combination of compulsions and addictions.

Compulsions

To experience shame and powerlessness is to be in unbearable pain. While physical pain is horrible, there are moments of relief. There is hope of being cured. However, when we believe we are defective, there is no cure. Shame is a defeated state. We have no relationship with ourselves or anyone else; we are totally alone. Relief from this intolerable pain must come, one way or another. We need someone or something to take away our profound loneliness and fear, and so we seek a mood-altering experience. We need an escape. Everyone has certain behaviors used as a way to "escape," but it is when we come to depend on them to relieve our unworthiness that these become compulsive in nature. And when we grow up in an environment of shaming, where the cause of pain is external, we develop the belief that the solutions to problems exist only externally through substances or behaviors that are medicators.

There are many different types of addictions and compulsions ranging from compulsively repeated activities to preoccupying thoughts to relationship dependencies. We may use some form of keeping busy to distance or to distract ourselves, to get our minds off our pain, our fear, or our anger. We keep busy to stay in control of our feelings and therefore to avoid feeling bad. Many behavioral compulsions would be otherwise harmless activities if they weren't exaggerated, destroying the balance in our lives. For example, exercise is a healthy activity until done so excessively that we actually injure our bodies.

Relationship addiction is the dependence on being in a relationship to validate our worth. That means we use other people to lessen our shame and to avoid truly facing our selves.

Sex addiction is the use of sexual stimulation to act as a distraction or medicator of pain; or it may be a false way of accessing power to overcome our sense of powerlessness. Compulsive sex experiences can temporarily offer us warmth and an appearance of love. Or we can act out sex as an expression of anger. These sex experiences may temporarily affirm that we are lovable and worthy, all the while compounding our belief in our defectiveness. Sex addicts vary in their focus, from obsessive masturbating, the use of pornographic materials, exhibitionism, obscene phone calls, voyeurism, to multiple affairs, use of prostitutes, and so on. For sex addicts, certain behaviors take on sexual meaning. They view objects and people through their sexual preoccupation.

Even though compulsive behaviors distract and alter feelings, feelings themselves can become compulsive in nature. We become dependent on certain feelings to mask and avoid experiencing what we are really feeling. We may become a rage-aholic, using rage as a release for all feelings. Fear can overwhelm us, where phobias, hyper-vigilance, and/or anxieties can control our lives.

While some compulsions are certainly more harmful to ourselves and our family, others may be considered only nuisances. Substances and behaviors can detract from our pain and, therefore, represent attempts to control whether or not we feel such pain. Yet any time we use a substance or become involved in a process or behavior that interferes with our honesty, our ability to be present with ourselves, it deserves our attention.

Rational or Cognitive Responses to Pain

While some people focus on controlling the pain itself, others attempt to control the source of the pain. Control is the key word here. These people hope to control the cause of the pain, as opposed to removing, releasing, or healing it. As with the emotional and behavioral responses discussed earlier, these cognitive or rational responses try to prevent potential abandonment and prevent the possibility of exposing a shameful self.

Perfectionism

A common rational or cognitive response to pain is perfectionism. Perfectionism is driven by the belief that if a person's behavior is perfect there will be no reason to be criticized and therefore no more cause for pain. However, perfectionism is a shame-based phenomenon because children learn that "no matter what they do, it's never good enough." As a result, in their struggle to feel good about themselves and relieve the source of pain, they constantly push to excel, to be the best.

Highly perfectionistic people are usually people who have been raised in a rigid family environment. The rigidity may be in the form of unrealistic expectations that parents have for their children and/or for themselves. In these situations, the children internalize the parents' expectations. Also, rigidity may be expressed as children feel the need to do things "right" in order to gain approval from their parent and to lessen fears of rejection. For most children, being "right" is perceived to mean there is no room for mistakes.

Let's look at the example of Teri, nineteen years old, in a therapy group and talking about being a perfectionist. "When I was in junior high school, in order to be able to visit with friends on Saturday afternoon I had to complete certain household tasks. So, every Saturday morning I would approach my father to get a list of what I needed to accomplish to be able to go out later in the day. I'd pick up his typewritten list and go on about my duties. When the list was completed, I'd return it to my father, but then he just gave me a second list. When I was done with that list, I was inevitably given a third list. Many times there was a fourth and fifth list."

As you can guess, Teri didn't spend a lot of Saturday afternoons with her friends. When Teri told this story, tears streamed down her cheeks. Then she paused and reflectively commented, "But we all come from some pretty crazy families. It could have been worse. Besides, I learned a few things. If you want something done, ask me. I know how to be quick." Then haltingly she added, "What I really learned, though, was that no matter what I do, it's never good enough."

That was the lesson for Teri. No matter what she did, it wasn't good enough. Nothing was good enough because it wasn't humanly possible to please her father. This Saturday ritual was not about Teri. It was about her father and his need to control, his need for power. Whether or not Terri was permitted to spend time with her friends was not about how well or how quick she was in her work. For her own well-being, Teri would need to acknowledge that. In doing so, she would be able to establish an emotional boundary, separating her worth from her father's severe criticism. In doing this she would be saying no to the shame she had internalized that told her she wasn't good enough. She can then start to counter the shame—based message by acknowledging her worth.

Unfortunately, most perfectionists have no internal sense of limits. With shame and fear nipping at their heels the entire time, they always perceive their performance as related to a standard or judgment outside themselves. As children, they were taught to strive onward. There was never a time or place to rest or to have inner joy and satisfaction.

Perfection as a performance criteria means you never measure up. Then, not measuring up is translated into a comparison with others of good versus bad, better versus worse. Inevitably you end up feeling the lesser for the comparison. Comparison with others is one of the primary ways that people continue to create more shame for themselves. You continue to do to yourself on the inside what was done to you from the outside. Since your efforts were never experienced as sufficient, adequate, or good enough, you did not develop an internal sense of how much is good enough.

As adults, we need to identify those areas where we once strived so hard for recognition, attention, and approval. Then we need to come to the understanding that not only did we do our best, we truly were good enough. The lack of acceptance we have felt is not about us or our worth, but a residue left from those who judged us and who sought power by threatening to reject us. While we were not able to understand that as children, we can come to terms with that today.

Procrastination and Ambivalence

Procrastination, such as starting but not completing a project, or considering a project but never initiating it, is often an attempt to defend against further shame. Perfectionism and procrastination are closely linked. It is easy to picture Teri, in the example given, never finishing her first list, realizing that she could not please her father. Teri, though, believed in herself a bit more strongly than most people who procrastinate. Often, the procrastinator has little confidence and more fear. The perfectionist is more apt to follow through because there is the possibility of the reinforcement of some sense of accomplishment. The procrastinator will not even see that possibility.

Some children received so little attention that they were not encouraged to initiate projects, let alone complete them. Too many times when these children did something, drew a picture or wrote a story and gleefully showed their parents, the parents barely looked at it and then set it aside, or maybe even lost it. When there is no positive reinforcement to complete school projects or homework, children perform with ambivalence. They believe that "No one else cares" and develop the attitude, "Why should I care?" The result is procrastination and ambivalence.

It was just as painful for children when their parents did pay attention, but were constantly critical, maybe making a joke of the children's work, possibly humiliating them in front of others. Sue, who was an average student in school, became very excited about a history project during her sophomore year of high school. "I worked hard on it all quarter, which was unusual for me, but I found this real interesting and the teacher liked me. For the first time in a long time I really wanted to do something well. One night I was at the dining room table putting all of the pages of my report in a notebook to be turned in the next day in class. I wasn't expecting my parents to come home for a few hours yet, so I was shocked when my mother and stepfather came in, both laughing loudly, both drunk. Mom asked what I was doing and then picked up my paper which was titled 'Did America Need To Be In World War II?' Suddenly, she was in a rage and calling me a communist, saying I wasn't patriotic.

"It was unreal. Within minutes, they were both screaming at me, calling me all kinds of names. They took my report and, in their words, threw the 'trash' into the fireplace. Well, there was no way I could tell the teacher what had happened. I just took a failing grade. It was pretty horrifying, but I should have known not to put that much effort into anything. Most things never worked out for me too much."

Sue's sense of defeat was a culmination of similar experiences. Whenever she put forth effort to achieve, she somehow always felt diminished. It was several years before she could put into perspective the report incident and all the smaller incidents that led her to believe even if she wanted to work at something, it probably wasn't worth the effort. As a result, Sue quit trying to achieve at a very young age.

When children are humiliated for their efforts, made to feel inadequate or stupid, they find ways to protect themselves so they cease involvement in any action that would prove they really are a failure.

In addition, children become discouraged when they are constantly compared to someone who "did it better" or might have done it better. Tom says he was always compared to his two older brothers. "My two older brothers were articulate. They were quick and did well in school. It took me longer to grasp things. I wasn't as interested in math and sciences as they were. I was more interested in my friends. So, with school being more of a struggle and having no real help from my parents, only the push that 'you should be like your brothers,' I just gave up. I wasn't like them and didn't want to be."

Also mixed into procrastination can be anger, expressed as an attitude of "I'll show you—I won't finish this," or "I'll only do it part way. I won't give my best." Inherent in this attitude is a challenge that insists, "Like me for who I am, not for what I do." In a family where rigidity is the rule, where it is not okay to make mistakes, not okay to take risks or be different, not okay to draw attention to yourself, you learn not to initiate, or not to finish what you started. For those of us raised this way, it is amazing that we get anything done.

Our pain, our choice of responses, and the consequences of our choices are summarized on the chart, "Pain from an Adult's Point of View." (Opposite page).

Understanding Your Defenses Against Pain

Rage, depression, victimization, addictions, compulsions, perfectionism, and procrastination—these are some of the responses to having lived with fear and pain. Such responses often became protectors. They offer ways to control the pain itself and/or control the source of the pain. Other protectors begin as common, everyday acts, but taken to extremes create negative outcomes in the long run. Some of these are intellectualization, physical isolation, humor, magical thinking, lying, silence, and withdrawal.

 What are the defenses you employ? Make a list of defenses you developed to defend against the pain. Are those still behaviors you use today? After you make your list, then ask yourself the following questions:

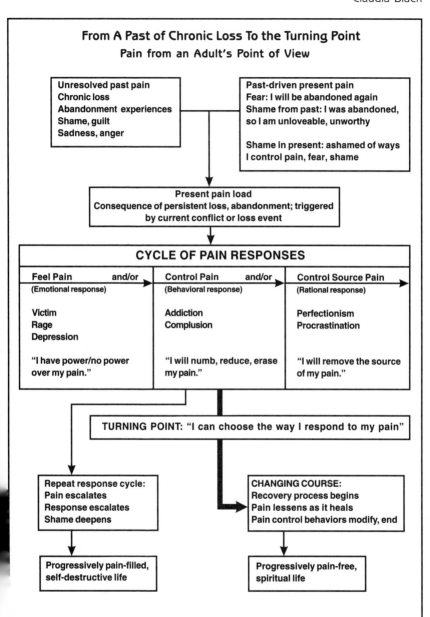

From A Past of Chronic Loss To the Turning Point
Pain from an Adult's Point of View

Unresolved past pain
Chronic loss
Abandonment experiences
Shame, guilt
Sadness, anger

Past-driven present pain
Fear: I will be abandoned again
Shame from past: I was abandoned, so I am unloveable, unworthy

Shame in present: ashamed of ways I control pain, fear, shame

Present pain load
Consequence of persistent loss, abandonment; triggered by current conflict or loss event

CYCLE OF PAIN RESPONSES

Feel Pain and/or	Control Pain and/or	Control Source Pain
(Emotional response)	(Behavioral response)	(Rational response)
Victim Rage Depression	Addiction Complusion	Perfectionism Procrastination
"I have power/no power over my pain."	"I will numb, reduce, erase my pain."	"I will remove the source of my pain."

TURNING POINT: "I can choose the way I respond to my pain"

Repeat response cycle:
Pain escalates
Response escalates
Shame deepens

CHANGING COURSE:
Recovery process begins
Pain lessens as it heals
Pain control behaviors modify, end

Progressively pain-filled, self-destructive life

Progressively pain-free, spiritual life

**Causes of past pain cannot be changed.
Responses to pain, both past and present, can change.
Changing responses to pain changes the course of pain in life.**

© *Changing Course*, Claudia Black

- What did it [the protective behavior] do for you in the past?
- What is it doing for you now?
- Would you like to let go of it?
- What do you need to do to let it go?
- What is interfering with your ability to let go of it?

Letting Go of the Past, Healing the Pain

Every one of us would like to rid ourselves of pain. The answer lies in being willing to admit and show your pain. That means facing the feelings. It means being willing to own the sadness, the hurt and the fears, embarrassments and anger about how you have had to live your life. It means being willing to be specific about all the ways you fought for emotional survivorship, how you attempted to compensate for powerlessness, and how you tried to gain control to overcome the incredible sense of shame and fear that have been so significant in your life.

 Ultimately, you will need to identify the loss events, conditions, and shaming messages in your adult life, as well as those in your growing up years, in order to be able to become separate from them. An adult loss graph, like the loss graph of your early years, is a very useful way to begin to identify the difference between who you are and what has happened to you. In the Appendix there is a Loss Graph form, with instructions, for you to record the losses in your adult years.

We Can't Go Forward Without Finishing the Past

To go forward, we must finish and let go of the past. Jill Johnston, author of *Mother Bound*, writes that as we let go of the past, "we alter the way we see ourselves in the present and the way we cast ourselves into the future...The notion of who has rights, whose voice can be heard, whose individuality is worthy, comes under revision...and the shame of difference will evaporate."

To let go of our pain, we must also acknowledge what we have been doing in the present to control our pain. Facing our own painful reality, both past and present, empowers us by giving us choice.

One option is that we can remain role-players, acting out old family roles, directed by negative judgments and false beliefs about ourselves. Choosing this option, of course, we are not really attempting to finish the past. Also, we are consigning ourselves to a future weighted down by the need to manage our shame and pain.

The other option we have is to become free agents, choosing to set our own course and act according to our own freely chosen beliefs, rather than the dictates of external standards. On this course we are able to finish the past because we are no longer being controlled by it.

Finishing the past does not mean that it disappears from our memories. Instead, it simply takes its rightful place as one significant dimension of our personal history.

Letting go of our pain doesn't mean that we will, or should, forget our suffering. That would be another kind of denial. In time we can learn to honor our past pain much as we would honor a soldier returning from war. We can also honor our experience as a significant part of our life's struggle to grow and survive.

Freeing ourselves from pain is what recovery is all about. Releasing ourselves from the past and freeing ourselves from the painful limitations of our past-driven present life is the process we go through as we turn to the new reality we want. Remember that recovery takes time. But it can be done. It can happen to you, to me, to all of us.

The awarenesses we now have bring us to another turning point to recovery:

The pain we feel is not only from the past, but also from the past-driven present.

We were powerless in the past, but we are not powerless in the present.

Another turning point comes with another awareness:

We are not our pain.

We are much, much more than mere embodiments of pain. Realizing that truth allows us to separate our selves from our emotional responses. Further, our own response is something we can affect, something we can make a choice about. As Steven Covey writes, "Responsibility is response-ability."

Together, these awarenesses lead us to the turning point that can put us on the path of freedom:

Our pain is our responsibility.

What we do about our pain is a choice we make.

Excerpted with permission from CHANGING COURSE, MAC Publishing, Inc., 2000

MORALITY IN COAs: Revisiting the Syndrome of Over-Responsibility

Sybil Wolin Ph.D.
Steven Wolin M.D.

Introduction

As a clinician, you are undoubtedly familiar with the clinical portrait of the overly responsible child of an alcoholic (4, 8, 22). The syndrome has been widely described; you have probably seen more than a few clients who fit the diagnosis. Variously called hypermature, co-dependent, responsible ones, or enablers, overly responsible children take charge when alcoholic parents abdicate their roles. These children respond to their parents' drinking by growing up fast. They react to the early signs of a parent's drunken rampage by putting pajamas on the younger kids and taking them to a neighbor's house to sleep. They do the weekly marketing and cook meals. They take care of the family's laundry. They clean the house and throw away their parents' broken liquor bottles. And they go out late at night to bring dad or mom home from the bar.

As a result of these children's efforts, some structure and consistency are achieved at home. However, according to conventional wisdom, the price they pay is great, amounting to no less than giving up significant parts of their youths. Often, as they grow into adulthood, overly responsible children become anxious, depressed, tense, and distant from others. They may enter into unhealthy relationships and overwork themselves to the point of exhaustion. Or attempting desperately to compensate for the lost pleasures of childhood, they may become excessively demanding and dependent. In all, overly responsible children bear the scars of their past.

We suggest that the pessimistic picture of overly responsible COAs, drawn above, is a partial truth which reflects a clinical bias toward identifying pathology in COAs. Having worked under the influence of a pathology bias, we know well that there are good reasons for it. Talking about pathology feels safe to clinicians; talking about strengths feels dangerous.

First, talking about deficits and symptoms gives us a professional legitimacy that talking about strengths does not. Second, our vocabulary of strengths is scant and pallid in contrast to the technical, high sounding lexicon available to us for discussing pathology. Third, the topic of strengths is difficult emotionally. Turning our attention away from forces that are harmful and dangerous to children violates our natural sympathies toward the young. To add to the matter, talking about their strengths instead can feel like excusing the inexcusable. Fourth, the topic feels politically risky. We are rightfully wary that professional acknowledgement of strengths in children of hardship could easily become justification for trimming the budget by withdrawing support services.

For all of these reasons, a bias toward pathology is understand-able. Nonetheless, it is also limiting and warrants our scrutiny. Emphasizing, as it does, problems and symptoms, a pathology bias diverts the clinician's interest away from clients' strengths. It can lull us into using such negatively tinged descriptors as "overly respon-sible," "co-dependent," and "enabler," and ultimately it leaves us with little to build on in therapy. Therefore, in this chapter, we invite you to examine the pathology bias by focusing on the usefulness of "over-responsibility" as a diagnosis and as a therapeutic term to be used with clients.

Morality vs. Defensiveness

The motivation of COAs who step into the roles abdicated by their parents has been typically attributed to the chaotic atmosphere that prevails in homes overrun by alcohol (1). This connection between the COAs' behavior and their disrupted home lives makes good sense and rests on well accepted precepts emerging from the field of child development.

We know that children need and want stability and structure. Families disrupted by the influence of alcohol, all too often, provide neither. Lacking basics such as food, clothing, safety and medical care, COAs learn that the adults around them cannot be counted on to provide. Consequently, many COAs act defensively to establish, by themselves, the structure that they and the rest of the family require.

Given the range of choices that are easier and perhaps more likely and natural for adolescents, we are struck by the widespread accep-tance of a diagnostic formulation which reduces taking over for an absent parent to a defense. Alternately, we suggest that such a choice can more accurately be seen as a moral achievement which, like any other achievement, comes at a price.

It does not seem farfetched to us that a strong sense of compassion, fairness, and decency, each of which we include in our concept of morality, account for bringing mom or dad home from the bar rather than letting either one be put out on the street at closing time. Nor does it seem hard to imagine that moral sentiments could prompt COAs into taking care of the younger kids in their families despite the personal costs. What does seem strange to us is that the moral sensibilities and the strength of character of many COAs can escape clinical attention, be misconstrued or even disparaged as pathology, or be spoken about primarily in terms of psychological costs.

A relevant perspective can be found in the work of Robert Coles, the noted child psychologist (4). Coles, has traveled around the world to interview children living in dire conditions. He wanted to know what course child development takes in environments commonly thought to bring out the worst in people.

Coles' work has taken him and his wife Jane to the American ghettos and migrant camps, the Brazilian favelas, and the South African mandated homelands. Where corruption and brutality are rampant, Coles found children who could judge right from wrong and who were honest, charitable, and fair. Coles marveled because there was little in the environment of these children which could account for their development.

Though Coles had been psychoanalytically trained, he did not even hint at a defensive component to the morality he observed among downtrodden children. Instead, he sees their morality as a positive, sustaining force that gives purpose and direction to their lives. Morality, according to Coles, is not an antidote to pain, nor does it prevent pain. Rather, morality is an accomplishment that makes life possible despite pain. We suggest that concept of morality, as described by Coles, has untapped value for organizing our clinical thinking and work with COAs. Consider the case of Terry and the injustice we would do her by diminishing the role of moral values in the choices she made.

Terry - A Case Study

Terry is a young woman in her twenties whom we interviewed for our video series "Survivor's Pride: Building Resilience in Youth at Risk" (11). By her own description, Terry played the role of mother in her family, meeting all the household and child care obligations that her alcoholic parents neglected.

Terry's earliest memory of her parents' drinking and her own abandonment dates back to kindergarten. The eldest of four children, she assumed more and more of the care of her young brothers and sisters throughout her elementary school years. By high school, she was totally in charge of the household, and while she was deter- mined to go away to college, and did go, separation from her family was a wrench. In her freshman year, when Terry's parents divorced, her mother left the home. The three younger children remained in the care of their father. Worried about their physical safety as well as their emotional well being, Terry interrupted her college career for two-and-a-half years to come home and hold the family together.

Terry told us that by choosing to return home, she was following the dictates of her conscience. She said further, that to this day, she felt good about what she had done. Nonetheless, she suffered. Being at home when she wanted to be in college was painful, and she began to drink.

At the time we interviewed Terry, she had not been drinking for over three years. She had some expectable symptoms related to her childhood, namely perfectionism, a recurrent feeling that she "could always do more," and some difficulty "playing." There was also a good deal that was positive in Terry's life. She was engaged to be married, had thought carefully and constructively about the nature of her relationship with her fiance, and could share her feelings with him freely. As she described it, they were "good friends."

Terry was also gratified to be completing an undergraduate degree in elementary education. She saw her career choice as a carryover from her past success with young children, both as a baby sitter and as an older sister. She said, "I love working with kids. A lot of my jobs were with kids... and I took care of my younger brother and sisters ... They thought I was their mother ... I babysat all over the neighbor- hood. Not just on my block because parents would refer me to other parents, and I'd get calls all the time. I was booked months in ad- vance. And those families still remember me and ask about me."

In addition to extending her early loving experiences with chil- dren, teaching offered Terry an arena for exercising her moral commitment. She saw in education the opportunity to have the same positive influence that her own teachers had on her. She said, "I've always wanted to be a teacher, and even more so now, realizing that I can make a difference , not only in academic education. I had some really kind supporting teachers I remember, and they definitely helped me."

Shortly before we interviewed Terry, she had seen her mother. She related the incident to us. Having recently achieved sobriety, Terry's mother wanted to repair relationships with her children. She contacted Terry with the intended goal of making amends. Accordingly, she acknowledged all the "terrible things" Terry was forced to do as a child. She then apologized and asked for Terry's forgiveness.

For Terry's mother, the apology had the likely effect of relieving guilt. For Terry, however, it hurt more than it helped, running afoul of her view of her self as a caring, decent, and competent person. Moreover, the apology robbed Terry of the pride she felt in her behavior as a child, and it undercut her efforts to rest her current decisions on her past accomplishments.

Terry explained, "Pride … hum … I get a lot of the opposite from my mom. She's always apologizing now that she's in recovery. And she feels that she made me responsible for so many things, and it's hard to be proud when she's saying that this was such a horrible thing. So it's kind of a dilemma for me cause I am proud. I did the right thing and I feel like I did a good job sometimes, the best I could, more than would be expected of a child. Then to have her tell me that she is so sorry and it was horrible and that's not the way it should have been. She's right, but … how about a pat on the back?"

The Damage Model

For clinicians to view Terry with a pathology bias, to dwell primarily on the psychological costs of her choices, to label her as overly responsible is to make the same error in judgement that her mother made. We call the mindset that spawns such pessimistic pathology-oriented thinking the Damage Model (10).

In the Damage Model (pictured below) troubled families, such as those with alcoholism, are seen as toxic agents, and offspring are regarded as victims of their parents' harmful actions.

COAs, according to the Damage Model, are vulnerable, and locked into the family. The best they can do is cope or contain the family's

THE DAMAGE MODEL

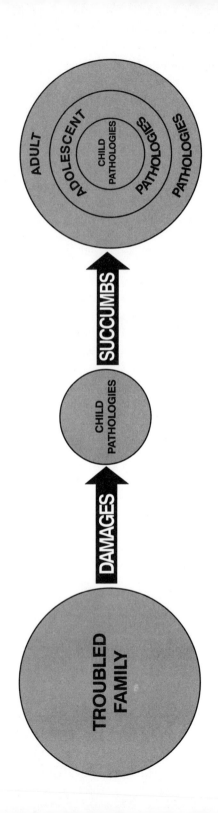

harmful influence at considerable cost to themselves. Inevitably, the accumulating price of coping takes its toll and results in symptoms and behaviors that make up the general category of pathologies. In adolescence and adulthood, pathologies are layered on pathologies, and eventually the child is no better off than his or her troubled parent.

The role of the therapist in this scenario is to uncover and give voice to the hurt feelings and anger in COAs such as Terry. Therapy aims to promote healing through the processes of grieving and of expressing hurt and anger. Biased toward disease and fixing what's wrong with the client, the Damage Model accommodates neither Terry's positive valuation of her own actions nor her resources to help herself. A different approach is required to understand Terry and others like her more fully.

The Challenge Model

The Challenge Model (pictured below) builds on the Damage Model (10). We intend it as an amplification or complement to the Damage Model and not as a refutation or replacement.

The Challenge Model starts, like the Damage Model, with the observation that troubled families can inflict considerable harm on their children. In the Challenge Model, however, two forces, represented by interlocking arrows, are at work as the child and the family interact. The troubled family is seen as a danger to the child, as it is in the Damage Model, and also as an opportunity. Children are vulnerable to their parents' harm, but they are also challenged to rebound by becoming active agents in their own lives. As a result of the interplay between damage and challenge, the children in troubled families are left with pathologies that do not disappear completely and resiliencies that limit the influence of their damage and promote their growth and well-being. The shaded and unshaded areas on the Challenge Model diagram represent the contrasting elements of strength and weakness in the inner life and outward behavior of COAs like Terry.

In the process of developing the Challenge Model, we interviewed adult children of troubled families, including children from alcoholic families. Our aim was to uncover both the strengths and the damage that resulted from their early, difficult experiences. Our analysis of the interview transcripts certainly revealed elements of pathology. But, unconstrained by a primary interest in sickness, we could also

THE CHALLENGE MODEL

TROUBLED FAMILY

DAMAGES

CHALLENGES

CHILD

PATHOLOGIES

RESILIENCIES

SUCCUMBS

REBOUNDS

ADULT

ADOLESCENT

CHILD

© Drs. Steven & Sybil Wolin
Project Resilience
Washington, D.C.

PATHOLOGIES

230

see common positive themes or clusters of strengths. We have called these clusters of strength resiliencies and have named them as follows: insight, independence, relationships, initiative, creativity, humor and morality. For the purposes of this paper, we will focus exclusively on morality.

The Developmental Unfolding of Morality

We define morality as the activity of an informed conscience (10). It is the wish for a good personal life grown large and inclusive. In adults, morality is defined as "serving" or devoting time and energy to improving institutions, community and the world. For example, choosing a career in teaching, as Terry did, because of the opportunity it offers for helping children; including charitable contributions in one's household budget; volunteering to tutor the illiterate; donating blood to a blood bank; supporting political reform; looking out for friends who are alone at holiday time; giving up a favorite activity to help a sick friend; reducing a standard fee for a needy client; writing a letter to the editor about biased reporting; or helping a mother search for a lost child on the beach. Morality is the capacity to move beyond self interest and act on the basis of a larger common good.

As the generous spirit of the people we interviewed revealed itself in these and other examples, we were deeply touched. We also wondered how those, given so little as children, had honed their moral sensibilities. Their explanations, which were similar, did not reflect an inclination to see themselves "as over-responsible" but rather as spiritual, mindful, generous, and moral people. For example, Noreen, an adult child of an alcoholic, said, "coming from the kind of home life I had . . . I'm left with a deep awareness of just how fragile the good things in life are and how easily they could disappear or just not be ... I have an abiding of appreciation for what I have—a sense of indebtedness and an obligation to repay."

Almost uniformly, the kind of sentiment expressed here could be traced back through early childhood and adolescence. Noreen, for example, said, "I knew my father was a mean machine. I didn't think that I or anyone else in the family deserved his violence. My father's brutality was his problem. In fact, that was one of the worst parts about growing up in my family. There was no rhyme or reason to him. What he did was so unconnected to what we did."

Noreen's words strongly suggest that, from a young age, she was capable of accurately judging the injustice of her parent's behavior. We suggest that, as children, many COAs had the same good judgement as Noreen. Indeed, applying a right/wrong standard to their parents was the first step in the achievement of their morality.

In keeping with a Damage Model, COAs are not normally credited with the early achievement of morality. Instead, the view has prevailed that young children are emotionally incapable of judging the rights and wrongs of their parents' behavior (2, 6, 7). Wanting and needing good parents in order to be safe in an overwhelming world, they are blinded to their parents' faults. Even when parents are abusive and neglectful, children will not hold them to account. Instead, they will blame themselves and construe the abuse and neglect as treatment they deserve. In short, on the basis of a pathology bias, abuse specialists (8) have become convinced that children will make themselves "bad" in order to preserve an image of their parents as "good."

More in keeping with the Challenge Model, our interviews revealed a **shifting** moral awareness among COAs, as children, rather than a **stable** sense of themselves as bad and their parents as good. At their neediest times, they succumbed and were, in fact, willing to accept the blame for their own abuse and neglect. At other times, however, they were able to be strong, to brave the world alone, and to see matters more clearly. They knew that abuse was bad and that they deserved better.

The research of Dr. Robert L. Selman confirms our impression (9). In a study looking at social development, Selman showed that young children **are** capable of acknowledging that parents are fallible. Asked hypothetical questions, seven-year-olds differentiated between the justifiable actions and the mistakes of their parents. In their opinion, punishment is not necessarily deserved because a parent metes it out. Rather, punishment can be warranted or unwarranted, fair or unfair. The seven-year-olds who spoke to Selman were capable, as the Challenge Model suggests, of skepticism toward parents, saying that it is wrong to punish children without considering the reasons for their behaviors.

In adolescence, the capacity for judging, found in our interviews and confirmed by Selman's research, develops into a coherent system of values, including decency, honesty, fairness, and justice. We suggest that this value system drives the behavioral pattern we have tagged as "over-responsibility." As Noreen told us, "It was a matter of tolerance. I saw all the suffering and I couldn't abide it. The worst was that my father would go after the younger kids, the little ones who couldn't defend themselves. I felt that I had to protect the little ones. It was a moral obligation, something I couldn't avoid, something any decent person would do."

Conclusion

In this paper, we have shown that the behavior of COAs who meet the obligations neglected by alcoholic parents has been seen commonly as a defense. As such, this behavior pattern is believed to serve an adaptive purpose for COAs when they are young but, ultimately, it becomes the foundation for pathology in adulthood. Alternatively, we have proposed that the COAs' evolving moral sensibilities underlie the willingness and capacity to step in for neglectful and/or abusive alcoholic parents. Therefore, their behavior, which has been commonly tagged as "overly responsible," would be more properly regarded as an achievement with a price rather than as a defense.

NOTES

1. Black C: Children of Alcoholics as Youngsters-Adolescents-Adults."It Will Never Happen to Me". New York, Ballantine Books, 1981

2. Bowlby J: On knowing what you're not supposed to know and feeling what you're not supposed to feel. Canadian Journal of Psychiatry 24: 403-408, 1979

3. Cermak TL: The Road to Recovery. A Time to Heal. Los Angeles, California, Jeremy P. Tarcher, Inc., 1976

4. Coles R: The Moral Life of Children. Boston, Houghton Mifflin, 1986

5. Friel J, Friel L: Adult Children. The Secrets of Dysfunctional Families. Pompano Beach, Florida, Health Communications, Inc., 1988

6. Kohlberg, L: The Philosophy of Moral Development. Volume I. San Francisco, Harper & Row, 1981

7. Miller, A: The Drama of the Gifted Child. New York, Basic Books, 1981

8. Rieker, PR & Carmen, E: The victim-to-patient process: The disconfirmation and transformation of abuse. American Journal of Orthopsychiatry 56: 360-370, 1986

9. Selman, R: The Growth of Interpersonal Understanding: Developmental and Clinical Analyses. New York, Academic Press, 1980

10. Wolin, SJ & Wolin S: The Resilient Self. How Survivors of Troubled Families Rise Above Adversity. New York, Villard Books, 1993

11. Survivor's Pride. Building Resilience in Youth at Risk. Verona, Wisconsin, Attainment Co., 1993

Children in Alcoholic Families: Family Dynamics and Treatment Issues

Hoover Adger, Jr., M.D., M.P.H.

Of an estimated 28 million Americans who are children of alcoholics, nearly 11 million are under the age of 18. Countless other children are affected by substance-abusing parents, siblings or other caregivers. Of the under-18 group, nearly three million will develop alcoholism, other drug problems, and other serious coping problems. Many of these children are exposed to chaotic family environments that lack consistency, stability or emotional support. Some of these children may be traumatized by accidental injury resulting from parental drinking or drug use, verbal abuse or physical abuse. Poor communication, permissiveness, under-socialization, neglect and violence, all potentially devastating, are common in children who live in families affected by alcoholism and other drug dependence (National Institute on Alcohol Abuse and Alcoholism, 1992, 1997; Bavolek and Henderson, 1990).

The cycle is frequently repeated. Approximately half of all children of alcoholics marry alcoholics; thus, there is a high likelihood of recreating the same kinds of highly stressful and unhealthy families in which these individuals grew up.

Children of substance-abusing parents are at increased risk because of both genetic and environmental factors (Begleiter and Porjesz, 1997; Anthenelli and Schuckit, 1990). Children who grow up with substance-abusing parents often develop unhealthy living patterns; for example, they may not learn to trust themselves or others, how to handle uncomfortable feelings, or how to build positive relationships. Children of substance-abusing parents who lack these skills also are at higher risk for school failure, depression, and increased anxiety, as well as trouble with alcohol and other drugs (Wegscheider, 1981; Black, 1982; Johnson and Rolf, 1988).

While genetic predispositions cannot be changed, unhealthy living patterns can be countered. Children of substance-abusing parents can learn to trust, to handle their feelings in healthy ways, and to build positive, nurturing relationships. Health care professionals can help children of substance-abusing parents understand their risks and learn better social and coping skills. All children have a right to be emotionally and physically safe. No child of an alcoholic or other substance-abusing parent should have to grow up in isolation and without support. Health professionals should play a vital role in helping to optimize the health, well-being and development of children and adolescents from these families and should address, as early as possible, any associated problems or concerns.

Effects of Alcohol and Drug Abuse on the Family

Families often tend to act in patterned and predictable ways when one member of the family is affected by alcohol or other drug abuse and dependence. Over time, affected families may move away from the supportive relationships that characterize healthy families and move toward increasingly dysfunctional or chaotic states. Denial, secretiveness, lack of trust and honesty, and suppression of feelings are patterns that are often observed.

Denial can be a powerful but maladaptive defense and may prevent individuals from recognizing the causes of a deteriorating family relationship. Hence, actions that are obvious indicators of problems related to alcohol or drug use may become accepted by the family as normal behavior. The family's denial may be even stronger than that of the affected individual and may be related to the amount of stigmatization felt by family members. Denial may be so pervasive that, even when an alcohol or other drug problem is suspected, affected family members may unconsciously mislead health practitioners into pursuing other causes of family stress (Estes and Heinemann, 1982). Because of the power of denial, the illness may progress while health practitioners are frustrated in their attempts to confirm a suspected diagnosis, and they might react by choosing not to pursue the issue. The importance of denial is underscored by the fact that it is not uncommon for a spouse or child in the family to feel that he or she is the cause of the deteriorating family relationship. Hence, the family history and attribution may be markedly distorted.

Once family members recognize that a parent, child or spouse has a problem with alcoholism or other drug abuse and dependence, they may attempt to adapt in a number of ways to insure the integrity of the family unit. They may not discuss the problem among themselves or with others outside the family. Even young children learn not to share painful and distressing observations; instead, family members hide the problem and their reactions from each other. The drinking or drug use is not mentioned. A spouse who is abused or battered by the affected individual may tell a child that he or she fell. And the family secret grows.

The isolation that develops around such a family is both social and emotional. Children may stop inviting friends to visit because of the unpredictability of the alcoholic's or addict's behavior. A spouse may refuse social invitations or make excuses for the impaired individual's absence from work. These behavior patterns—denial, secretiveness, lack of honesty, and suppression of feelings—are amazingly similar and parallel to those of the alcoholic or drug dependent individual. The boundaries around such families can become rigid and impermeable, restricting the flow of information into and out of the family. In such situations, normal needs may be gratified in abnormal ways. For example, several studies have documented the association between child physical, emotional, and sexual abuse, neglect, family violence, and substance abuse in the family. Often the family members suffer in silence and do not reveal such abuse for many years.

Family Roles. As the family becomes increasingly preoccupied with the addicted person's drinking or drug use, there may be attempts to reorganize, and in this process various adaptive roles may be assumed. Stereotypic roles in the alcoholic family (and dysfunctional families in general) were first described by Wegscheider (1981) and since have become popularized in the lay literature. They include the alcoholic or drug addict, the "enabler," the "scapegoat," the "lost child," and the "mascot".

The *alcoholic* or *addict* is the central character in the family's drama. The *enabler*, frequently the spouse, takes control of the family and protects the affected person from the consequences of his or her actions by assuming the alcoholic's or addict's responsibilities and by shielding him or her from outside scrutiny. While the enabler usually is perceived as extremely responsible and strong-willed, he or she can harbor a number of negative feelings. Frustration, anxiety and stress-related symptoms are an understandable corollary of enabling behaviors.

The *hero* often is a high achiever and brings pride to the family through successes at school or at work. While portraying an image of self-confidence and success, the hero may feel inadequate and experience the same stress-related symptoms as the enabler.

The *scapegoat* diverts attention away from the alcoholic by acting out his or her anger. The scapegoat is considered to be at high risk for addiction because of his or her association with risk-taking activities and peers, and may be progressively involved in self-injurious and delinquent behaviors.

The *lost child*, often characterized as quiet and shy, withdraws from the family and social activities to escape the family's problems. The *mascot* seeks attention by being cute or funny, demonstrates immature behavior, and may have difficulty learning in school. While laughing on the outside, he or she may be quite sad on the inside.

For the physician, the importance of understanding these roles lies not only in the insights they provide into the dynamics of the alcoholic's or addict's family, but also their usefulness in identifying the health problems that are related to maladaptive behaviors (Duggan, Adger et al., 1991). Although the roles are stereotypical, patients may describe themselves in these terms. Hence, the physician can be more supportive of such patients if he or she understands the terms and the concepts they represent. An understanding and appreciation of family dynamics also places the physician in a better position to help patients learn more functional coping strategies.

Often, the behavior exhibited by children of substance-abusing parents brings them to professional attention before alcohol or other drug abuse or dependence is diagnosed in the parent or other family member. The impact of an alcoholic or drug-abusing parent on the child can be devastating. The younger a child is when the drinking or drug abuse begins, the more serious is its potential impact on the child's subsequent adult life (Duggan, Adger et al., 1991). When family alcohol and other drug abuse is untreated, children often carry the family rules and role-related behaviors into adulthood.

It is important to understand that, while numerous studies emphasize the illness or damage that can occur to children of substance-abusing parents, the majority of children in such families become healthy, well-adjusted adults. It appears that there are protective mechanisms that enable many children to grow into emotionally healthy adults. Children of substance-abusing parents and other drug abusing parents who do not develop serious coping problems are distinguished from their peers by more attention from a primary caretaker early in life and the absence of prolonged separation from parents. These resilient children appear to have more affectionate temperaments in childhood, have at least average intelligence, possess adequate communication skills, maintain a positive self-image, and have a more internalized locus of control (Werner, 1986).

Familial Responses. Steinglass and colleagues have found that families differ in their responses to the effects of alcoholism. Their research has highlighted that the family's rituals, priorities and behavioral styles and their use of resources and energy are altered by alcoholism. Many families are successful at maintaining their primary tasks and are not identified as problematic. In families where the alterations are the greatest, learned behaviors may be passed on to the next generation. When the family is able to resist the full effects of the disease, the children do not necessarily recreate the same kinds of highly stressful and unhealthy families in which they grew up (Steinglass, Bennett et al., 1987; Wolin, Bennett et al., 1980).

Physicians who understand these behaviors and associated symptoms can be helpful in uncovering the problem of alcoholism and other drug dependence. They can be instrumental in explaining to the family how they might be affected by the problem and can provide valuable assistance to the family and the alcohol or drug-dependent individual.

Intervention and Treatment

Understanding the many ways in which alcohol and other drug abuse affects families can be helpful in formulating a plan for intervention and treatment. The family can be instrumental in initiating treatment. Even when the alcoholic or drug abusing family member is highly resistant or unwilling to participate in treatment, the clinician may have another highly motivated patient: the family.

The first step in intervention and treatment is identification (Graham, 1990; Macdonald and Blume, 1986; Duggan, Adger et al., 1991). The National Association for Children of Alcoholics (NACoA) recently developed a set of core competencies to serve as a specific guide to the core knowledge, attitudes, and skills that are essential in meeting the needs of children and youth affected by family substance abuse (The White House, 1997). These competencies set forth three levels for professional involvement with children who grow up in homes where alcohol and other drugs are a problem.

Level I. For all health care professionals with clinical responsibility for the care of children and adolescents:

1. Be aware of the medical, psychiatric, and behavioral syndromes and symptoms of children and adolescents in families with substance abuse present.
2. Be aware of the potential benefit, to both the child and the family, of timely and early intervention.
3. Be familiar with community resources available for children and adolescents in families with substance abuse.
4. As part of the general health assessment of children and adolescents, health professionals need to include appropriate screening for family history/current use of alcohol and other drugs.
5. Based on screening results, determine family resource needs and services currently being provided so that an appropriate level of care and follow-up can be recommended.
6. Be able to communicate an appropriate level of concern and offer information, support and follow-up.

Level II. In addition to Level I competencies, health care providers accepting responsibility for prevention, assessment, intervention and coordination of care of children and adolescents in families with substance abuse should:

1. Apprise the child and family of the nature of alcohol and other drug abuse dependence and its impact on all family members and strategies for achieving optimal health and recovery.
2. Recognize and treat, or refer, all associated health problems.
3. Evaluate resources-physical health, economic, interpersonal, and social-to the degree necessary to formulate an initial management plan.
4. Determine the need for involving family members and significant other persons in the initial management plan.
5. Develop a long-term management plan in consideration of the above standards and with the child or adolescent's participation.

Level III. In addition to Level I and Level II competencies, the health care provider with additional training, who accepts responsibility for long-term treatment of children and adolescents in families with substance abuse should:

1. Acquire knowledge, by training or experience, in the medical and behavioral treatment of children in families affected by substance abuse.

2. Continually monitor the child or adolescent's health needs.
3. Be knowledgeable about the proper use of consultations.
4. Throughout the course of health care treatment, continually monitor and treat, or refer for care, any psychiatric or behavioral disturbances.
5. Be available to the child or adolescent and the family, as needed, for ongoing care and support.

The complexity and diversity of problems encountered in many children of substance-abusing parents require early and comprehensive intervention. The addiction specialist needs to be acquainted with health professionals in the community who can be enlisted to assist in the evaluation, assessment and treatment of affected families. Common intervention strategies—which include delivering developmentally and age appropriate education, connecting patients with social support networks, offering training in skills development and addressing the socio-emotional needs of affected individuals—should be familiar to health practitioners.

Conclusions

Addiction medicine specialists and other clinicians are in an ideal position to identify early alcohol- and other drug-related problems in children, adolescents and families. While it is easiest to identify alcohol and other drug-related problems in those patients who are most severely affected, the challenge is to identify individuals early in their involvement and to intervene in a very timely and meaningful manner.

References

Anthenelli, R.M. and Schuckit, M.A. (1990). Genetic studies of alcoholism. International Journal of Addiction 25:81-94.

Bavolek, S.J. and Henderson, H.L. (1990). Child maltreatment and alcohol abuse: Comparisons and perspectives for treatment. In R.T. Potter-Efron and P.S. Potter-Efron (eds.) Aggression, Family Violence and Chemical Dependency. Binghamton, NY: Haworth Press, 165-184.

Begleiter, H. and Porjesz, B. (1997). Event-related potentials in COAs. Alcohol Health and Research World 21-3:236-240.

Black, C. (1982). It Will Never Happen to Me. Denver, CO: Medical Administration Company.

Duggan, A.K., Adger H., McDonald, E.M. et al. (1991). Detection of alcoholism in children and their families. American Journal of Disease of Children 145:613-617.

Estes, N. and Heinemann, M. eds (1982). Alcoholism, Development, Consequences, and Interventions, Ed. 2. St. Louis, MO: C.V. Mosby Co.

Graham, A.V. (1990). Family Issues in Substance Abuse. Project SAEFP, Society of Teachers of Family Medicine, DHHS No. 240-89-0038.

Johnson, J. and Rolf, J.E. (1988). Cognitive functioning in children from alcoholic and non-alcoholic families. Journal of Addictions 83:849-857.

Macdonald, D.I. and Blume, S.B. (1986). Children of alcoholics. American Journal of Diseases of Children 140:750.

National Clearinghouse for Alcohol and Drug Information (1995). Alcoholism Tends To Run in Families (DHHS publication No. (ADM) 92-1914). Bethesda, MD: National Institutes of Health.

National Institute on Alcohol Abuse and Alcoholism (1997). Ninth Special Report to the U.S. Congress on Alcohol and Health (NIH Pub. No 97-4017). Bethesda, MD: National Institutes of Health.

Steinglass, P., Bennett, L.A., Wolin, S.J. and Reis, D. (1987). The Alcoholic Family. New York, NY: Basic Books, Inc.

Wegscheider, S. (1981). Another Chance. Palo Alto, CA: Science and Behavior Books, Inc.

Werner, E.E. (1986). Resilient offspring of alcoholics: A longitudinal study from birth to age 18. Journal of Studies on Alcohol 47:34-40.

The White House (1997). Conference Proceedings, Core Competencies: Involvement of Health Care Providers in the Care of Children and Adolescents in Families Affected by Substance Abuse, The White House, September 15.

Wolin S.J., Bennett, L.A., Noonan, D.L. and Teitelbaum, M.A. (1980). Disrupted family rituals: A factor in the intergenerational transmission of alcoholism. Journal of Studies on Alcohol 41:199-214.

This paper is reprinted with permission from Principles of Addiction Medicine Second Edition, American Society of Addiction Medicine, Inc. 1998.

The Development of Alcoholic Subtypes
Risk Variation Among Alcoholic Families During the Early Childhood Years

Robert A. Zucker, PH.D., Deborah Ellis, PH.D.,
C. Raymond Bingham, PH.D, and
Hiram E. Fitzgerald, PH.D.

Lifetime differences in antisocial behavior among alcoholic men historically have been useful in distinguishing alcoholic subtypes. However, the usefulness of this subtyping strategy for identifying differences in families that may put offspring at risk for developing later alcoholism has not been previously documented. Findings from a prospective study on the development of vulnerability for alcoholism among (initially) preschool-age children showed that children from families with antisocial alcoholism differ on a number of indicators of child risk, including measures of risky temperament, externalizing behavior problems, and hyperactivity. Risk differences among children from these family subtypes appear to be sustained into middle childhood. Differences between nonantisocial alcoholic families and nonalcoholic control families were less distinguishable in both early and middle childhood. KEY WORDS: disorder classification; AOD dependence; risk assessment; risk factors; high risk group; familial alcoholism; children of alcoholics; childhood; child; family environment; family dynamics; antisocial behavior; hyperactive behavior; aggressive behavior; behavioral problem; adolescence; longitudinal study; prospective study.

The diagnostic system most widely used for classifying psychiatric disorders is the *Diagnostic and Statistical Manual of Mental Disorders* (i.e., the DSM criteria). The most recent version of this manual, the fourth edition (American Psychiatric Association 1994), provides two categories in which to classify alcohol-use disorders: (1) alcohol dependence, which generally involves symptoms of tolerance and withdrawal, along with a host of other symptoms indicative of chronic and compulsive alcohol use, and (2) alcohol abuse, which involves symptoms that are less chronic and severe. Instead, the critical identifying feature for alcohol abuse is a pattern of use characterized by recurrent and significant adverse consequences. Close examination of the DSM criteria shows that even within these two categories, a multiplicity of different symptom complexes and outcomes exists. Both researchers and clinicians have been aware of the diversity of alcohol abuse and alcoholism (i.e. its heterogeneity) for well over a century (Babor and Lauerman, 1986), and the DSM-IV classification system is the most recent, albeit imperfect, attempt to sort these varied symptoms in a meaningful way.

Alcohol abuse involves a complex of behaviors. These behavior characteristics are less severe and they change rapidly (i.e. are more transitory) compared with the characteristics of alcohol dependence. As a result, the use of two distinct categories for classifying people with alcohol problems seems justified. In addition, as noted in the DSM-IV, abuse does not invariably lead to dependence. Moreover, signs of early alcohol dependence do not necessarily indicate that an individual will continue this pattern of behavior over time (Skog and Duckert, 1993). Because such heterogeneity exists within this classification system, scientists continue to speculate that the causes underlying the apparently single disorder of alcohol abuse-dependence amy actually involve multiple processes (Cloninger 1987; Cloninger et al., 1986; Hesselbrock, 1995; Schuckit, 1985; Zucker, 1994). Scientists continue to look for other categorization approaches that would better reflect the variability that exists within the alcohol abuse-dependence framework. This is the rationale behind the research for subtypes.

One study that has documented the heterogeneity found within alcohol abuse and dependence is the Epidemiologic Catchment Area (ECA) Study. This study provided a survey of the distribution of psychiatric disorders. Using this data, scientists have been able to project the prevalence of alcohol abuse-dependence within the U.S. population as well as begin to make estimates of the extent to which this disorder is associated (i.e., the degree of aggregation) with other psychiatric syndromes, such as antisocial personality disorder (ASPD) (Helzer and Pryzbeck, 1988; Regier et al., 1990). The ECA study has documented that significant variation exists in the degree of aggregation of alcohol abuse-dependence with other psychiatric disorders. For example, although ASPD occurs in only 4 percent of the U.S. male noninstitutional population, it is 12 times more common among those with alcohol abuse-dependence than it is among those without the alcohol-use disorder. Less dramatic, but also suggestive of aggregation, is the association, particularly in women, between mania and alcohol abuse-dependence. Mania occurs in less than 1 percent of the general population of women; however, the chances of depression being present are nine times greater among women with alcohol abuse-dependence. These aforementioned associations may be possible indicators of different alcohol-disorder subtypes (Babor and Dolinsky, 1988; Zucker, 1994). If this is the case, the comorbid psychiatric disorders would help in identifying alcoholism subtypes[1] that are clinically more alike (i.e. homogeneous).

Several possible theories exist to explain how alcohol abuse-dependence may be linked to other psychiatric disorders. One hypothesis states that because alcohol abuse-dependence and other disorders occur together, these disorders must share a common developmental process (i.e. etiology). An alternative possibility, and one that must be ruled out to fully understand the co-occurrence of these disorders, is that the psychiatric symptoms are simply a result of the alcoholism, rather than a marker of a common causal process. Still another possibility is that the symptoms of alcoholism and other psychiatric disorders occur independently but share a common factor that contributes to the development of both disorders.[2] By determining how alcoholism relates to psychiatric symptoms, researchers may be able to determine which explanation is more likely. Researchers would then come closer to identifying the subtypes that best reflect the heterogeneity of the disorder. Such specific descriptions would be useful as indicators of potential differences in the course and causes of the disorder and could possibly assist in the development of prevention and treatment strategies.

In both men and women, alcoholism is associated most strongly with the comorbid disorder ASPD. This disorder is characterized by a pervasive disregard for and violation of the rights of others and is evident during both childhood and adulthood. The presence or absence of symptoms composing ASPD is a major distinguishing feature of virtually all of the alcoholism subtyping schemes developed during the past generation (Babor and Dolinsky, 1988; Cloninger et al., 1981; Hesselbrock et al., 1984; Babor et al., 1992; Zucker et al., 1994). Although it is less commonly acknowledged, children from families with alcoholic adults who have antisocial symptoms (i.e. who have high levels of antisocial symptomatology) are at greater risk of becoming alcoholic later in life than other children. (For a definition of risk, see sidebar.) The risk factors include having a greater number of alcoholic relatives (i.e., a denser family

A NOTE ABOUT LIFE-COURSE VARIATION AND THE DEVELOPMENT OF RISK

The concept of risk refers to the statistical probability that a specific (usually negative) outcome will occur at a later date (Zucker, 1989). Thus, when identifying risk characteristics for the later emergence of alcoholism among children, researchers understand that they are making a similar probability statement that-all other things being equal-a given pattern of influences will increase or decrease the probability of a later harmful outcome. The phrase "a pattern of influences" implies that a number of factors are present and that they must operate in concert, rather than in opposition, for the disorder to ultimately appear. Consequently, in families with alcoholism in which antisocial characteristics also are high, potential influences found in early childhood might include a heightened genetic vulnerability for alcoholism, a temperament that generates problematic responses from others, a rearing environment that may encourage problem alcohol use, and a family structure with conflict within its boundaries. Such influences, in turn, are related to the presence or absence of other psychiatric symptoms in one or both of the parents. The phrase "all other things being equal" refers to the fact that time passes, and as it does, other influences appear that also may affect outcome. As the child grows older, school provides another rearing environment, as do peer relationships outside the family. Social conditions do not always exacerbate problematic temperamental styles; they sometimes operate to dampen such behavior (Forehand and McMahon, 1981). Only when these factors operate together are the outcomes likely to be of the highest risk, the greatest damage, and the earliest appearance of difficulty.

High-Risk Longitudinal Studies

Tracking and understanding how risk factors operate together is a significant challenge. The influences (i.e., the causal structures) that must be assessed are not available all at once. In fact, these influences are likely to emerge gradually at different points during the life course. The impact of each influence also may be seen only gradually, as patterns of behavior become shaped and consolidated.

The research method of choice for mapping the structure of such influences is the longitudinal study. To highlight specific processes, investigators use the high-risk longitudinal study. In such studies, individuals are selected who are known to differ in their likelihood of later showing signs of the disorder-in this case, alcoholism. The causes for the ultimate outcome are not known; the selection of risk groups is based on the statistical likelihood of developing the disorder, rather than on an understanding of how the risk status is manifested. Statistically speaking, outcome is predictable only at the study group level. By choosing a network of variables that, optimally, includes those factors which are the ultimate causes for the disorder and by tracking study participants over time, researchers are able to document earlier characteristics that influence the later disorder, characteristics that might be protective and insulating against it and characteristics that ultimately are irrelevant to later clinical outcome.

-Robert Zucker

References

Forehand, R., and McMahon, R. Helping the Non-Compliant Child: A Clinician's Guide to Effective Parenting. New York: Guilford Press, 1981.

Zucker, R.A. Is risk for alcoholism predictable? A probabilistic approach to a developmental problem. Drugs and Society 4:69-93, 1989.

history of alcoholism), which, in turn, will increase the probability that the children will have some genetically mediated vulnerability for alcoholism; more severe alcoholic symptoms and more nonalcoholic psychiatric symptoms among the parents; and a greater likelihood that a variety of relational problems (e.g., marital and legal problems) exist within the family (Hesselbrock et al., 1984; Lewis, 1990).

The variations in antisocial symptoms found in adult alcoholics offer a potentially powerful framework (i.e., construct) on which to base future subtypes. A collaborative group of researchers from three Michigan universities have been working together to further evaluate and refine this construct. The goal of this research effort is to better define the variations in symptoms found in individual adult alcoholics and to delineate the differences that exist among the families (i.e. familial variations). The hypothesis guiding this research is that these families will develop alcohol problems or alcoholism later in their lives.

The Michigan State University/University of Michigan Longitudinal Study

The Michigan State University - University of Michigan (MSU-UM) Longitudinal Study (Zucker 1987; Fitzgerald et al. 1995) began as a pilot study in 1982, and researchers began regular data collection in 1985. The MSU/UM study was set up according to a high-risk design structure (see sidebar), and it is tracking high-risk families that include a heterogeneous group of 220 alcoholic men, their initially preschool-age (i.e., 3 to 5 years old) sons, and the boys' biological mothers. The plan is to continue the study well into the children's adulthood. When the study began, the mothers' drinking status ranged from alcoholic to nondrinker. Families were excluded from participating, however, if the child displayed signs of fetal alcohol effects. Mothers and fathers had to be living together at the beginning of the study; however, as is common in alcoholic families, separation and divorce occurred at high rates. Even in such cases, the study continues to follow both biological parents. If a custodial parent has remarried, the custodial stepparent is added to the study. In addition to this high-risk group, the study includes a contrast group of 91 families with similar structures located in the same neighborhoods as the high-risk families; however, in these families, both parents were free of alcoholism and other drug (AOD) dependence.

Boys initially were selected as the target group because in the general population alcoholism is approximately five times more common in men than in women. In addition, sons of alcoholic fathers are about 1.5 times more likely to develop alcoholism than the offspring of non-alcoholics (Russell, 1990). A parallel study tracking the risk for alcoholism among girls would require a much greater number of subjects and, consequently, a much more expensive design. Nonetheless, the outcome for girls from alcoholic homes is an equally important area of investigation, given the broad range of other difficulties that female children of alcoholics (COA's) experience (Cloninger et al., 1986; Goodwin et al., 1977; Widom, 1993). An addition to the study has allowed the project to include one daughter from each of the families studied in cases where this option is available. It is still too early, however, to evaluate the data obtained from these girls.

Families are assessed at 3-year intervals. Although the study has continued for more than a decade, all parents but one continue to participate, including those who have moved away from the study's primary field site.[3] At each time point, or wave, of data collection, family members participate in a nine-session schedule in which an extensive set of measures is used. These measures include interviews; self-report questionnaires; reports by collateral informants, such as spouses, parents, and teachers, as well as the children's reports of their experiences with their parents; observer ratings; and data obtained from videotaped interactions. Some research is conducted at the university laboratory, but most data are collected in the respondents' homes to ensure cooperation from a study population that is known for its waywardness and chaos. Data collectors do not know the families risk status.

EARLY RESULTS FROM THE MSU/UM LONGITUDINAL STUDY

Although the study's ultimate outcome can be determined only after the children reach adulthood, a number of influencing structures are likely to play a role in shaping the development of alcoholism. These influences include differences in genetic vulnerability;[4] rearing environment variations; cultural, community, and socioeconomic influences associated with risk for alcoholism (i.e., macro level environmental factors); and, most important, the child's personal characteristics that may put him at risk for an alcoholic outcome. To assess these influences, the study uses a number of measures that are proxy indicators of risk load. So far, the indicators being used are measures of externalizing behaviors (e.g. aggression, hyperactivity, and delinquency) because these characteristics are known to be precursors to antisocial deviance, which, in turn, has repeatedly been shown to be a precursor to the development of AOD abuse in adolescence (see Kandel 1978).

Early Risk Variation Among the Families

Using data from the MSU/UM study's initial assessment period (i.e. when the children were ages 3 to 5), a series of analyses evaluated differences in the home rearing environments and in the presence and extent of externalizing behavior in the children from the alcoholic (i.e., high-risk) versus the nonalcoholic (i.e., low-risk) families. These analyses demonstrated a number of significant differences between the high - and low-risk groups, as follows:

- Alcoholic parents exhibited greater levels of psychopathology (e.g., depression and antisocial symptomatology) than nonalcoholic parents.
- The quality of the home rearing environment, as assessed by an interview and observation measure of the cognitive, social, and emotional stimulation available to the child, was poorer in the high-risk than in the low-risk families (Fitzgerald et al., 1993; Noll et al. 1992; Whipple et al., 1995).
- Although both groups were recruited from the same neighbor-hoods, high-risk families were lower on indices of social functioning and access to societal opportunities than were the low-risk families (i.e., the high-risk parents were of a lower socioeconomic status and had less education) (Fitzgerald and Zucker, 1995).
- Although they were still preschoolers, the COAs could more readily identify alcoholic beverages. They also were more likely to expect male adults to choose alcoholic drinks as the beverages of choice in everyday social situations. These findings show that the COAs have a more developed cognitive structure concerning alcoholic bever-ages. Thus, despite their young age, the two groups of children already differed in their rudimentary alcohol expectancy structure (Zucker et al., 1995a).

Subtyping of Alcoholic Families

As previously described, significant differences were found be-tween the high- and low-risk families. They study's interest in identifying different patterns of risk variation led the investigators to explore whether risk aggregation might be even more concentrated if the parents' alcoholism were subtyped. The subtyping scheme used was a classification based on the presence or absence of differences

Table 1   Differences Among Families With Different Alcoholic Subtypes and Nonalcoholic Controls in Indicators of the Offspring's Early Vulnerability for Alcoholism[1]

Indicators of Offspring's Vulnerability	Degree to which Indicator Is present in Family
Family history of alcoholism	AAL>NAAL> Control
Paternal intellectual functioning	AAL<NAAL< Control
Maternal intellectual functioning	AAL<NAAL= Control

[1]The indicators were measured when the children were preschool age (i.e., ages 3-5). AAL= Antisocial alcoholics. NAAL= Nonantisocial alcoholics. Control= Matched nonalcoholics recruited from the same communities. SOURCE: Adapted from Ellis et al., 1994 and Zucker et al., in press.

in each father's antisocial behavior in conjunction with his alcoholism. Theory based on the developmental psychopathology literature (see Cicchetti and Cohen, 1995) indicates that family risk should be greatest when the parent's psychopathological risk structure has been in place for most of his or her lifetime. On these grounds, and given the investigators' interest in the role of parents' antisocial behavior, a special variation (i.e., a developmental stipulation) was added: The distinction between sub-groups had to be made not on the basis of an ASPD diagnosis but on the basis of the presence or absence of a sustained, high-level history of antisocial behavior during both childhood and adulthood. Men with a pattern of alcoholism in adulthood and a sustained lifetime history of high antisocial behavior were categorized as antisocial alcoholics (AALs). Those without such a sustained history were classified as non-antisocial alcoholics (NAALs).

Although this subtyping approach is similar to one based on an adult diagnosis of ASPD, it approaches the problem developmentally. It also takes into account a theory concerning the processes involved in the acquisition of alcohol abuse-dependence with this particular type of comorbidity pattern. A long history of research on the development of drinking problems has noted the occurrence of a variety of other forms of deviant behavior, including rule breaking, trouble making and antisocial problem behavior, along with the drinking (Zucker et al., 1995b; Zucker et al., in press). In fact, this connection has been a central part of the dominant theories on the development of problem drinking behavior in adolescents (Kandel, 1978). What is less well known is that for a subset of adolescents, this pattern begins substantially before adolescence and appears to continue into early adulthood and beyond. For another subset of youth, the pattern begins in adolescence but ends with the transition to adulthood, work roles, and marriage (see Zucker et al., 1995b for an extensive discussion of this literature).[5]

If it is effective, the AAL–NAAL subtyping strategy should reflect differences in the fathers' lifetime AOD use (i.e., early and sustained involvement versus later onset and more transitory involvement). The AAL–NAAL subtypes also should serve as a marker for a variety of other influences that have shaped the early learning of the fathers' alcohol-seeking and alcohol-using behavior. Thus, it would be expected that the AALs, more often than the NAALs, come from families with dense family histories of alcoholism and have been reared in environments that encouraged or caused them to seek the company of early AOD-using peers (Pihl and Peterson, 1994; Johnson et al., 1995). If this typing strategy works, it also may prove useful as a marker of the different parenting activities of these men and their partners, which then may help to identify variations in their children's risk for later alcohol problems.

The AAL–NAAL classification, based solely on the father's alcoholism, was used to chart individual and familial characteristics pertaining to alcohol use and familial and social functioning. The classification strategy produced findings that largely were as predicted. Other derivative findings also emerged that supported the scheme's

Table 2 Differences in Indicators of the Early Rearing Environment of Children From Families With Different Alcoholic Subtypes and From Nonalcoholic Control Families[1]

Indicator of Rearing Environment	Degree to Which Indicator Is Present in Family
Paternal Psychopathology	
Paternal current depression	AL>NAAL=Control
Paternal worst-ever depression	AAL>NAAL>Control
Paternal lifetime alcohol problems	AAL>NAAL>Control
Maternal Psychopathology	
Maternal antisocial behavior	AAL>NAAL> Control
Maternal current depression	AAL>NAAL= Control
Maternal worst-ever depression	AAL=NAAL> Control
Maternal lifetime alcohol problems	AAL=NAAL> Control
Rearing environment	
Family socioeconomic status	AAL<NAAL< Control
Maternal aggression toward spouse	AAL>NAAL= Control
Paternal aggression toward spouse	AAL>NAAL= Control

[1]The indicators were measured when the children were preschool age (i.e., ages 3-5). AAL = Antisocial alcoholics. NAAL = Nonantisocial alcoholics. Control = Matched nonalcoholics from the same communities. SOURCE: Adapted from Ellis et al., 1994 and Zucker et al., in press.

validity. The analyses indicated that the scheme sorted out differences among the parents that likely will serve as markers of differing vulnerability for the children (see table 1). Moreover, the AALs and NAALs differed on several measures of the rearing environment that are apt to have an effect on the children's socialization (see table 2). For example, the AAL men had denser family histories of alcoholism, lower levels of intellectual functioning, and significantly higher levels of nonalcoholic psychopathology than did the NAAL men (Bingham et al., 1996; Ellis, 1994; Ichiyama et al., in press; Zucker et al., 1994; Zucker et al., in press). In addition, results provided evidence for the aggregation of risk by way of assortative mating[7] among the AAL families. For example, the wives of AAL men had higher levels of antisocial behavior than did the wives of NAAL or control men. The AAL wives also had more nonantisocial psychopathology and higher lifetime levels of alcohol-related problems than did the wives of the control men, although they did not differ on these characteristics from the NAAL wives. Finally, the AAL parents displayed more aggressive behavior and conflict and were lower in socioeconomic status than were the NAAL and control families. Other analyses have shown that this is a result of downward social mobility rather than differences in social origin between the AALs and the NAALs (Zucker et al., in press).

Although the pattern of these findings is of considerable interest, concerns among scientists who have debated subtype issues focus on three vital questions. First, given that the two alcoholic types differ in level of antisocial behavior, what evidence exists that these differences are particular to the alcoholism? To answer this question one needs to determine if a sustained antisocial life-course subtype also exists among nonalcoholic populations. Current evidence indicates that this is highly unlikely, at least in this culture; because the link between antisocial behavior and alcoholism is so close, sustained antisocial behavior among nonalcoholics statistically is a rare occurrence (Zucker et al., in press).

Second, because the AALs and the NAALs differ in their levels of sustained antisocial behavior, is it more parsimonious to regard the high and low levels of antisocial behavior as extremes on a continuum, rather than as distinct types with similar (i.e., clustered) attributes? Several types of analysis, using sophisticated statistical techniques, have focused on this issue, including one analytic technique called configural cluster analysis (Zucker et al., in press) and another called structural equation modeling (Ellis 1994; Zucker et al., 1994), discussed below.

Results from the configural cluster analysis indicate that in addition to the close link between antisocial characteristics and alcoholism, one other distinct clustering, or type, is present. This type, called the nonantisocial alcoholic group, involves the coaggregation of alcoholism and a lifetime of continuous, low-level antisocial behavior. In other words, a pattern of continuous, high-level antisocial behavior is found in association with alcoholism; a pattern of continuous low-level antisocial behavior is clustered with alcoholism.

Third, nonantisocial psychopathology as well as antisocial behavior varies across the two alcoholic subtypes. On these grounds, what evidence exists that the AAL–NAAL classification primarily involves higher versus lower levels of antisocial behavior, rather than variations in general psychopathology that occur over the life course? This is a central issue, because one of the major alcoholism subtyping schemes currently in use, the type A-type B categorization (Babor et al., 1992), is a framework that heavily categorizes alcoholism based on the level of psychopathology. To test this competing hypothesis, statistical analyses were conducted that removed the effects of general level/severity of psychopathology (Ichiyama et al., in press). The results still held, confirming the unique importance of the antisocial categorization.

Outcomes Among the Children of Different Alcoholic Subtypes

The findings described in the previous section focus on parents in alcoholic families. These findings are consistent with other reports of differences between antisocial and nonantisocial forms of alcoholism in adults, and they expand on previous studies of family functioning. However, when considering factors that contribute to a child's risk for later becoming alcoholic, one also needs to explore what impact the child's functioning has within this family framework of risk. The proxy indicators being tracked by the MSU–UM study include measures of externalizing behavior problems (e.g., aggression and delinquent activity) as well as measures of internalizing behavior problems (e.g., schizoid/anxious, depressed, obsessive-compulsive, and uncommunicative behavior), hyperactivity (e.g. restlessness, short attention span, and fidgeting) and risky temperament (i.e., a composite index

Table 3 Differences in Childhood Risk Indicators Among Boys From Families With Different Alcoholic Subtypes and From Nonalcoholic Control Families

Childhood Risk Indicators Is Present in Children	Degree to Which Indicator
Preschool Years (ages 3-5)	
Child externalizing behavior problems[1]	AAL>NAAL> Control
Child internalizing behavior problems[2]	AAL>NAAL= Control
Child hyperactivity index[3]	AAL>NAAL= Control
Child risky temperament	AAL>NAAL= Control
Early School Years (ages 6-8)	
Child externalizing behavior problems	AAL>NAAL> Control
Child internalizing behavior problems	AAL>NAAL= Control

[1]Externalizing behavior problems include aggressivity and delinquency.
[2]Internalizing behavior problems include depressed or uncommunicative behavior.
[3]The hyperactivity index measures characteristics such as restlessness and a short attention span.
AAL= Antisocial alcoholics.
NAAL = Nonantisocial alcoholics
Control = Matched nonalcoholics from the same communities
SOURCE: Adapted from Bingham et al., 1996 and Ellis et al., 1994.

based on high activity level, emotional reactivity, and approach to life situations). To date, the study has collected data on the children and their families from two age periods: during preschool (i.e., ages 3 to 5) and during the early school years (i.e., ages 6 to 8).

Results show that during both early childhood and the early school years, significant behavioral differences exist between the children from families with different alcoholic subtypes (table 3) (Bingham et al., 1996; Ellis, 1994, Zucker et al., 1994). For example, externalizing behaviors, the foremost proxy indicator of the emergence of earlier and more problematic adolescent alcohol use, and internalizing behaviors are greatest among the children of AALs at both assessment periods. In addition, as preschoolers, the AAL boys showed more signs of hyperactivity and scored higher on a measure of risky temperament than did the boys from the NAAL and control families. Other analyses indicate that these differences exist not only in the level of overall group effects but in extremes of behavior. That is, significantly more boys from AAL homes than from the NAAL or control homes were classified in the clinical range on externalizing behavior problems (Jansen et al., 1995; Ellis, 1994; Zucker, et al. 1994). Finally, using a technique called structural equation modeling, researchers have found that separate process models for the AALs, NAALs, and control families better describe the interrelationships among the different variables than does one overall model. This finding implies that the pathways of influencing structure differ among the three groups and tentatively suggests that the mechanisms of risk development may be specific to subtypes. The latter finding has only been established at the first wave of data collection and will need to be replicated in later longitudinal analyses.

The Broader Structure of Risk: Conclusions and Outlook

The typological classification described in this article and the derivative findings from the ongoing longitudinal sutdy highlight observations from other investigators (e.g., Jacob and Leonard, 1986), which indicate that not all alcoholic families are equally problematic and not all COAs function in a manner that distinguishes them from nonalcoholic families or is indicative of a potentially troubled later outcome. For example, some elements of family functioning that are thought to be associated with alcoholism (e.g., aggression within the family) appear to be manifestations of only one subtype (i.e., AALs). Similarly, not all COAs exhibit behaviors that differ from those of non-COAs. Children from NAAL families occupy this intermediary position. From a practical standpoint, findings to date have indicated that NAAL families often are less identifiable as sources of developmental trouble, and the risk differences observed emphasize the possibility that NAAL children will be less at risk as they move into adolescence. The ability of researchers to determine more finely detailed and subtle differentiations within the alcoholic disorder is one aspect of the usefulness of subtyping.

The findings summarized here, which involved determining the families' alcoholism subtypes as well as showing significant differences in childhood risk patterns related to the subtypes, were determined when the children were ages 3 to 5. It would be a serious mistake to conclude that all effects of subtyping and problematic outcome have appeared by the time these at-risk children have reached middle childhood. Evidence continues to indicate that both school and later peer influences play important roles in shaping a child's risk status (Johnson et al., 1995); moreover, later positive or negative parental influences probably continue to sustain or alleviate child risk (Wills et al., 1996). Not all alcoholics remain actively alcoholic, and it is possible that the family subtype classifications used here will evolve over the course of childhood. Moreover, parents in alcoholic families frequently divorce, and new family structures may be formed that shape a child's behavior in different ways from when he or she was young. This is a *probabilistic* framework for viewing how risk increases and decreases over time. It is important to keep this framework in mind, even as we discover that not all family structures carry the same risk burden.

At the same time, risk variation within subtypes is not random over time (Bingham et al., 1996), and the contextual structure that sustains and may even enhance an individual's risk does not vary randomly either (Zucker et al., 1995b). Some social environments heavily restrict the range of opportunity; and, within these contexts, risk appears to be more heavily aggregated. Such restricted environments include poverty areas, frequently inhabited by disenfranchised minorities. The term "nesting environment" has been used to describe this restricted range of opportunity and the nonrandom aggregation of factors (i.e., nesting) that sustain individual risk. Under conditions of nestedness, when environment and biological risk coincide, subtypes are most likely to develop (also see Wills et al., 1996).

Two additional features of this research warrant some comment. First, not all aspects of early childhood functioning varied with familial subtype. For example, although preschool children from alcoholic families were more precocious in their ability to identify alcoholic beverages and exhibited a more highly developed conceptual understanding about alcohol as a drug, its effects, and who should use it, the subtype differences in the children's development of these schemes were not evident (Zucker et al., 1995a). This finding was unexpected, given the earlier onset of drinking and drinking problems among adult AALs. It remains to be seen whether subtype differentiation will appear as the children grow older.

Second, the research carried out thus far has been guided by the proposition that one alcoholic subtype, marked by the sustained life-course presence of antisocial behavior, would differ from other forms of alcoholism in life-course functioning, in the rearing environment available to the offspring, and in childhood characteristics indicative of level of risk for later alcohol problems. Contrasts have been made against a heterogeneous group of other alcoholic families (NAALs), who in some respects are even indistinguishable from nonalcoholic families. Given the variety of other comorbid symptoms found among alcoholics in the general population, other subtypes may exist that display different distinguishing characteristics and which create different rearing and risk environments for their children. The comorbidity literature suggests that these characteristics may exist (Helzer et al., 1991; Zucker, 1994), but other variants (e.g. alcoholism without comorbidity and developmentally limited alcoholism) have received much less attention in the typological literature. Accordingly, future research needs to better characterize these other variations among both fathers and mothers and to assess their influences on the development of risk among the children. Finally, researchers must determine the extent to which the effects of parental alcoholism subtype on the risk status of male COAs can be generalized to female children from the same families.

Footnotes

[1]Throughout the remainder of this article, the term "alcoholism" is used to represent the clinical diagnosis of both alcohol abuse and alcohol dependence.

[2]Because this alternative ultimately ties back to a common causal process for both disorders and thus would contribute to understanding subtypes and their outcomes, it can be considered a variant of the first alternative described.

[3]In 1 percent of the families, a parent has died. When the study began, the researchers expected some attrition because of the lack of interest and an inability to locate families. However, the skill of the project's clinically trained research staff and the regular contact through newsletters and birthday and Christmas cards have allowed the study to sustain this high level of family involvement.

[4]The term "genetic vulnerability" specifically describes the measurement of particular genetic attributes.

[5]The same two identifiably different life-course paths (i.e. trajectories) also have been noted in literature on the development of antisocial behavior (Moffitt, 1993) and have given rise to a parallel taxonomy of subtypes with different onsets, life trajectories, and correlates.

[6]The manner in which parental IQ differences contribute to a child's risk is less obvious than for some of the other variables described here. However, lower IQ is related to the use of less reasoned and more authoritarian forms of child discipline and lesser parent agreement about child rearing and also may be related to specific differences in child-rearing practices, such as deficits in monitoring, that ultimately may contribute to the development of antisocial behavior in the child (Davies et al., 1989). Lower IQ also may be a low-level indicator of neural regularity deficits that may be a part of the genetic disposition that contributes to the non-alcohol-specific differences in impulsivity noted among COAs (Martin et al., 1994).

[7]Assortative mating is a nonrandom choice of a partner based on personal characteristics (e.g., an alcoholic is more likely than a non-alcoholic to have an alcoholic partner).

References

American Psychiatric Association. Diagnostic and Statistical Manual of Mental Disorders, Fourth Edition. Washington, DC: the Association, 1994.

Babor, T.F., and Dolinsky, Z.S. Alcoholic typologies; Historical evolution and empirical evaluation of some common classification schemes. In: Rose, R.M., and Barret, J., eds. Alcoholism: Origins and Outcome. New York: Raven Press, 1988. pp. 245-266.

Barbor, T.F., and Lauerman, R.J. Classification and forms of inebriety: Historical antecedents of alcoholic typologies. In: Galanter, M., ed. Recent Developments in Alcoholism. Vol. R. New York: Plenum Publishing Corp, 1986. pp. 113-144.

Barbor, T.F.; Hofmann, M.; Del Boca, F.K.; Hesselbrock, V.; Meyer, R.E.; Dolinsky, Z.S.; and Rounsaville, B. Types of alcoholics: I. Evidence for an empirically derived typology based on indicators of vulnerability and severity. Archives of General Psychiatry 49:599-608, 1992.

Bingham, C.R.; Zucker, R.A.; and Fitzgerald, H.E. Risk Load Variation and its Association with Problem Behavior Development Among the Sons of Alcoholics. East Lansing and Ann Arbor, MI: Michigan State University-University of Michigan Longitudinal Study, 1996.

Cicchetti, D., and Cohen, D.J., EDS. Developmental Psychopathology: Volume 2. Risk, Disorder, and Adaptation. New York: Wiley, 1995.

Cloninger, C.R. Neurogenetic adaptive mechanisms in alcoholism. Science 236:410-416, 1987.

Cloninger C.R.; Bohman, M.; and Sigvardsson, S. Inheritance of substance abuse: Cross-fostering analysis of adopted men. Archives of General Psychiatry 38:861-867, 1981.

Cloninger, C.R.; Von Knorring, A-L.; Sivardsson, S.; and Bohman, M. Symptom patterns and causes of somatization in men: II. Genetic and environmental independence from somatization in women. Genetic Epidemiology 3:171-185, 1986.

Davies, W.H.; Zucker, R.A.; Noll, R.B.; and Fitzgerald, H.E. Parental psychopathology and childrearing practices in young alcoholic families (abstract). Alcoholism: Clinical And Experimental Research 13:338, 1989.

Ellis, D.A. "Typological Differences in Patterns of Risk Among Young Alcoholic Families." Doctoral dissertation, Department of Psychology, Michigan State University, East Lansing: MI, 1994.

Fitzgerald, H.E., and Zucker, R.A. Socioeconomic status and alcoholism: The contextual structure of developmental pathways to addiction. In: Fitzgerald, H.E.; Lester, B.M.; and Zuckerman, B., eds. Children of Poverty. New York: Garland, 1995. pp. 125-148.

Fitzgerald, H.E.; Sullivan, L.A.; Ham, H.P.; Zucker, R.A.; Brucknel, A.; and Schneider, A.M. Predictors of behavioral problems in three-year-old sons of alcoholics: Early evidence for onset of risk. Child Development 64:110-123, 1993.

Fitzgerald, H.E.; Zucker, R.A.; and Yang, H-Y. Developmental systems theory and alcoholism: Analyzing patterns of variation in high risk families. Psychology of Addictive Behaviors 9:8-22, 1995.

Goodwin, D.W.; Schulsinger, R.; Knop, J.; Mednick, S.; and Guze, S.B. Psychopathology in adopted and nonadopted daughters of alcoholics. Archives of General Psychiatry 34: 1005-1008, 1977.

Helzer, J.E., and Pryzbeck, T.R. The co-occurrence of alcoholism and other psychiatric disorders in the general population and its impact on treatment. Journal of Studies on Alcohol 49:219-224, 1988.

Helzer, J.E.; Burnam, A.; and McEvoy, L.T. Alcohol abuse and dependence. In: Robins, L.N., and Regier, D.A., eds. Psychiatric Disorders in America: The Epidemiologic Catchment Area Study. New York: The Free Press, 1991. pp. 81-115.

Hesselbrock, V.M. The genetic epidemiology of alcoholism. In: Begleiter, H., and Kissin, B., eds. Alcohol and Alcoholism. Vol 1. New York: Oxford University Press, 1995.

Hesselbrock, M.N.; Hesselbrock, V.M.; Babor, T.F.; Meyer, R.E.; Stabenau, J.R.; and Weidenman, M.A. Antisocial behavior, psychopathology and problem drinking in the natural history of alcoholism. In: Goodwin, D.W.; Van Dusen, K.T.; and Mednick, S.A., eds. Longitudinal Research in Alcoholism. Dordrecht, the Netherlands: Kluwer Academic Publishers, 1984. pp. 197-214.

Ichiyama, M.A.; Zucker, R.A.; Fitzgerald, H.E.; and Bingham, C.R. Articulating subtype differences in self and relational experience among alcoholic men via structural analysis of social behavior. Journal of Consulting and Clinical Psychology, in press.

Jacob, T., and Leonard, K. Psychological functioning in children of alcoholic fathers, depressed fathers and control fathers. Journal of Studies on Alcohol 47:373-380, 1986.

Jansen, R.E.; Fitzgerald, H.E.; Ham, H.P.; and Zucker, R.A. Pathways into risk: Temperament and behavior problems in three- to five-year-old sons of alcoholics. Alcoholism: Clinical and Experimental Research 19:501-509, 1995.

Johnson, E.O.; Aria, A.M.; Borges, G.; Ialongo, N.; and Anthony, J.C. The growth of conduct problem behaviors from middle childhood to early adolescence: Sex differences and the suspected influence of early alcohol use. Journal of Studies on Alcohol 56:661-671, 1995.

Kandel, D.B. Convergences in prospective longitudinal surveys of drug use in normal populations. In: Kandel, D.B., ed. Longitudinal Research on Drug Use. Washington, DC: Hemisphere, 1978.

Lewis, C.E. Alcoholism and antisocial personality: Clinical associations and etiological implications. In: Parvez, S.; Burov, Y.; Ollat, H.; and Parvez, H., eds. Progress in Alcoholism Research: Volume 2. Alcohol Behavior: Basic and Clinical Aspects. Netherlands: VNU Science Press, 1990. pp. 15-37.

Martin, C.S.; Earleywine, M.; Blackson, T.C.; Vanyukov, M.M.; Moss, H.B.; and Tarter, R.E. Aggressivity, inattention, hyperactivity, and impulsivity in boys at high and low risk for substance abuse. Journal of Abnormal Child Psychology 22(2): 177-203, 1994.

Moffitt, T.E. Adolescent-limited and life-course-persistent antisocial behavior: A developmental taxonomy. Psychological Review 100:674-675, 1993.

Noll, R.B.; Zucker, R.A.; Fitzgerald, H.E.; and Curtis, W.J. Cognitive and motoric functioning of sons of alcoholic fathers and controls: The early childhood years. Developmental Psychology 28: 665-675, 1992.

Pihl, R.O., and Peterson, J.B. Attention-deficit hyperactivity disorder, childhood conduct disorder, and alcoholism: Is there an association? Alcohol Health and Research World 15:25-31, 1994.

Regier, D.A.; Farmer, M.E.; Rae, D.S.; Locke, B.Z.; Keith, S.J.; Judd, L.L.; and Goodwin, F.K. Comorbidity of mental disorders with alcohol and other drug abuse. Journal of the American Medical Association 19:2511-2518, 1990.

Russell, M. Prevalence of alcoholism among children of alcoholics. In: Windle, M., and Searles, J.S., eds. Children of Alcoholics: Critical Perspectives. New York: Guilford Press, 1990.

Schuckit, M.A. The clinical implications of primary diagnostic groups among alcoholics. Archives of General Psychiatry 42:1043-1049, 1985.

Skog, O-J., and Duckert, F. The stability of alcoholics' and heavy drinkers' consumption: A longitudinal study. Journal of Studies on Alcohol 53:178-188, 1993.

Tarter, R.E.; Moss, H.B.; and Vanukov, M.M. Behavior genetic perspective of alcoholism etiology. In: Begleiter, H., and Kissin, B., eds. Alcohol and Alcoholism. Vol. 1. New York: Oxford University Press, 1995.

Windom, C.S. Child abuse and alcohol use and abuse. In: Martin, S.E., ed. Alcohol and Interpersonal Violence: Fostering Multidisciplinary Perspectives. National Institute on Alcohol Abuse and Alcoholism Research Monograph No. 24. NIH Publication No. 93-3496. Bethesda, MD: the Institute, 1993. pp. 291-323.

Whipple, E.E.; Fitzgerald, H.E.; and Zucker, R.A. Parent-child interactions in alcoholic and nonalcoholic families. American Journal of Orthopsychiatry 65:153-159, 1995.

Wills, T.A.; McNamara, G.; Vaccaro, D.; and Hirky, A.E. Escalated substance use: A longitudinal grouping analysis from early to middle adolescence. Journal of Abnormal Psychology 105:166-180, 1996.

Zucker, R.A. The four alcoholisms: A developmental account of the etiologic process. In: Rivers, P.C., ed. Nebraska Symposium on Motivation: Volume 34. Alcohol and Addictive Behaviors. Lincoln, NE: University of Nebraska Press, 1987. pp. 27-83.

Zucker, R.A. Is risk for alcoholism predictable? A probabilistic approach to a developmental problem. Drugs and Society 4:69-93, 1989.

Zucker, R.A. Pathways to alcohol problems and alcoholism: A developmental account of the evidence for multiple alcoholisms and for contextual contributions to risk. In: Zucker, R.A.; Boyd, G.; and Howard, J., eds. The Development of Alcohol Problems: Exploring the Biopsychosocial Matrix of Risk. National Institute on Alcohol Abuse and Alcoholism Research Monograph No. 26. NIH Publication No. 94-3742. Bethesda, MD: the Institute, 1994. pp. 255-289.

Zucker, R.A.; Ellis, D.A.; and Fitzgerald, H.E. Developmental evidence for at least two alcoholisms, I: Biopsychosocial variation among pathways into symptomatic difficulty. Annals of the New York Academy of Sciences 708:134-146.

Zucker, R.A.; Kincaid, S.B.; Fitzgerald, H.E.; and Bingham, C.R. Alcohol schema acquisition in preschoolers: Differences between children of alcoholics and children of nonalcoholics. Alcoholism: Clinical and Experimental Research 19:1011-1017, 1995a.

Zucker, R.A.; Fitzgerald, H.E.; and Moses, H.D. Emergence of alcohol problems and the several alcoholisms: A developmental perspective on etiologic theory and life course trajectory. In: Cicchetti, D., and Cohen, D.J., eds. Developmental Psychopathology: Volume 2. Risk, Disorder, and Adaptation. New York: Wiley, 1995b. pp. 677-711.

Zucker, R.A.; Ellis, D.A.; Fitzgerald, H.E.; Bingham, C.R.; and Sanford, K. Other evidence for at least two alcoholisms, II: Life course variation in antisociality and heterogeneity of alcoholic outcome. Development and Psychopathology, in press.

This paper was adapted from the authors' article of the same title published by the National Institute on Alcohol Abuse in ALCOHOL HEALTH AND RESEARCH WORLD, Vol. 20, No. 1, pp.46-54.

Alcoholism and the Family

Robert J. Ackerman

Living with an alcoholic is a family affair. Because it subjects all members of a household to constant stress and fears of various kinds, it has often been referred to as a "family illness." To one degree or another, all members of the family are affected. However, not all alcoholic families, nor all members of the same family, are affected in a similar manner.

The Collective Mind

To assume that all family members are equally and identically affected is to assume that the family possesses a "collective mind." The "collective mind" assumes that the entire family shares the same feelings about the alcoholic and alcoholism. Additionally, this would mean that all alcoholic families are alike. This is not true. To understand the effects of alcoholism on the family, we need to look at the individual members of the family. The individual is the beginning unit of analysis to understanding family dynamics in an alcoholic home. This is true for the alcoholic as well as the non-alcoholic family members.

There are many factors that can affect members of alcoholic families differently. These include: whether or not a parent is recovering from alcoholism or still drinking (Callan & Jackson, 1986: Moos and Billings, 1982); sex of the child and sex of the alcoholic parent (Ackerman, 1987; Werner, 1986; Steinhausen et al., 1984); age of the child (Ackerman, 1987; Werner, 1986); race (Ackerman, 1987); ordinal position (Keltner et al., 1986); socio-economic factors of the family (Parker and Harford, 1987); and offsetting factors which can be either people or institutions that have had a positive impact on the children (Ackerman, 1987).

Additionally, three other factors should be considered. These are the degree of alcoholism, the type of alcoholic in the home, and the individual perception of potential harm from living with an alcoholic.

The degree of alcoholism refers to the severity of the problem. How often does the drinking occur? Is the alcoholic a binge drinker once a month, intoxicated daily, or totally unpredictable? Can the alcoholic be relied upon to function socially and for performance of his or her normal duties? Is the alcoholic employed or capable of working in and outside the home?

Closely related to the degree of alcoholism is the type of alcoholic that lives with the family. One type of alcoholic is the belligerent type who is verbally abusive and is consistently looking for an argument. The recipient of these attacks is exposed to high degrees of verbal and emotional abuse.

Another type of alcoholic may be jovial after drinking. This person likes to laugh a lot and is preoccupied with entertaining. Being around this alcoholic, although not physically or verbally harmful, may be emotionally stressful, due to inappropriate joking, or the inability to express himself or herself seriously.

These are a few examples of the many types of alcoholics. Obviously, these differences can be manifested in a variety of forms for non-alcoholic family members. A child growing up with a physically abusive alcoholic parent may have a very different perspective on alcoholism, as opposed to a child living with a highly passive alcoholic.

The variables of degree and type relate to the alcoholic. The third variable—and perhaps the most important for non-alcoholic family members—is their perception of the situation.

Does the non-alcoholic family member perceive the situation as harmful? Often, our perception dictates our reactions. Whatever we perceive to be real, we react to as if it is. Reality may be secondary to perception. In an alcoholic home, some non-alcoholic members may feel minimally affected, because they perceive that the alcoholism is not harmful to them. However, in the same family, others may be totally devastated because they feel that they are living in a crisis situation.

In summary, although we are concerned with alcoholism in the family, we need to be even more concerned with the effects of alcoholism on the individual members of a family. Each family member requires his or her own individual analysis of the situation. To understand the individual situation, the degree of alcoholism, the type of alcoholic in the family, and the non-alcoholic's perceptions must be considered.

Which Parent is Addicted?

Do we have a higher probability that the father is alcoholic or that the mother is alcoholic in a family? To answer this question, we must consider several factors.

In our society today, if a woman is married to a male alcoholic and there are children under the age of 18 in the family, nine out of ten women will stay with the alcoholic. However, if the situation is reversed, and she is the alcoholic, only one out of ten males will stay. In fact, an alcoholic wife has a nine times greater chance of divorce than an alcoholic husband (Kinney, 2000). Many of the women's reasons for staying range from a lack of viable alternatives to denial. Additionally, the norms of society must be considered. For example, a male can become inebriated and engage in drunken behavior, and still be permitted to feel masculine. It is difficult for a woman to become inebriated and engage in drunken behavior and feel feminine. For the male, there exists a complementary norm of excessive drinking and masculinity. However, for the female, there exists a conflicting norm regarding excessive drinking and femininity. Where a complementary norm exists, there is a higher probability of its continual occurrence and a higher level of social acceptance.

Another factor may be that if a woman has children, and she is suspected of having a drinking problem, one of the first things that may be said about her is that she is an "unfit" mother. It is unlikely that the male will stay in this situation. However, how long does male alcoholism continue before we hear that he is an "unfit" father?

Finally, there simply is a greater number of male alcoholics than female alcoholics in our society. Some estimates indicate that 76% of problem drinkers are men, and only 24% are women (SAMHSA, 1997). Although we are currently discovering female alcoholics at a faster rate than male alcoholics, it is doubtful that given societal values and socialization patterns, alcoholism will become an "equal opportunity" destroyer (Kinney, 2000).

In summary, if the alcoholic family is physically residing in the same house, there is a higher probability that the alcoholic in the family is the father. The percentage of cases where both spouses are alcoholics represents only 20% of the alcoholic homes in America (Ackerman, 1987). The majority of intact alcoholic homes, therefore, have a higher probability of only one spouse being alcoholic, and this spouse is usually the father.

Family Responses to the Alcoholic Parent

Responses to alcoholism in the family can be divided into four phases. These are called reactive, active, alternative and family unity phases. These different periods are distinguished by several characteristics which dominate the particular phase. Not all alcoholic families experience these conditions similarly, however, nor are these universally progressive: that is, not all families will progress from one phase to the next. Many families, unfortunately, remain in the first phase and never reach the fourth state of sobriety and family growth.

Phase I—The Reactive Phase

The reactive phase is characterized by the behavior of non-alcoholic family members reacting to the alcoholic's behavior. During this time, most family members become extremely cautious in their behavior, in order to avoid further complicating the existing problems of alcoholism. However, by being reactive, they are constantly adapting their behavior in order to minimize or survive an unhealthy situation. Much of that adaptation will not only have detrimental effects on those who are adjusting, but also indirectly allows and supports the continuing alcoholism. During the reactive phase, three typical family characteristics emerge: family denial, coping strategies, and social disengagement.

Family Denial

It is ironic that family members deny a drinking problem in their family, because this is exactly what the alcoholic does. We know that, for the alcoholic, denial is functional for the continuation of the drinking. As long as the alcoholic denies that he/she has a problem, there is no reason to seek a solution. Non-alcoholic family members also deny, but their denial is totally dysfunctional to meeting their needs. Everyone in the family denies that anything is wrong, yet no one feels right. Family denial of alcoholism occurs in at least three ways: as systemic denial; as protection against exposure; and, as the primary patient philosophy.

1. *Systemic Denial*

Systemic denial means that the entire system denies the existence of a problem. Certainly the family is analogous to a system which is a pattern of inter-relationships. Within the family system, denial usually occurs when the family members do not want to admit that one of them is an alcoholic, or because they perceive alcoholism as some sort of reflection upon themselves. This is particularly true in the case of non-alcoholic spouses who are women. For example, in American society, if the husband has a drinking problem, often there is a connotation that the wife is partly responsible. Statements such as "she drove him to drink" are typical. Even though these statements are not empirically correct, the woman may perceive them as true and that she may be somehow responsible for the development of his alcoholism. Therefore, as long as she denies that her husband has a drinking problem, she can deny that she had anything to do with causing the problem.

An additional form of systemic denial occurs at the societal level. The family itself is also part of a larger system, which is the community or society in which it resides. Our society does not readily admit to alcohol problems. Although we accept alcoholism as a disease, there still are many who attach a moral stigma of deviancy status to alcoholism. Consequently, we cannot blame a family for covering up a condition that is not understood by society.

Another consideration is that the family is in an unfortunate position of "negative anonymity;" that is, being anonymous has a negative implication for the family. They are in a "no win" situation. To deny, on the one hand, keeps others from knowing or judging, but, on the other hand, keeps the family from getting help. This situation is similar to the alcoholic who covers up his or her drinking, but is also different if getting help is considered. For example, the alcoholic who wants help may join Alcoholics Anonymous. In this instance, his anonymity works for him, but for the non-alcoholic family members, their anonymity works against them. One of the paramount problems for families of alcoholics is in being recognized as individuals in need of assistance. If they are to overcome denial, they must overcome anonymity.

2. Protection Against Exposure

A second form of family denial is protection against exposure. Protection means not talking about the problem as a method of sheltering oneself from the situation. Exposure means not only experiencing the problem, but recognizing it, discussing it, and overcoming any effects. In the alcoholic home, the non-alcoholic spouse will often attempt to protect the children from exposure. A common mode of protection is to treat the situation as if it does not exist. This is impossible in an alcoholic home, but it is not uncommon for the non-alcoholic parent to say, "I have to cover up because I want to protect my children." Usually this means that the situation is never discussed, particularly with the children. This would be fine if protection were the problem, but trying to protect the children when they are exposed continually is a form of denial. In essence, the exposure is denied, any effects from the exposure are denied, and, more importantly, their need for help is denied. If we are going to help non-alcoholic family members, we must concentrate our efforts not on protection, but on overcoming the effects from exposure. To assume that children in an alcoholic home do not know and feel the effects of alcoholism is naïve. They know. They may not understand, but they know. Living in an alcoholic home is not a "spectator sport." Everyone is involved to one degree or another, including the passive participants. This cannot be denied away.

3. *Primary Patient Philosophy*

The third form of denial is the "primary patient philosophy." In the past, when alcoholism existed in a family, it was assumed that the alcoholic was the primary concern. The alcoholic was to be helped first. The majority of alcoholics do not quit drinking, however, and while we are waiting for sobriety to occur, families fall apart, marriages may collapse, and children grow up and leave home. As long as we consider the alcoholic the primary concern, we again deny intervention for the non-alcoholic family members. Non-alcoholic family members should be considered the primary interest, not the alcoholic. This is not to ignore the alcoholic, but to insure that we do not ignore the effects of alcoholism on the family while the drinking is occurring. Additionally, as mentioned earlier, there are far more non-alcoholic family members than alcoholics, and their needs cannot be denied.

Coping Strategies

The key to surviving in an alcoholic home is adaptation. You learn to adapt your behavior in order to minimize the effects of alcoholism. A method of adaptation is to develop coping strategies. In the alcoholic home, these strategies are developed, even though the family denies the existence of alcoholism. The denial within the home is no longer as strong perhaps, but it is maintained outside of the household. For this reason, coping strategies are "home remedies." They are efforts by non-alcoholic family members to survive a situation while denying its existence to others. These strategies are severely limited, and seldom work. Coping strategies can be either verbal or behavioral attempts, and at best they provide a brief, but anxious, respite.

1. Verbal Coping Strategies

Verbal strategies are efforts by non-alcoholic family members to communicate effectively with the alcoholic about alcoholism—efforts which usually are interpreted by the alcoholic as "nagging" or persecution. As a response, the non-alcoholic resorts to morality lectures, pleas for self-respect, threats, promises, and statements such as "How could you do this to us?" Unfortunately, most verbal strategies do little to motivate the alcoholic, but do a lot to increase everyone's anxiety.

Verbal communication between non-alcoholic family members may be helpful, though in most homes no one wants to talk about the addiction, hoping that silence means non-existence. Although it is true that the problem cannot be talked away, discussing verbally and sharing the "family secret" is a positive beginning for non-alcoholic family members in their attempts for recovery. Family members often develop verbal strategies in only one direction, which is from the non-alcoholic to the alcoholic. Thus, there is no possible positive reciprocal effect for them. Verbal interaction among non-alcoholic family members is an available strategy, if they are willing to risk the sharing of information and feelings with each other.

2. Behavioral Coping Strategies

The second type of coping strategy is behavioral. The behavioral strategies are behaviors that non-alcoholic families knowingly—or unknowingly—adopt to cope with their situation. Typical behavioral strategies are hiding alcohol, refusing to buy alcohol, marking bottles, avoiding the alcoholic or other family members, staying away from home, and isolating oneself. Many families deny that they have developed coping strategies, but it is difficult to deny their unusual behavior. In a home where drinking is permitted, and is within normal acceptable limits, family members do not engage in this unusual behavior. Where drinking is abnormal, there exists abnormal non-alcoholic behavior as coping mechanisms. As a result of these coping strategies, non-alcoholic family members become socially disengaged from friends, family, community, and themselves.

As stated earlier, many non-alcoholic family members deny—or are unaware of—their participation in coping strategies. The following questionnaire has been developed for non-alcoholic family members to help to overcome their denial of the effects of alcoholism on their lives. Note that most of these questions pertain to the behavior of non-alcoholic family members.

Family members should answer these questions with as much honesty as possible. The questions were developed by Betty Reddy, Program Specialist, Alcoholic Treatment Center, Lutheran General Hospital, Park Ridge, Illinois.

1. Do you lose sleep because of a problem drinker?
2. Do most of your thoughts revolve around the problem drinker or problems that arise because of him or her?
3. Do you exact promises about drinking that are not kept?
4. Do you make threats or decisions and not follow through on them?
5. Has your attitude changed toward this problem drinker (alternating between love and hate)?
6. Do you mark, hide, dilute, and/or empty bottles of liquor or medication?
7. Do you think that everything would be O.K., if only the problem drinker would stop or control the drinking?
8. Do you feel alone, fearful, anxious, angry, and frustrated most of the time? Are you beginning to feel dislike for yourself, and to wonder about your sanity?
9. Do you find your moods fluctuating wildly as a direct result of the problem drinker's moods and actions?
10. Do you feel responsible and guilty about the drinking problem?
11. Do you try to conceal, deny, or protect the problem drinker?
12. Have you withdrawn from outside activities and friends because of embarrassment and shame over the drinking problem?
13. Have you taken over many chores and duties that you would normally expect the problem drinker to assume—or that were formally his or hers?
14. Do you feel forced to try to exert tight control over the family expenditures with less and less success—and are financial problems increasing?
15. Do you feel the need to justify your actions and attitudes and, at the same time, feel somewhat smug and self-righteous compared to the drinker?
16. If there are children in the house, do they often take sides with either the problem drinker or the spouse?

17. Are the children showing signs of emotional stress, such as withdrawing, having trouble with authority figures, rebelling, acting-out sexually?
18. Have you noticed physical symptoms in yourself, such as nausea, a "knot" in the stomach, ulcers, shakiness, sweating palms, bitten fingernails?
19. Do you feel utterly defeated–that nothing you say or do will move the problem drinker? Do you believe that he or she can't get better?
20. Where this applies, is your sexual relationship with the problem drinker affected by feelings of revulsion; do you "use" sex to manipulate—or refuse sex to punish him or her?

Here are some additional questions specifically for children of alcoholics to help assess their feelings about alcoholism (Brooks, 1981).

1. Do you worry about your mom or dad's drinking?
2. Do you sometimes feel that you are the reason your parents drink so much?
3. Are you ashamed to have your friends come to the your house, and are you finding more and more excuses to stay away from home?
4. Do you sometimes feel that you hate your parents when they are drinking, and then feel guilty for hating them?
5. Have you been watching how much your parent drinks?
6. Do you try to make your parents happy so they won't get upset and drink more?
7. Do you feel you can't talk about drinking in your home—or even how you feel inside?
8. Do you sometimes drink or take drugs to forget about things at home?
9. Do you feel if your parents really loved you, they wouldn't drink so much?
10. Do you sometimes wish you had never been born?
11. Do you want to start feeling better?

Social Disengagements

Social disengagement is the withdrawing of family members from interaction with others. The family literally denies itself the support structure that it needs. This withdrawal is exacerbated because the family feels that it must protect itself, has been embarrassed, or fears future encounters with others where the alcoholic is present. The family becomes isolated and, at this point, feels there is a lack of available alternatives. The home becomes a "habit cage." Families of alcoholics need not become isolated if they do not choose to be. Most families rarely feel they have a choice, however; they see their only response as withdrawal. This social disengagement can occur as either physical or emotional withdrawal.

1. *Physical Disengagement*

Physical disengagement occurs when the family stops receiving and giving invitations for social interaction. The family is pulled back from physical contact with others. Children, for example, no longer invite their friends to their homes. Non-alcoholic spouses hide invitations to functions involving alcohol to avoid any confrontations or embarrassment. Fewer people stop by to visit because of the unpleasantness or tension from a previous visit. The family becomes significantly separated as a unit from others. This physical isolation can lead to emotional disengagement.

2. *Emotional Disengagement*

Emotional disengagement is a decline in positive emotional relationships. In the alcoholic home, this decline is replaced with an increase in negative emotions. The longer the alcoholism continues, and the more the family withdraws, the greater the probability that negative emotions, such as tension, anxiety, despair, and powerless-ness, will emerge. One method of handling these negative emotions is to attempt to become "non-feeling," that is, to deny and minimize negative feelings to prevent further pain. Thus, avoidance becomes the norm for handling negative emotions, even though avoidance can lead to the denial of benefits of positive relationships which could be offsetting factors for the negative ones. The goals of positive relation-ships are sacrificed for the "comfortableness" of isolation within the family. As stated earlier, not all family members are affected equally; however, some members are able to overcome the internal negative emotions by outside non-family relationships. In research with children of alcoholics, it was found that children who were able to establish primary relationships outside the home were not as likely to become alcoholic in their adult lives as children who did not establish these relationships (Ackerman, 1978). This is particularly relevant, considering that approximately 50% of alcoholics come from an alcoholic home.

Of all the problems encountered by non-alcoholic family members, emotional isolation may be the greatest. It affects not only the non-alcoholic life within the family, but also outside the family. Healthy relationships are denied or postponed to survive an unhealthy situation. Most non-alcoholic family members never assess the negative impact of this approach; they do what they believe makes the most sense at the time. The real impact may be found outside of the family or, for the children, in their adult lives. This is particularly true when considering that the children of alcoholics are dispropor-tionately represented in juvenile courts, family courts, spouse and child abuse cases, divorce, and within populations plagued with psychological or emotional problems as adults.

Unfortunately, many families of alcoholics do not go beyond the reactive phase. They deny that the problem drinker is alcoholic, they helplessly hope for recovery, or they passively participate in the alcoholism syndrome. This stagnation at the reactive phase is likely to lead to these common effects on the alcoholic, the non-alcoholic spouse, and the children (Coates, 1979).

During the Reactive Phase,

The alcoholic:

- Denies the alcohol problem, blames others, forgets and tells stories to defend and protest against humiliation, attack and criticism from others in the family;
- Spends money for day-to-day needs on alcohol;
- Becomes unpredictable and impulsive in behavior;
- Resorts to verbal and physical abuse in place of honest, open talk;
- Loses the trust of family, relatives, and friends;
- Shows deterioration of physical health;
- Experiences a diminishing sexual drive;
- Has feelings of despair and hopelessness; and,
- Thinks about suicide and possibly makes an attempt.

The spouse:

- Often tries to hide and deny the existing problem of the alcoholic;
- Takes on the responsibilities of the other person, carrying the load of two and perpetrating the spouse dependence;
- Takes a job to get away from the problem and/or maintain financial security;

- Finds it difficult to be open and honest because of resentment, anger, and hurt feelings;
- Avoids sexual contact;
- May over-protect the children, neglect them, and/or use them for emotional support;
- Shows gradual social withdrawal and isolation;
- May lose feelings of self-respect and self-worth;
- May use alcohol or prescription drugs in an effort to cope.

The children:

- May be victims of birth defects;
- May be torn between parents; being loyal to one, they arouse and feel the anger of the other;
- May be deprived of emotional and physical support;
- Avoid peer activities, especially in the home out of fear and shame;
- Learn destructive and negative ways of dealing with problems and getting attention;
- Lack trust in anyone;
- May lose sight of values, standards and goals because of the absence of consistent, strong parenting.
- Suffer a diminishing sense of self-worth as a significant member of the family.

Phase II—The Active Phase

The main differences between the active and reactive phases are the responses of the non-alcoholic family members, even though the alcoholic is still drinking. Rather than being passive to the effects on themselves from alcoholism, they begin to take an active interest in themselves. No longer do they perceive themselves as totally under the alcoholic's control, and they attempt to gain some control over their own lives. In this manner, the family begins to "de-center" itself from alcoholism. In addition, family denial of alcoholism is not as strong. A major step into the active phase is the overcoming of denial by family members. They begin to realize that the problem cannot be denied away. Likewise, they are willing to abandon their anonymity in exchange for help and a viable alternative to the way they have been existing. The two predominant characteristics of the active phase are awareness and being normal.

Awareness

During the active phase, the family develops a growing awareness about alcoholism, their family and themselves. Some of the awareness that develops is:

- they are not responsible for the alcoholism;
- they do not have to live like this, that alternatives are available;
- they recognize the need for help;
- they realize that help is available; and,
- they are not alone and do not have to be alone.

Much of this active time for non-alcoholic family members is becoming involved in their own recovery. They begin to become involved in various educational, counseling, and self-help programs that are available to them. During this time, they may begin to realize that they, too, are important, and that even the failure of the alcoholic to stop drinking should not necessarily prevent them from getting help. During the reactive phase, they may have assumed that nothing could be done until the alcoholic received help. Now, in the active phase, they realize that to wait may be futile, denies their own needs, and only perpetuates and reinforces the impact of alcoholism on their lives.

Being Normal

During this period, the non-alcoholic family members, particularly the non-alcoholic spouse, attempt to stabilize the alcoholic home. Despite active alcoholism, i.e., the alcoholic is still drinking, it is decided to "get on with" normal family activities as much as possible. Even though it is desirable for the alcoholic to quit drinking and become a part of the normalizing process, sobriety is not a prerequisite. True, this will impede the process, but what is actually happening during the normal stage is an open and honest attempt to make the best of a negative situation inside and outside of the home, in order to overcome the negative impacts of alcoholism. The idea that families can begin their recovery process and become involved in normal activities that once were avoided, begins to take hold.

These activities may include supporting children to become involved in school and group activities, joining self-help groups, encouraging family conversations, and the sharing of feelings. These endeavors do not necessarily pertain to alcoholism and recovery, which is significant in itself, but also, and perhaps more important, is that they pertain to normal activities of children who are not from alcoholic homes. These "other" activities have their benefits, not only in the activities themselves, but also in the separation from alcoholism. These can serve as positive, outside factors offsetting to a negative home environment, as well as contribute to building better family interaction patterns. Again, paramount to this phase is overcoming denial, risking the loss of anonymity, and once again taking an active interest in their lives by the non-alcoholic family members. These steps begin with awareness of the desire to feel normal.

Phase III—The Alternative Phase

The alternative phase now begins, when all else has failed. The family now faces the painful question of whether or not separation is the only viable alternative to survive alcoholism. It is not necessary that a family progress through both of the previous phases. Some families will go directly from the reactive phase into the alternative phase, while others will attempt the active phase before making the decision to separate. The characteristics of the alternative phase are polarization, separation, change, and family re-organization.

Polarization

Prior to separation, many alcoholic families go through the process of polarization, that is, family members begin to withdraw from each other, and are often forced into "choosing sides." Parents may begin to make threats to each other, or statements to the children that they are considering a legal separation or divorce. For the children, this means many things, but ultimately it means that they will not be living with both parents. The effects of alcoholism on their lives now have become even greater; it has now led to a divorce. Unfortu-nately, alcoholism contributes to approximately 40% of family court cases, and thus, many children of alcoholics experience the "double jeopardy" of being not only children of alcoholics, but also children of divorce. Polarization is also the process leading up to a separation. In many cases, this time of decision is long and painful, and in some cases may be more traumatic than the actual separation. For the children, it is a time of impending change, and is often accompanied by feelings of confusion, torn loyalties, fear, resentment, anger, and increased isolation.

Separation

For some families, the only viable alternative left to them will be family separation. For others, the separation will only compound existing problems, and still others will only exchange one set of problems for a new set of problems. In short, for some life will get better, for others it will be about the same, and for still others it will get worse. For many children, separation will be life without daily contact with the alcoholic. Even within the same family, this change may be greeted with different feelings. For younger children, the loss of the parental role is of more concern than the loss of the alcoholic parent, but for older children it may be the opposite. They may perceive that although they may be losing the parental role, it was lost anyhow for all intents and purposes, and that they will no longer be affected by all of the family alcoholic problems. Much of their reaction will depend upon how the individual family members perceive this change in their lives.

Change

There is a belief that change is, in and of itself, always traumatic. What should be considered when assessing the impact of change, however, are the rates and directions of change. If the rate of change occurs too rapidly, it can be traumatic, because of the inability to adjust quickly enough. On the other hand, change that occurs too slowly can also be anxiety-producing. For example, not only may the separation be painful, but also the manner in which the separation has occurred. In some alcoholic families, the process of polarization may have been a long and tedious affair; whereas, in other families, polarization occurred too rapidly, and the decision to separate was made in haste. In some instances, however, it may be that the family members perceived that it was time for a much-needed change, and that the time was now. Thus, the rate of change can help or hinder the alternative phase.

Additionally, the direction of change becomes critical for each family member. Individual family members see the new change to their advantage or disadvantage. If a child perceives that he or she will be worse off after the separation, then the child views the change as undesirable, and is opposed to it. If a child perceives that his or her life will improve, however, then the change is not problematic. Life without the alcoholic is seen as better than life with the alcoholic. In reality, for some members of the alcoholic family this will be true, and for others it will not. Much depends upon how the new family grows and is re-organized.

Family Re-Organization

For alcoholic families that have chosen the alternative phase, several things can occur when re-organization takes place. The family begins to re-organize, pull together, and grow. In these families, family members may begin to seek help for themselves, or become further involved in their recovery process. Family members will begin to feel good about themselves, and establish healthy relationships within and outside of their family.

For other families, re-organization will involve new and additional roles. The custodial spouse now faces the single-parent role alone, whereas in the past, even though the alcoholic parent was often absent at times, he/she helped in parenting. In addition, children may find themselves in roles with added responsibilities. All of the family members' new roles can, however, be impeded by old feelings and behavior, such as their feelings of resentment, anger, guilt, abandonment, failure, and doubt about alcoholism, and about being the child or the spouse of an alcoholic. These feelings can be coupled with the old behavior of continually talking about the alcoholic, blaming the problems on alcoholism, or holding the alcoholic solely responsible for their lives.

Re-organization can be complicated further by recurring visits of the alcoholic parent, particularly if the alcoholic is still drinking. For example, the alcoholic can use the children to "get at" the non-alcoholic spouse. The children may become pawns between the spouses, a situation which can be further complicated by the alcoholic's seeking support from the children for a reconciliation. Even within the same family, however, this idea can receive mixed reactions. Younger children, again, may favor the idea more than the older children, because they may not have been exposed to the longevity of the alcoholism. One of the main problems of re-organization will be the tendency to fall back into many of the patterns of the reactive phase. A family will need to be supported during the alternative phase, if the alternatives are to become viable solutions.

Phase IV—Family Unity Phase

Unfortunately, many alcoholic families never reach the family unity phase, because of continuing alcoholism. There are no definitive progressive patterns that lead to the unity phase. Some families will proceed directly from phase one to phase four, others will go through the first two phases and then onto four, and still others may go through all the phases on their way to family unity. When they arrive, however, the family will face three concerns which are characteristic of this phase: sobriety, the "dry drunk," and family growth.

Sobriety

Central to the family unity phase is the maintaining of sobriety by the alcoholic, but sobriety alone may not be enough. Certainly, it is superior to inebriation, but acceptance of the sober alcoholic back into the mainstream of the family is not automatic. Sobriety does not guarantee family growth; it only makes it possible. Just as the family does not cause alcoholism, sobriety does not cause an immediately healthy family. The initial stages of sobriety may contain some pitfalls. For example, the family has probably waited a long time for sobriety to occur, and now that it has expects to enter "paradise." The longer the alcoholism continues, in many alcoholic families, the higher the probability that all family problems are blamed on the bottle. Therefore, the family expects other problems to end when the drinking ends, but difficulties continue to exist, as they do in all families. Difficulties which were formerly believed to be related to alcoholism surface as ordinary, normal, family disagreements. In the past, these problems may have been denied, as was the alcoholism, but now new ways of dealing with normal family problems will be needed. Some families have heard promises of sobriety before, and adapt a "wait and see" attitude before committing themselves to the family recovery process. Other families, however, will be more active and supportive of the new-found sobriety, and will be eager for many of the normal family behaviors that have been missing.

The Dry Drunk

For those families who are not able to join the recovery process from alcoholism, much of their lives will remain the same. That is, even though sobriety has occurred, no other changes in the family are taking place, because the results of the previous breakdown in family communications continue to take their toll on the emotions of family members. Unless the family is able to adapt to the sober alcoholic and themselves, and can establish and grow as a unit, the family may find itself on a "dry drunk." In such cases, tension, anxiety and conflict persist, because other problems have not been solved. The family needs to understand that throughout the drinking period, family relationships were deteriorating, and were never sufficiently established. Some children in the "dry drunk" situation are unable to remember anything but drinking behavior on the part of one or both parents. The recovering alcoholic may, in fact, be trying to parent properly, but since this is a new or strange behavior, it may not be entirely trusted within the family when the drinking stops. The family must be incorporated in a new adaptive process. To ignore the role of the family in helping the recovering alcoholic support his or her sobriety is to ignore the emotional impact that alcoholism has had on the family.

Family Growth

For those family members who can integrate the alcoholic back into the family, and emotionally integrate themselves, their lives will get better. With this integration comes the potential for family growth. This family growth will mean that the family does not dwell on the past, nor hide the past, but has learned from it. The growing family is one that goes beyond the past. It continues to change and improve, moving toward the goal of healthy family relationships. It is a family that is overcoming the negative influences of alcoholism, and is united. Unfortunately, this does not happen enough, as we noted earlier.

Family Interrelationships

What are the effects of all this adaptation and change? Many alcoholics are not aware of the emotional hazards they unthinkingly cause for their young. These effects, if considered at all, are seen as latent in the home, but may be seen as manifest by others outside the home. In order to consider the impacts of these effects, some of the dynamics occurring in the home should be noted. It is critical to consider whether or not both parents are alcoholic. In cases where both parents are involved in alcoholism, physical as well as emotional needs of the children may be unmet. When parents are unable or unwilling to assist in the home, their children consistently may be forced to organize and run the household. They may be picking up after parents, and assuming extremely mature roles for their ages.

The time of onset of parental alcoholism is also an important consideration. Were the children born into an alcoholic home, or did parental addiction occur later in their lives, and at what age? It is fairly well agreed upon in various educational studies that the impact of emotional crises upon children are more detrimental at some ages than at others. Many children will experience an emotional separation from their parents, often feeling rejected by both parents, even though only one is alcoholic. The inability to discriminate between love as a noun and love as a verb, and the lack of emotional security take their toll on many children of irresponsible parents. Alcoholic behavior in the family can prohibit intimate involvement and clearly impede the development of essential family bonds. When children's emotional needs have been stunted by neglect or destroyed by cruelty, the traditional function of parents as mentors and guides for their offspring becomes a farce. Clearly, the generally agreed upon effect of the positive influence of parents in early education of children becomes questionable (Brookover and Erickson, 1975). It cannot be assumed that the proper parental roles toward education are being met, let alone attempted, in the alcoholic home.

The roles their parents play in the family are of critical importance in the development of children. When a parent is alcoholic, his or her parental roles too often are marked by inconsistency, and both the alcoholic and the non-alcoholic parent exhibit inconsistency. The alcoholic parent behaves like several individuals, with conflicting reactions and unpredictable attitudes. Often his or her role perfor- mance is dictated by successive periods of drunken behavior, remorse, or guilt, followed by high degrees of anxiety, tension, and finally, complete sobriety. Children may learn through experience to adapt themselves to such inconsistency in roles, and even to develop some form of predictability, but they develop very little emotional security. What emotional security is attained is usually attained only during periods of sobriety, and often only if other family issues are not producing tension.

A typical example of this kind of cycle goes as follows. On Friday night, and all day Saturday, the alcoholic is drunk. Sunday and Monday are hangover and recovery days, commonly marked by some degree of guilt or remorse. The middle of the week is the most normal. As the next weekend approaches, the alcoholic is being dominated by increasing anxiety and tension, precipitating another drinking episode. The children in such a situation learn that whatever is needed, physically or emotionally, must be obtained in the middle of the week. These become the "getting" days, when the getting may be optimal, because it is at this time, if any, that parenting or positive stroking by the alcoholic will occur. This is also the time when many unrealistic, as well as realistic, promises are made, which may or may not be kept. Normal promises made on good days may go unfulfilled because the collection day is one of inebriation. Sometimes this results in the making of still bigger and more elaborate promises, which are, in turn, broken. Occasions when promises are kept are sporadic, and thus cannot be relied upon, again adding to inconsistency. The alcoholic may show exaggerated concern or love one day, and mistreat the child the next. It is little wonder that a major problem for such children is a lack of trust and security in relationships with an alcoholic parent.

The non-alcoholic parent is hampered in attempting to fulfill the needs of the children, because he or she is usually under constant tension over what is happening, or may happen. Even when the alcoholic is sober, the spouse tends to suspect that the situation is tenuous, and consequently cannot support the alcoholic's attempt to win respect and approval—knowing that the probability of consistency is low. The non-alcoholic parent, who is subjected to, and controlled by, the inconsistent nature of the alcoholic, may be so engrossed in trying to fulfill two roles, that he or she or she is unable to fulfill one role adequately and consistently. Just as the alcoholic fluctuates between different levels of sobriety and emotionalism, so does the non-alcoholic react to these varying positions. As a result, the non-alcoholic parent may be just as guilty as the alcoholic in showing too much concern for the children at times, and too little at other times. In addition, the non-alcoholic spouse, worried about the effects of alcoholic behavior in the family situation, is apt to become too protective of or fearful for the children. This protection is often misunderstood by the children, especially when it is negatively administered in the form of unexplained warnings against certain places and people.

Perhaps, most of the non-alcoholic spouse's parental concern is justified by the fact that as many as 28% or higher of the children of alcoholic parents become alcoholics themselves (Ackerman, 1987; Kinney, 2000). Much has been written about the causal factors for this phenomenon. The question is centered around the nature-

The strength of this systemic organizing principle is illustrated in family rules. One of our clients explained:

"There were two rules in our family: The first was 'there is no alcoholism' and the second was 'don't talk about it'." (Beletsis & Brown, 1981)

Maintaining the unhealthy, pathological system requires a reactive stance and a dominant emphasis on accommodation and defense. What may be most visible and obvious, and is certainly most central, the drinking, is also most vehemently denied <u>and</u> explained as something else.

Why would anyone go along with this kind of blatant denial or even subtle distortion? We know from experts in child development (Kagan 1984; Miller, 1981; 1984) that all children need a very close human bond, what is called a primary attachment, in order to survive. Most often a parent fulfills this role. We also know that the preservation of this bond is of utmost importance to the developing child. Any threat or disruption in the parent-child bond will cause tremendous fear and anxiety in a child (Kagan, 1984; Lidz, 1973; Bowlby, 1980; 1985).

One of the greatest threats to family attachment and solidarity is the challenge of the family's denial about parental alcoholism. Children and adults will readily accept the secret keeping, joining the parents in the denial and distortion, in order to maintain family ties. Everyone in the family fears that telling the truth about drinking will result in loss of love, abandonment and perhaps the breakup of the family.

The realities of the traumatic out-of-control environment and the dominance of pathological systems dynamics take precedence over opportunities for healthy individual development. Indeed, one of the major consequences of family alcoholism is the sacrifice of healthy individual development to the greater need of maintaining the pathological system (Brown, 1988; 1991).

inappropriate, incorrect popular terminology), is often a highly functional, but rigid and unhealthy system (Brown, 1991; Steinglass et al, 1987).

The family's dominant need for defense results in a tight, rigidly controlled, and narrow system. There are strict limits on behavior and what can be known and named. The realities of out-of-control behavior, tremendous cognitive and affective denial and distortion, and role confusion contribute to a rigidly regulated system with restricted access in and out (Steinglass et al, 1987; Guidano and Liotti, 1983; Brown, 1988). The alcoholic dominates the system, setting the shifting rules to which everyone else must adjust. The child's needs, feelings and behavior are subjugated to, and regulated by, the needs of the drinker.

How Does it Work?

John, an ACA in group therapy, recalled his childhood home and how the system worked:

> "In my family alcohol was at the head of the table. My father's drinking organized our whole lives, but everyone would tell you that it wasn't true. My father was drunk every night, but no one could talk about what was happening. We all knew that Dad had a difficult job and drinking was his way of relaxing and giving him some relief from the stresses of work. In some way, we all believed that Dad was entitled to behave this way because of what he put up with every day and all he did for us."

The alcoholic family becomes dominated by the presence of alcoholism and its denial as John illustrates. Maintaining this secret, the reality of alcoholism, while denying it at the same time, becomes the central double-bind focus around which family life is ordered.

Each individual develops the same behavioral and thinking disorder as the alcoholic: They are controlled by the reality of alcoholism and they must deny that reality at the same time. To preserve this inherent contradiction, all family members must adapt their thinking and behavior to fit the family's "story," that is, the explanations that have been constructed to allow the drinking behavior to be maintained and denied at the same time. The "story" includes core beliefs which family members share and which provide a sense of unity and cohesion, often against an outside world perceived as hostile or unsafe.

nurture controversy surrounding alcoholism. Is alcoholism genetically based, or are there other factors present? This author believes the nurturing aspects play the more prominent role, and the damage inflicted on the child is not limited to preadolescence or adolescence, but has long-range implications. Although not directly related to drinking practices, additional evidence that the nurture impact is the stronger influence is shown by the fact that children of alcoholic parents are more affected by the disharmony and rejection in the home life than by the drinking. They see that drinking stops once in awhile, although the fighting and tension continue. This constant state of agitation affects personality development. More particularly, children observe the use of alcohol as a method of dealing with uncomfortable situations. Although the children may vow not to drink, and are cognizant of the potential harm of alcohol abuse, this position may give way to use of drinking as a means of escape during real or perceived crisis in later life.

The two-parent family, in which alcoholism affects one or both partners, cannot provide a healthy parental relationship. A single, non-alcoholic parent can give children a healthier atmosphere. In a family where one of the parents is alcoholic, the other parent will not be able singly to overcome all of the impacts of the other's drinking; he or she cannot provide a separate environment because both parental roles are distorted or inconsistent. The non-alcoholic parent devotes energy in trying to deal with the alcoholic at various phases of adaptation, leaving little energy for the needs of offspring. Often, the children are forced into a position of increased responsibilities and unfamiliar roles. The eldest child may be put in charge of smaller children, or be drawn into the role of confidante for the non-alcoholic parent.

Sometimes children find themselves abandoned in the middle, or forced to choose sides, either of which can lead to withdrawal and a preference to be left alone. It was earlier mentioned that family disengagement from contact with others is a form of adapting behavior to the alcoholic problem. Disengagement can also occur within the family itself. The children avoid family contact as often as possible, having learned that minimal contact may mean minimal discomfort. Such children want only to be left alone, and no longer feel close to either parent. The need to be isolated from their parents' conflicts may carry over to their attitudes toward other adults. Such children associate solitude with the absence of conflict. Thus, being alone is not always as feared as one might expect; it may be viewed as a pleasant time of relaxation. Affection or emotional support outside the home is a vital aspect in helping such children, a topic which will be considered in subsequent chapters.

Many families can become recovered or recovering families, but not without assistance from others. Outside support is critical to this process, especially when we remember that there may be no support from within the family. Often children need help in acquiring or regaining a sense of trust in their parents and others. Also vital to the children is the acquisition of self-awareness and self-esteem. Basic to a family recovery program is the question of whether the children can grow up to face life successfully. Will they be able to achieve a sense of security, to be able to grow while accepting their circumstances, and, more importantly, to feel good about themselves? When working with the children of alcoholic parents, we must remember to address the many manifestations of alcoholism, not just those directly related to the alcoholic. We must bring the entire picture into focus, and examine and address the not-so-visible symptoms as well as the easily visible ones, with concern for how they manifest themselves in each individual in the family.

References

Ackerman, R.J. Children of Alcoholics. 2nd Ed., Simon & Schuster, New York, 1987.

Ackerman, R.J. "Adult Children of Alcoholics: The Effects of Background and Treatment on ACOA Symptoms" The International Journal of the Addictions, 26(11), 1159-1172, 1991.

Ackerman, R.J. Let Go and Grow. Health Communications, Deerfield Beach, FL, 1987.

Ackerman, R.J. Perfect Daughters. Health Communications, Deerfield Beach, FL, 1989.

Ackerman, R.J. Silent Sons. Simon & Schuster, New York, NY, 1993.

Brookover, W., and Edsel L. Erickson. Sociology of Education. Dorsey Press, Illinois, 1975.

Brooks, C. The Secret Everyone Knows. Operation Cork, CA, 1981.

Callan, V.J. and Jackson, D. Children of alcoholic fathers and recovered alcoholic fathers: Personal and family functioning. Journal of Studies on Alcohol, 47, 180-182, 1986.

Coates, M. and Paich, G. Alcohol and Your Patient: A Nurses Handbook. Addiction Research Foundation, Canada. 1979.

Gondolf, E.W. and R.J. Ackerman. "Validity and Reliability of an 'Adult Children of Alcoholics' Index" The International Journal of the Addictions, 28(3), 257-269, 1993.

Hindman, M. "Children of Alcoholic Parents." In: Alcohol World Health and Research. NIAAA, Rockville, MD, Winter, 1975-76.

Keltner, N.L., McIntyre, C.W. and Gee, R. Birth order effects in second generation alcoholics. Journal on Alcohol Studies, 47, 495-497, 1986.

Kinney, J. Loosening The Grip, sixth edition. McGraw-Hill, New York, NY 2000.

Moos, R.H. and Billings, A.G. Children of alcoholics during the recovery process: Alcoholic and matched control families. Addictive Behaviors, 7, 155-163, 1982.

National Institute on Alcohol Abuse and Alcoholism. Facts about Alcohol and Alcoholism, Rockville, MD, 1980.

Parker, D.A. and Harford, T.C. Alcohol related problems of children of heavy drinking parents. Journal on Alcohol Studies, 48, 265-268, 1987.

Reddy, B. "Alcoholism, A Family Illness," Lutheran General Hospital, Park Ridge, Illinois.

Steinhausen, H.C., Gobel, D. and Nestler, V. "Psychopathology in the offspring of alcoholic parents". Journal of American Academy of Child Psychiatry, 23, 465-471, 1984.

Substance Abuse and Mental Health Services Administration: National Household Survey on Drug Abuse, Rockville, MD., 1997.

Werner, E.E. Resilient offspring of alcoholics: A longitudinal study from birth to age eighteen. Journal of Studies on Alcohol, 47, 34-40, 1986.

ABOUT NACoA

The National Association for Children of Alcoholics (NACoA) believes that no child of an alcoholic should grow up in isolation and without support.

NACoA is a national nonprofit membership and affiliate organization working on behalf of children of alcoholics. NACoA defines children of alcoholics as those people who have been impacted by the alcoholism or other drug dependence of a parent or another adult filling the parental role.

The Mission of NACoA is to advocate for all children and families affected by alcoholism and other drug dependencies.

For more information on children of addicted parents or NACoA, contact:

National Association for Children of Alcoholics
11426 Rockville Pike, Suite # 100
Rockville, MD 20852
Phone: (301) 468-0985
FAX: (301) 468-0987
e-mail: nacoa@erols.com

Or

Visit the NACoA site on the World Wide Web:

http://www.nacoa.org